NEW MERMAIDS

NEW MERMAIDS

General editor: Brian Gibbons
Professor of English Literature, University of Münster

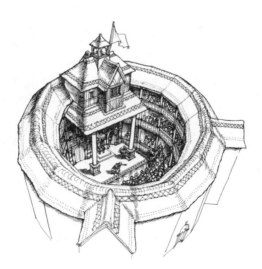

Reconstruction of an Elizabethan theatre
by C.Walter Hodges

NEW MERMAIDS

Thomas Middleton
& William Rowley

The Changeling

edited by Joost Daalder

**Professor of English
Flinders University of South Australia**

A & C Black • London
W W Norton • New York

Second edition 1990
Reprinted 1991, 1992, 1994,
1995, 1997, 1998, 1999, 2000
Published by A & C Black (Publishers) Limited
35 Bedford Row, London WC1R 4JH
ISBN 0–7136–3280–1

© *1990 A & C Black (Publishers) Limited*

First New Mermaid edition 1964
by Ernest Benn Limited
© *1964 Ernest Benn Limited*

Published in the United States of America by
W. W. Norton & Company Inc.
500 Fifth Avenue, New York, N. Y. 10110
ISBN 0–393–90061–4

CIP catalogue records for this book
are available from the British Library
and the Library of Congress.

Printed in Great Britain by
Whitstable Litho Printers Ltd,
Whitstable, Kent

CONTENTS

PREFACE

WHEN *The Changeling* was first entered in the Stationer's Register on 19 October 1652 it was described as a comedy by William Rowley. Our century has been more inclined to view it as a tragedy by Middleton. I have no wish to belittle Middleton's contribution, but I have paid more attention to Rowley's than is customary, and not only to the comic aspects of it. It is simplistic to think of the play as a tragedy which happens to have a comic sub-plot, and it is significant that Rowley wrote not only the so-called comic scenes but also the first and last scenes of the main plot. It is the nature of the connection between the two plots which is truly important, and on which I have placed special emphasis in both the introduction and the running commentary on the text, even if not always explicitly.

To me *The Changeling* is as exciting a play, in its profound understanding of human conduct and its artistry, as any I know outside the Shakespeare corpus, and I believe that it offers things which we do not find in Shakespeare. Its grasp of the nature of madness is particularly noteworthy, and is presented with the utmost skill and originality.

I have tried to present a modernized text which is both responsible and lucid. But there has been a much more drastic departure in the area of annotation. I agree with those who feel that the play 'does not rely upon explicit statement or direct speech but upon implication' (M. C. Bradbrook), and this means that as an editor I have had to pay close attention to the language and just what it is likely to imply rather than merely what it says quite obviously. This is particularly – but not uniquely – true in the many cases where the play offers two meanings, of which one is sexual. As Christopher Ricks pointed out in 1960, the play centrally depends on the need for us to be aware of the two levels in these instances, yet editors have done little to elucidate them. The matter is not just one of wit (though it is that too), but more significantly one of what the play is chiefly concerned with, such as (especially) the difference between what we are conscious of and what is in reality more important although not apparent to us because it resides in 'the unconscious', to use Freud's term. In the area of sexual meanings, I have been crucially aided by Ricks' work, but even more by that of Eric Partridge and of James T. Henke.

I have learned something from every previous edition of the play, but most from those to which I repeatedly refer, especially those by Dilke, Dyce, Bawcutt, Williams, and Black. I owe an incalculable debt to the publishers and general editors of 'New

Mermaids', who have twice given me the opportunity to edit a text for the series. On this occasion, I am particularly grateful to the present general editor, Brian Gibbons, for his persistent support, advice and generosity. Over the years I have also been helped tremendously by the editors of *Essays in Criticism*, and they gave me my first chance to publish on *The Changeling*; I have to some extent drawn on my 1988 article for the journal. I should further like to thank, for help and acts of kindness, Professor J. R. Mulryne and two former students, Antony Telford-Moore and Leigh Sutton, as well as, of course, my wife, Truus Daalder, not least as a fellow interpreter of the text. I also acknowledge with gratitude a large debt to Flinders University, and notably its Research Committee.

The edition by Brian Loughrey and Neil Taylor, *Thomas Middleton: Five Plays* (1988), appeared too late for me to make systematic use of it; although I have been able to read it, it has not influenced my own work.

Although I am indebted to many people, I alone of course remain responsible for any shortcomings in this edition.

Adelaide, 1989   JOOST DAALDER

NOTE TO THE FIFTH IMPRESSION (1995)

Since the first impression of this edition appeared in 1990 there have been a few corrections and, especially, some significant additions.

I would now point out in the note to II.ii.77, *scurvy,* that De Flores's skin condition is as likely to be due to syphilis as any other disease. To a Jacobean audience, *scurvy* would have meant much the same as *scabby* or *scabbed,* and could thus readily have indicated the presence of syphilis (cf. H, *scabbard,* etc.). It is, as De Flores points out, not his physical condition which has changed, but Beatrice's attitude to him. When she talks airily about 'the heat of the liver' (line 80) she is ironically unaware that it is no doubt indeed De Flores's sexual passion which has, quite literally, caused his disease.

Adelaide, 1995   J.D.

ABBREVIATIONS

Editions of *The Changeling*

Bawcutt	N. W. Bawcutt, ed., *The Changeling* (1958)
Black	M. W. Black, ed., *The Changeling* (1966)
Dilke	C. W. Dilke, ed., *Old English Plays* Vol. 4 (1815)
Dyce	Alexander Dyce, ed., *The Works of Thomas Middleton* Vol. 4 (1840)
Ellis	Havelock Ellis, ed., *Thomas Middleton* Vol. 1 (1887)
Frost	D. L. Frost, ed., *The Selected Plays of Thomas Middleton* (1978)
Gomme	A. H. Gomme, ed., *Jacobean Tragedies* (1969)
Harrier	R. C. Harrier, ed., *An Anthology of Jacobean Drama* Vol. 2 (1963)
Neilson	W. A. Neilson, ed., *The Chief Elizabethan Dramatists* (1911)
Sampson	M. W. Sampson, ed., *Thomas Middleton* (1915)
Spencer	Hazelton Spencer, ed., *Elizabethan Plays* (1934)
Williams	G. W. Williams, ed., *The Changeling* (1966)

Other Abbreviations

Abbott	E. A. Abbott, *A Shakespearian Grammar* (3rd rev. ed., 1870)
Craik	T. W. Craik, emendations proposed in *NQ*, March–April 1977, 120–2, and August 1980, 324–7
H	J. T. Henke, *Renaissance Dramatic Bawdy (Exclusive of Shakespeare): An Annotated Glossary and Critical Essays*, 2 vols. (1974)
M	Middleton
NQ	Notes and Queries
ODEP	*The Oxford Dictionary of English Proverbs* (3rd ed., 1970)
OED	*The Oxford English Dictionary* (1st ed.)
PDS	Eric Partridge, *A Dictionary of Slang and Unconventional English*, 8th ed., rev. Paul Beale (1984)
PSB	Eric Partridge, *Shakespeare's Bawdy* (3rd rev. ed. 1968)
Q	the 1653 quarto of *The Changeling*, esp. 162.k.10 in the British Library

R	Rowley
Reynolds	John Reynolds, *The Triumphs of God's Revenge against ... Murder* (1621)
Ricks	Christopher Ricks, 'The Moral and Poetic Structure of *The Changeling*', *Essays in Criticism* 10 (1960), 290–306
sd	stage direction
Slater	A. P. Slater, 'Hypallage, Barley-Break, and *The Changeling*', *The Review of English Studies* n.s. 34 (1983), 429–40
Tilley	M. P. Tilley, *A Dictionary of the Proverbs in England in the Sixteenth and Seventeenth Centuries* (1950)

Shakespeare references are to Peter Alexander's edition (1951).

INTRODUCTION

THE AUTHORS

THOMAS MIDDLETON WAS born in 1580, the child of a prosperous bricklayer. His father died in 1586, leaving property and bequests to his wife and children. His mother soon after remarried, but her second husband was an adventurer, and quarrels and lawsuits followed when the stepfather, mother and children sought control over the estate. Middleton matriculated in 1598 at the Queen's College, Oxford, but probably did not take a degree. A document of early 1601 describes him as being 'here in London daily accompanying the players'.[1] These players were probably Philip Henslowe's Admiral's Men (the rivals of the company to which Shakespeare belonged: the Lord Chamberlain's Men, later the King's Men). Middleton's early, often collaborative, pieces were written for Henslowe. In 1602 or 1603 Middleton married the sister of an actor in Henslowe's company.

Although Middleton's connection with Henslowe continued, in one way or another, for many years after, his earliest really successful work was done for the boys' companies, especially the Children of Paul's. Plays like *Michaelmas Term* and *A Trick to Catch the Old One* were 'citizen comedies' written for boy players between 1604 and 1606. Broadly speaking, such plays mercilessly satirize and expose the attitudes and actions of contemporary Londoners, especially their greed. From about 1606 the children's companies declined, and with them citizen comedy as a genre. By 1609 there was a growing demand for romantic tragi-comedies in the Beaumont and Fletcher mould. Middleton wrote a number of such plays over the next decade, chiefly for the King's Men. One admires *A Fair Quarrel* (c. 1615), written in collaboration with Rowley. However, for all its psychological interest (something for which Middleton is renowned), few like it as much as *A Chaste Maid in Cheapside* (c. 1613), which, although part of this new stage of Middleton's career, is best viewed as a magnificent city comedy. During the last major phase of his career Middleton concentrated on tragedy, especially *Women Beware Women* (c. 1621) and *The Changeling* (with Rowley, 1622). From 1613 he had written pageants and entertainments for city occasions, and in 1620 he became City Chronologer. His last important play is *A Game at*

---

[1] Unless otherwise indicated, spellings have been modernized.

Chess, a political satire which caused much stir when it was performed in 1624. Middleton died in 1627.[2]

Although Middleton's star has been rising in recent decades, it is not easy to point at a critical consensus as to just what kind of writer he is or how high a ranking his total output deserves. My sketch above is, of course, only very crude. But it would in any case be very different, as an outline and an assessment, if it included *The Revenger's Tragedy* (c. 1606). The play does not neatly fit into the common view of Middleton's development, but that is no reason for believing that he did not write it. In fact, the internal evidence for Middleton's authorship now appears to be so strong that I agree with the scholars who are moving towards the view that the onus for proving that it is *not* Middleton's has come to lie with those who continue to cling to the traditional belief that Tourneur was the author. This is not the place to argue the matter, but it seems safe to say that, if Middleton's authorship comes to be generally accepted (as I think it will be), our view of his complexity as a writer will be significantly affected, while his reputation – high though that already is – would be boosted so as to make him without doubt one of the leading dramatists of the Renaissance. As things stand, his output is generally seen as uneven, and only his very best work could be regarded as on a par with the best of writers like Shakespeare, Jonson and Marlowe. And, interestingly, the play for which he is best known – and which many would see as one of the greatest tragedies of the age – was not solely his product: *The Changeling* is a tragedy in which Rowley had a substantial, though much disputed, part as co-author.

William Rowley's life (c. 1585–1626) and works are less well known than Middleton's. He was known as an actor and man of the theatre, a member of the Duke of York's (later the Prince's) men, whose leader he had become by 1616; in 1623 he joined the King's Men. He was particularly good at acting the role of a fat clown. In some cases he appears to have written such a part as well as acted it. His gift for creating this type of character is certainly obvious from his portrayal of Lollio in *The Changeling*.

Rowley wrote a few plays under his own name – e.g., *All's Lost by Lust* (c. 1619) – which at present are, to my mind unjustly, neglected. His chief talent, however, appears to have been for collaboration, and his hand has been detected (or claimed to be present) in a very large number of plays. Middleton was by no means his only distinguished co-author, though the collaboration between the two seems to have been particularly fruitful. Accord-

---

[2] For a fuller survey of Middleton's life (and of his works), R. H. Barker's *Thomas Middleton* (1958) still remains useful. See also, as a good introduction offering a more modern approach, J. R. Mulryne's *Thomas Middleton* (1979).

ing to the late seventeenth-century stage historian Gerard Langbaine, Rowley was 'beloved by those great men, Shakespeare, Fletcher, and Jonson.' The judgement of posterity clashes most oddly with that of leading playwrights contemporary with Rowley. One reason is no doubt that we are not altogether sure of the nature of Rowley's contribution, but more probably he is the victim of some strange misunderstandings, such as the thought that a collaborator is automatically inferior to someone who writes a play completely on his own, and, in the case of *The Changeling*, that something both intrinsically difficult and hard to relate to the remainder of the play must somehow be defective. There are signs that the prevailing attitude to his work is becoming less negative, and it is likely that his contribution will be revalued as it becomes better understood.

DATE AND SOURCES

The Changeling was written in 1622. The earliest information on its existence is that it was licensed to be acted by the Lady Elizabeth's Servants at the Phoenix, 7 May 1622; but it must have been composed (at least in part) after 11 March, as one of its sources – Digges' book, see below – was then entered for printing. Clearly the dramatists worked fast.

The major source for the play (inasmuch as it deserves the epithet 'major') was John Reynolds' *The Triumphs of God's Revenge against the Crying and Execrable Sin of Wilful and Premeditated Murder*, Book I, History IV. Reynolds' book (1621) is a collection of thirty 'Tragical Histories', in all of which greed and adultery prompt murder and result in death for the perpetrators.

In Reynolds, Alsemero falls in love with Beatrice when he meets her in a church. However, her father wants her to marry Alonzo. Beatrice returns Alsemero's love, and persuades De Flores (described as a gallant young gentleman) to murder Alonzo – something De Flores is willing to do because he is himself in love with her. As a reward De Flores receives many willing kisses from Beatrice, but she gets married to Alsemero. However, after three months Alsemero becomes inexplicably jealous of Beatrice. His actions alienate her, and this provides De Flores with an opportunity. Alsemero kills the lovers when he finds them in adultery. Alonzo's brother, Tomazo, challenges Alsemero, who kills him treacherously. He is caught, and at his execution confesses that Beatrice and De Flores killed Alonzo; their bodies are taken up out of their graves, then burnt, and their ashes thrown into the air.

Even this bare outline will show that there are broad similarities, but also significant differences. In Reynolds, Beatrice does not find De Flores at all unattractive, and her later love for him develops naturally enough once Alsemero shows himself jealous. Alsemero is much less respectable than in the play. The characters are flat and contrived; there is little by way of convincing (leave alone profound) psychological treatment; and the plot (which is not firmly related to the characters) is crudely manipulated for its banal moral purpose. Although several detailed similarities could be quoted, the general effect of *The Changeling* is totally unlike that of Reynolds' story, and in all important respects the dramatists owe little to him.

Some elements in the plot were derived from Leonard Digges' *Gerardo The Unfortunate Spaniard*, a translation from a Spanish tale. One of the characters is somewhat like De Flores, but it is especially the way in which a substitute is used on the wedding night and then murdered which reminds one of *The Changeling*. Again, some detailed similarities exist, but again they are ultimately trivial.[3]

No source has been found for the sub-plot. The idea of using scenes set in a lunatic asylum is not unique; neither is the motif of the jealous elderly husband. Some points may have been derived from close observation of the practices in the leading madhouse of the day, Bethlehem Hospital, just outside London. But the overall concept of the sub-plot appears to be novel, as is the way its relationship with the main plot is handled. The truth is that *The Changeling* is a highly original play, and even the odd verbal borrowing from Shakespeare, for example, does not show any marked derivativeness, especially as the vision and presentation of the dramatists appear to be inspired and fresh throughout.

THE MIDDLETON-ROWLEY COLLABORATION

Who Wrote What?

According to the evidence of modern scholarship there was no dramatist with whom Middleton collaborated so extensively and intensively as Rowley; their collaboration lasted for several years and resulted in the co-authorship of five dramatic works, of which *The Changeling* was the last.

Some of the nineteenth-century readers of the play had a pretty shrewd idea of the division of authorship in *The Changeling*. Indeed, F. G. Fleay very nearly gave the division which has since been accepted by almost all scholars.[4] His attempted attribution is

[3] For relevant excerpts from Reynolds and Digges, see Bawcutt.
[4] *A Biographical Chronicle of the English Drama, 1559–1642* (2 vols, 1891), vol. 2, p. 101

the more remarkable because it does not appear to have been based on any systematic investigation of facts. Such an investigation was subsequently carried out by P. G. Wiggin, in *An Inquiry into the Authorship of the Middleton-Rowley Plays* (1897). Wiggin agreed with Fleay that the division of labour was:

Rowley:	I; III. iii; IV. iii; V. iii
Middleton:	the remainder

In other words, Rowley wrote the first and last scenes, and the whole of the sub-plot (of which I. ii is part).

Much of what Wiggin argues seems to me by itself debatable. On the other hand, some of her evidence remains compelling even now. For example, she was right to point out that Middleton was inclined to use feminine endings more often than Rowley, though I think she exaggerates what she sees as the rhythmical irregularity of the latter. Few appear to have accepted Wiggin's large and loose assertion that, compared with Middleton, Rowley believed in 'the essential dignity and beauty of human nature'; one difficulty about this type of remark is that, even if one agreed that Rowley's scenes showed such an attitude, it would be impossible to be sure that what is conveyed is anything other than the result of a dramatic strategy which the dramatists jointly adopted. Yet Wiggin goes so far as to contend that Middleton actually changed his attitude to life, as expressed in this play, under Rowley's influence.[5]

A much more rigorous and responsible attitude to the problems of authorship which have surrounded the Middleton canon has been adopted by a number of recent scholars whose work will in my view prove difficult to refute. Of great excellence has been the work of Cyrus Hoy; for our purposes, it is sufficient to refer to his article 'The Shares of Fletcher and his Collaborators in the Beaumont and Fletcher Canon (V)'.[6] Hoy's approach was essentially the one adopted, and successfully applied to a large body of evidence, by D. J. Lake in *The Canon of Thomas Middleton's Plays* (1975) and by M. P. Jackson in *Studies in Attribution: Middleton and Shakespeare* (1979). Starting with work which one can feel confident is Middleton's (such as *A Game at Chess*, which survives in his hand and which all external evidence firmly establishes as his), these scholars have tried to identify certain linguistic traits which, especially when taken together, set Middleton apart in the way a fingerprint would. They avoid tellingly expressive phrases

---

[5] Uneven though her approach is, Wiggin does seem to point to several features which are characteristic of each author. Rowley is approached in a similar vein by D. M. Robb, in 'The Canon of William Rowley's Plays', *Modern Language Review* 45 (1950), 129–41.

[6] *Studies in Bibliography* 13 (1960), 77–107

which might readily be produced by imitators and concentrate instead on seemingly insignificant features such as, for example, the form *I've* for *I have*. In *The Changeling, I've* occurs 7 times and only in the sections of the play traditionally considered Middleton's. In the five plays which Middleton and Rowley wrote together, Middleton appears to have used *I've* 28 times and Rowley never. Conversely, in those same plays, Jackson found that *hath* occurs 29 times in the Rowley sections but only twice in the Middleton portions; parentheses are used 120 times by Rowley, but only 25 times by Middleton.[7]

The point is not, of course, that a single occurrence of, say, *hath* immediately identifies a scene as Rowley's. The evidence gathers weight, however, not only when each context is considered in which *hath* occurs, but when it is also found that *hath* tends to occur in the same contexts as parentheses, etc. In this way, combinations of features are found which are hardly likely to be accidental; extensive comparisons with the works of other dramatists of the period show that such combinations can, in fact, confidently be associated with certain individuals and no others. Moreover, these linguistic habits are not conditioned, it appears, by literary considerations, for example, character. The forms in question are truly *authorial*, and are found in quite different literary environments. And it is impossible to attribute their occurrence to the habits of scribes or printing houses: on the contrary, it is remarkable to note that authorial forms of this nature frequently survive in printed texts which materialized in a variety of ways.

It does not matter that Wiggin's division remains largely unaltered (in fact, the only change is that we are to accept IV. ii. 1–16 as Rowley's) – we can feel secure, now, that her attribution has been confirmed by a more objective method than some, at least, of those which she employed. In this edition, I give the authorship of each scene in my commentary on the text, but it may be useful to have it set forth here as well:

Rowley: I. i (main plot), ii (sub-plot); III. iii (sub-plot); IV. ii. 1–16 (main plot); IV. iii (sub-plot); V. iii (main plot)
Middleton: the remainder (main plot)

What Was the Nature of the Collaboration?

It is a measure of Hoy's quality as a scholar that despite all his work on questions of authorship he was able to write: 'The criticism of collaborative drama, however, has yet to catch up with – to make any real use of – the scholarly gains that have been made over the

[7] Jackson, pp. 130–1

past quarter of a century in the work of defining authorial shares which is the necessary prerequisite to any informed critical appraisal of this body of drama.'[8] Interestingly, he mentioned *The Changeling* as perhaps the finest product of collaboration which the Jacobean theatre produced.

It does appear to be fairly generally agreed that in this play each dramatist wrote better than at any other time, as though the sum of the collaborative process transcends the parts – presumably because each author was inspired to do something which he would normally have been incapable of doing on his own. Yet the obvious good sense of this assumption is constantly eroded by a critically unsympathetic attitude to Rowley. It is no longer necessary to take seriously the suggestion that Rowley merely revised a play written by Middleton, or that he was no more than a 'pupil-assistant' (a view proposed as late as 1970).[9] But the view of, for example, Samuel Schoenbaum, in *Middleton's Tragedies: A Critical Study* (1955), still seems to be the general one. He holds that 'Middleton is responsible for the characterization of the principal figures and the general conduct of the main action' and that 'Rowley was entrusted with the composition of the first and last scenes and the minor plot' (pp. 216–17). Clearly Middleton is here seen as the controlling genius; inasmuch as Rowley was 'entrusted' with the composition of the first and last scenes of the main plot he obviously worked under the guidance of Middleton, to whom the actual credit for what matters in the main plot is due. Of late, the argument has assumed a rather different form. Following the early suggestions of William Empson in *Some Versions of Pastoral* (1935) and M. C. Bradbrook in *Themes and Conventions of Elizabethan Tragedy* (1935), the 'minor' plot (which people like Schoenbaum saw as the play's 'worst blemish') is treated with less disrespect. Several critics have traced detailed resemblances between the two plots and acknowledge that the sub-plot contributes something of importance to the general impact of the play.[10]

I believe that critics have still not been willing to take the sub-plot as seriously as they should. Major aspects of it, as well as

---

[8] 'Critical and Aesthetic Problems of Collaboration in Renaissance Drama', in *Research Opportunities in Renaissance Drama* 19 (1976), 3–6

[9] By D. M. Holmes, in *The Art of Thomas Middleton* (1970), p. 217

[10] See especially Richard Levin's searching volume *The Multiple Plot in English Renaissance Drama* (1971), pp. 34–48, and M. E. Mooney, ' "Framing" as Collaborative Technique: Two Middleton-Rowley Plays', *Comparative Drama* 13 (1979), 127–41. A useful earlier essay remains K. L. Holzknecht, 'The Dramatic Structure of *The Changeling*', *Renaissance Papers* (1954), 77–87; reprinted in Max Bluestone and Norman Rabkin, eds, *Shakespeare's Contemporaries* (1961). There are also some good pointers in L. S. Champion's *Tragic Patterns in Jacobean and Caroline Drama* (1977), pp. 166–79.

several matters of detail, still remain unexplored. The real nature of the relationship between the two plots has not been given enough thought, even if there is an awareness of many parallels and of the general fact that the sub-plot offers some sort of ironically comic version of the main plot. The sub-plot is an indispensable part of the play. Likewise, the idea of Middleton as the instructor must be abandoned. Quality is of course more important than quantity, but we do well to realize that Rowley wrote about 54% of the play, and Middleton no more than 46%. (These figures, incidentally, are not inconsistent with those for the collaboration in the five plays now held to be their joint work, of which Middleton is supposed to have written 5000 lines and Rowley 6500.)[11] More importantly, it is a fact that Rowley wrote the very substantial first and last scenes of the play. It is just as plausible that *he* was the main originator of what the play should contain as that Middleton was. If Middleton was the *auctor intellectualis*, one would have expected him to write these crucial scenes, not Rowley. If, as I believe, the play is concerned especially with madness and shows that through an intimate connection between the two plots, it becomes virtually impossible to believe that Middleton first invented that connection and then expected Rowley to give effect to it. More probably, Rowley thought of the way in which the theme of madness could be introduced by connecting the two plots, and then implemented his idea by writing the first two scenes: I. i as part of the main plot immediately establishing psychological disjunction in Alsemero and particularly Beatrice (notably when she drops her glove), and I. ii to illuminate what otherwise might not be understood in the main plot. Of course the authors would have discussed their collaboration thoroughly, and Middleton shows in what follows that they are working towards the same purpose.

It will never be possible to work out exactly how the collaboration may have proceeded, and I do not think that, from a critical point of view, we need to know, or to try and establish who was the more important author. On the contrary, I think we should approach the play as a fully integrated artefact. With due respect to Hoy and his followers, I therefore do not see the question of authorship as ultimately very significant. It is likely that most readers who do not read the play with the fact of dual authorship in mind will experience it as though it was the product of one unified sensibility. That, in essence, is how T. S. Eliot saw it when he wrote his early essay 'Thomas Middleton'.[12] At the end of his piece, Eliot says: 'Incidentally, in flashes and when the dramatic

---

[11] Jackson, p. 131

[12] 1927; reprinted in, e.g., *Elizabethan Dramatists* (1963)

need comes, he is a great poet, a great master of versification', and, by way of example, he then quotes V. iii. 149–57. The passage which he cites to make an important point about Middleton was, however, written by Rowley. Eliot's error is no doubt one that would have delighted the dramatists, who obviously did not intend us to ask such questions as 'Who wrote what?' and 'What was the nature of the collaboration?'

THE PLAY

In the main, *The Changeling* offers us a picture of the operation of folly and madness within the mind. In doing so it explores 'abnormal' mental states. While the focus is on what happens within the individual, the impact on others is not ignored. Madness is of greater concern than folly, and is presented particularly in association with sex.

It is impossible to understand the play adequately without grasping what happens in the sub-plot, and how that provides a pointer to the significance of the main plot. The presentation of madness (or for that matter folly) in the main plot is so subtle that generations of critics who have paid insufficient attention to the sub-plot have failed to detect it.[13] Admittedly the play is difficult in this regard. One of its chief points is that madness at a sophisticated level of society – i.e., in people like Beatrice and those of her class – is not noticed by most people, as it lurks under the surface of people's actions and words. With careful attention, a perceptive observer can nevertheless discover the signs of madness before it violently erupts. In order to direct our attention to the symptoms, notably in Beatrice, the authors leave no doubt that madness is their central concern by making it prominent in the sub-plot. The same is true of folly, but this is less significant within the play, and one of the chief reasons why the dramatists show its essence is that this way they make their picture of 'abnormal' psychology more comprehensive, and – perhaps yet more importantly – understandable.

For the distinction between madness and folly is emphatic and crucial. As in Bethlehem Hospital ('Bedlam'), Alibius' madhouse in the sub-plot has two wards, one for fools and one for lunatics. There is one counterfeit fool in the sub-plot, Antonio, and one counterfeit madman, Franciscus (though Isabella also briefly

---

[13] Nicholas Brooke, in *Horrid Laughter in Jacobean Tragedy* (1979), is exceptional in seeing both Beatrice's genuine madness and, in part, its composition. And in all respects his discussion (pp. 70–88) is among the most perceptive ones, though I disagree with him about the connection between the two plots (and some other matters).

assumes the role of a lunatic). One of the purposes of these disguises is that by implication it enables the dramatists to say: 'When
you consider these characters you will know what we mean by
fools and madmen, for we are using labels to separate the two
categories (and those and "normal" people); and when a character
acts the part of a fool, we can all study it in isolation from such a
complex mixture as an individual's mind might offer us in real
life.'

The basic distinction which the authors make between fools and
madmen was one officially recognized by their society: 'For the
purposes of the Court of Wards and Liveries the difference
between idiots (natural fools) and lunatics (*non compos mentis*)
rested simply on the congenital nature of the condition; natural
fools were those "mentally subnormal from birth" and lunatics
were those "whose intellect and memory [failed] sometime after
birth."'[14] Antonio acts the role of someone whose intelligence is
subnormal from birth. As 'Tony', he can answer certain simple
questions correctly, or at least without making a mistake. In
III. iii, his keeper Lollio asks him 'How many is five times six?' to
which he replies: 'Six times five'; but the answer to 'How many is
one hundred and seven?' eludes him – his simple but defective
logic leads him to say 'Seven hundred and one' (ll. 156–61). There
is a touch of pathos in the fact that he cannot do better than this,
comic though the situation is at the same time. But the play is not
primarily concerned with provoking an emotional response on our
part; rather, it gives us facts as they are.

Within its larger framework, too, the play is clinically objective
towards folly rather than emotional, although, again, it does not
seem to show itself harsh towards it. We must realize, of course,
that the characters are not of below average intelligence. Inasmuch
as we are shown any 'real' patients in Alibius' hospital, they are
lunatics, and in Vermandero's castle there are no congenital fools
either. Rather, those who are foolish lapse into folly temporarily,
and under the impact of emotion. In this respect, we can see some
similarity with those who are mad, but those people are seriously
out of touch with reality, and either institutionalized because their
disease is easy to recognize or dangerous because it is not. In the
case of essentially normal people, folly is a relatively innocuous
lapse. Antonio decides, as he is sexually attracted to Isabella, to
disguise himself as a fool, and in so doing he does not just act a role
but for the time being *is* a fool. However, this state is largely harmless and one which is curable. It is for this reason that people like

---

[14] See my essay 'Folly and Madness in *The Changeling*' (containing an earlier and more
elaborate discussion of these matters), *Essays in Criticism* 38 (1988), 1–21. This quota-
tion occurs on p. 6.

him at the end are part of a 'comic', i.e., a happy, ending. Even those who are not seriously mad can partake in that, as their madness, too, shows in temporarily foolish behaviour but is not ultimately incurable or as dangerous as that of, especially, Beatrice.

Even so, we should recognize the 'semi-mad' for what they are. In the sub-plot, the most striking example is ironically (and almost predictably) the 'psychiatrist', Alibius, who is in charge of the insane while his keeper, Lollio, has the humble task of looking after mere fools. Alibius' insanity is a form of what we would now popularly call 'paranoia'. He is old and married to an attractive young wife, and comes to imagine that she will be unfaithful to him if ever he is absent. In a state of temporary folly brought on by this mad fantasy, he locks her up in his madhouse, asking Lollio to look after her. He is out of touch with reality in more than one way. Above all, he is wrong to mistrust his wife, for, although she is subjected to temptation and human enough to experience it and almost to succumb,[15] she is essentially trustworthy, and probably the sanest person in the play, even though she is surrounded by people 'officially' considered mad, and tempted by Antonio, Franciscus, and ironically Lollio himself. Certainly Alibius' action subjects Isabella to considerable discomfort and humiliation; on the other hand, she has so constructive an attitude to life that she ends up improving the mental health of curable people around her and enjoys much of her experience.

In the main plot, Alibius' comparatively innocuous insanity is paralleled by that of Alsemero. In essence Alsemero is quite a normal man. The play shows, however, how even such a person can, so to speak, lose his head under the influence of his libido. To begin with, Alsemero develops a somewhat unhealthy intensity when he allows himself to be infatuated with Beatrice. We see an incipient madness in the way he does not recognize his own sexual impulse for what it is, but rationalizes it as though it were something totally different – in fact spiritual and noble. Even so, we can perhaps regard his decision to marry her as a foolish act rather than a mad one. But his behaviour comes to resemble that of Alibius when once his marriage has come about. The dramatists obviously imply, not so much that sex is bad (though they do appear to see it as almost by definition harmful), but that it is particularly dangerous when we do not understand it, yet act upon it and then allow it to dominate our lives; someone who has taken a definite step based on this urge by forming a relationship is bound to be in a particularly perilous state. At the beginning of the play, we learn from Alsemero's servant, Jasperino, that Alsemero had never been

[15] In a minor way and temporarily she does succumb, but not seriously and not when a real test comes.

interested in women; yet at the beginning of Act IV it turns out that he has something like a private laboratory which will enable him to test whether his wife is still a virgin, or even whether she is pregnant. Critics have attacked this circumstance as improbable, but that is because they have read the play as though it should be 'realistic'. Renaissance drama asks us to use our imagination and not to be surprised if things happen very quickly; but, more importantly, Alsemero's unhealthy interest is perfectly under- standable if we view him, as we should, from a psychological point of view, and understand that at this point *he* is a pathological case and has no reason (as allowed by the evidence at his disposal) for being suspicious of his wife. In other words, Alsemero, like Alibius, shows himself paranoid: jealous in the absence of facts that justify his fantastic assumption. A difference with Alibius' situation is that in the end Alsemero's jealousy does come to match the facts, and in his defence we can say that he felt instinctive discomfort when he came to know Beatrice at the beginning of the play. But the difference is one of situation rather than character: Alsemero, like Alibius, can be saved because fundamentally he is a normal person, and thus on the one hand he is absorbed into the 'comic' ending while on the other hand, as he loses Beatrice and his happiness, his ending is also 'tragic'. (We shall return to the ques- tion of what is 'comic' versus 'tragic' later in this discussion.)

The key point to remember in our consideration of madness will be that it has nothing to do with stupidity *per se*: on the contrary, it is likely to affect someone who has the kind of imagination for which intelligence is required (there is not much that a stupid person can imagine), and who is capable of such rationalization as will be persuasive to the self as well as others. Someone truly mad, in the terms of this play, bases an unrealistic belief on a powerful – usually sexual – emotion which prompts the person's fantasy towards a distorted view that the intellect embraces on the strength of spurious but plausible and seemingly clever reasons.

The character who most clearly allows us to see what the play- wrights mean by madness is Franciscus, whose psychology is totally different from Antonio's if we study him as though he were truly mad. For example, Franciscus addresses Isabella thus when he first meets her:

> Hail, bright Titania!
> Why stand'st thou idle on these flow'ry banks?
> Oberon is dancing with his Dryadës;
> I'll gather daisies, primrose, violets,
> And bind them in a verse of poesy.   (III. iii. 49–53)

The immediate effect is one of exuberant bizarreness. But the passage should not be dismissed as showing no more than that (effective though it is as such). Nor should we be content to note that Franciscus pays Isabella an exaggerated, flirtatious compliment underneath his 'madness' and tries to seduce her while pointing out that Alibius (Oberon) is sporting elsewhere with his 'nymphs' (Dryadës). The passage in fact tellingly reveals to us what real madness is like. The difference between 'Tony' and this 'madman' is that the latter lives in a fantasy world. The cardinal point is that the speaker persuades himself of the existence of a 'reality' quite different from what we know to be true on the basis of fact and reason, and is so convinced of the accuracy of his belief that he acts on it. Of course, if someone in our presence does act in this way we realize the madness, and that is why such people end up in asylums. Much of the main plot is concerned with the exploration of more subtle, less identifiable forms of madness which nevertheless are similarly based on a confusion of fantasy and reality as commonly perceived.

The play pays some attention to the question as to how 'the madman' Franciscus came to be mad, and it is an important point in both plots that while fools are subnormal from birth, someone who goes mad is likely to do so as a result of experience. It is not implied, of course, that all of us react to experience the same way; nor are we all subjected to identical events. The sub-plot gives us an indication of what the dramatists think does happen, for example in Lollio's comment in I. ii. 207–9: 'There's no hope of recovery of that Welsh madman was undone by a mouse that spoiled him a permasant; lost his wits for't.' The Welshman must have had an inclination towards madness anyway, or else the incident would not have affected him so grievously. (There is of course a joke here, to the effect that *all* Welshmen might go mad if deprived of cheese, but the very absurdity of that suggestion leads us to a more accurate appraisal of this particular individual.) What we are to understand is that a person like this might remain sane under propitious circumstances but will become mad if some particular event brings on the condition. Thus, although it would be quite wrong to suggest that, in the main plot, Beatrice goes mad as a simple result of external events, they do play a part. The wayward nature of the sub-plot enables the dramatists to make a crucial observation like this in a way which is fully dramatic yet clear, and it helps us to understand the main plot.

Yet, informative though the sub-plot is about folly and madness, its world is quite different from that of the main plot. We never see the real fools supposedly cared for by Lollio, and the implication is that they are both psychologically easy to understand and harmless. We do get some slight glimpse of the lunatics, and it is obvious, after analysis, what the nature of their disease is. This does provide interesting psychological insight, but they too are not dangerous. For the remainder, there are Antonio and Franciscus, the former just a little foolish and the latter just a little mad, but predominantly just play-acting and no real threat to anyone. Isabella is in fact a model of sanity. Lollio is more complex. He is certainly sex-obsessed, and as such some discomfort to Isabella, but no worse than that, and capable of understanding his own libido and that of others. He is certainly not mad. Neither is he a fool in the sense that he lacks intelligence. Yet to say that in general he is sane and perceptive is not to say that he is altogether free from a tendency towards madness or folly. None of these characters can be regarded as people who should be institutionalized because they are a danger to themselves or others. Those who are more seriously mad are to be found outside the asylum, and this is no doubt one reason why the dramatists present Alibius as spending so little time inside it.

It would be too simple to suggest that the sub-plot contains a sane woman within a madhouse and the main plot an insane woman in a sane world. Beatrice's Alicante, for one thing, would be viewed much too idealistically. Still, something like this ironic mirror-image is offered to us in the main plot, and the contrast between the two women, at any rate, is largely of this nature.

Environment does not appear to be the chief thing to set them apart in their conduct. Being surrounded by lunatics, Isabella might well have caught their madness, but she does not, and much the same goes for the sexual temptation to which she is subjected. By contrast, Beatrice's world is on the surface much easier to contend with, and it would be impossible to argue that what is below the surface and outside her is responsible for what she is and does. Of course, such external factors are not to be ignored. She has a father who on the one hand has materialistically spoiled her yet on the other hand is keen to get her married, without contradiction, to a suitor whom he likes. But critics are often too sentimental and partisan about this latter supposed handicap. It is quite plain from the evidence – and Beatrice herself never denies – that she was a very willing party in her engagement to Alonzo. It makes more sense to see her wish to get her own way in everything as at least partly something for which her background is responsible. The fact that she is confronted with attractive young men like Alsemero is nothing remarkable, and does not explain her conduct at all fully. On the other hand, De Flores is a more extraordinary creature to contend with, but again it would be quite wrong to blame him for everything she does. For one thing, many of the people around her do not respond to him the way she does, either positively or negatively.

It should be clear that, from the beginning of the play, there is something very wrong about Beatrice which escapes the attention of many around her, but to which Alsemero instinctively responds:

> 'Twas in the temple where I first beheld her,
> And now again the same. What omen yet
> Follows of that? None but imaginary:
> Why should my hopes of fate be timorous?   (I. i. 1–4)

Many would, like Alsemero, reject what their instinct tells them. After all, what is the evidence for his misgivings? What the dramatists imply, however, is that one's instinct may at times be a far more reliable guide than we are usually prepared to believe. Everything that follows makes it evident that Alsemero should have trusted it.

The quality in Beatrice which frightens Alsemero is present also, in a different form, in De Flores. Beatrice's reaction to De Flores is in this regard similar to Alsemero's response to her. In both instances, the reaction says something about those inspiring it, namely Beatrice and De Flores, and also about those affected. Beatrice's reaction to De Flores is the peculiarly interesting one, as it is so very bizarre. Only she expresses extraordinary loathing for De Flores, although later Tomazo de Piracquo's feelings approximate to hers somewhat (in a much milder form). For one thing, then, Beatrice's attitude to De Flores is somehow abnormal.

What inspires it? At a positive level, one might say that she is capable of an instinctive response which most are not equipped for, and which is similar to Alsemero's at the beginning of the play. But she is also similar to Alsemero in feeling attracted to the person about whom she feels misgivings. The similarity thus establishes tellingly one of the main facts of the play that we might readily overlook – and will overlook if we take things at face value – namely, that Beatrice is attracted to De Flores without knowing it. The attraction is 'unconscious': it exists in a part of her mind which she refuses to acknowledge, and her 'conscious' attitude is to deny what her unconscious[16] tells her. It is precisely because her feeling for De Flores is so sexual and strong that she vehemently describes him as a poison (in a play which regularly associates food and sex).

But on the whole Beatrice's attitude at the beginning of the play seems almost normal. It is perhaps only with the wisdom of hind-

---

[16] I am uneasily aware of the fact that at times I slip into using the language of psycho-analysis. This, however, is for want of a better vocabulary, and not because I believe the play to match a modern intellectual system. There is, nevertheless, some considerable overlap between a Freudian view of things and that of *The Changeling*, and I agree with Freud himself that the poets and philosophers before him discovered the unconscious. But such an analysis as Emil Roy's 'Sexual Paradox in *The Changeling*', *Literature and Psychology* 30 (1975), 124–32, seems to me fanciful and mistaken.

sight that we find her amorous shift from Alonzo to Alsemero very sudden. Its significance, however, appears to be that her sexual impulse is stirred quite easily. She knew little about Alonzo, and when she meets Alsemero she says: 'This was the man was meant me. That he should come / So near his time and miss it!' (I. i. 84–5). She imputes her change of heart to having relied on her eyes before, not judgement. But in fact she is almost as ill-acquainted with Alsemero as with her fiancé, and clearly this new love is accepted by her as a result of rationalization. What propels her is her libido, and it will be directed very rapidly towards De Flores.

The erotic basis of her feeling for him becomes obvious to us at the end of I. i, if we have not been able to guess at it before. She says to herself 'Not this serpent gone yet?' (l.223), and then drops a glove. The serpent, De Flores, is an image for the devil, and in her conscious mind Beatrice rejects him. But the dropping of the glove constitutes a sexual invitation that she extends unconsciously. It is clear that she is not aware of her action because her father draws her attention to the fact that her glove has fallen. That the glove has to be seen as sexual is something of which De Flores is at least partly aware, for, as he understands her action, it expresses extreme distaste for him, to the extent that

> She had rather wear my pelt tanned in a pair
> Of dancing pumps than I should thrust my fingers
> Into her sockets here. (ll. 230–2)

In other words, she would rather see him dead and step on him than admit him into her body. The imagery of 'fingers' thrusting into various kinds of holes is plainly sexual throughout the play, and traditional as such. De Flores is correct in thinking of Beatrice's gesture as sexually expressive, but he misunderstands its unconscious purpose, which is to establish sexual contact with him, not to repel him.

The dramatists must signpost the development of Beatrice's sexual urge in this way since it is fundamental in their design that it is unconscious and thus part of Beatrice's insanity while yet it will inevitably run its course and thus should not seem quite arbitrary to us later in the play. The critics who think that Beatrice's later willingness to copulate with De Flores arises merely from his 'blackmailing' her clearly miss the point – that action only provides a trigger and her unconscious sexual interest in him should be apparent to us long before. The ugliness of his face and inner being appears to mesmerize her.

By the end of I. i her fascination with him has been revealed to us. But in her conscious mind, Beatrice remains attracted to Alsemero, and this leads her, ironically, to invite De Flores to kill

Alonzo (her official fiancé) on her behalf. At this point we should begin to realize that Beatrice has a profound link with De Flores not only in that both are intensely sexual, but also in that they are violent whenever their sexual drive is thwarted. Again, of course Beatrice is not aware of this aspect of her psychology. She just acts on her irrational impulses, and thus we find her flattering De Flores in II. ii. This has an unfortunate impact on De Flores of which she is not conscious: he understands that he himself is a sexual creature (and is thus much saner than she), but he misinterprets Beatrice's attitude to him as showing that she too is consciously aroused. It may well be, of course, that ironically Beatrice finds it easier to flirt with De Flores because of the unconscious passion which she has been developing towards him. But if so the fact is not within her conscious mind, which still rejects De Flores; and the latter – whom critics often credit with such full insight as he does not possess – is dangerously (even if understandably) deluded in supposing that she seeks his help because she wishes to be united with him. In fact, at the end of this scene both characters are shown as living in a fantasy world. Beatrice thinks that she will be able to rid herself of both Alonzo and De Flores – the former by his death, and the latter by bribing him to live elsewhere. De Flores imagines her in his arms already. However, that notion is more firmly rooted in reality than Beatrice's idea that she can expect him to kill Alonzo for her, and to be flattered, without intensifying his longing (which she knew of before).

To Beatrice, murder is merely something one thinks about in abstract terms, not as a reality, and when De Flores shows her the finger with the ring upon it in III. iv, she exclaims: 'Bless me! What hast thou done?' (l. 29). Her mind's refusal to accept the murder for what it is is combined with her horror of sex at this point as the finger is not only that of a dead man but also phallic (ironically held fast by her ring, symbolic of her vagina). In what follows De Flores makes her aware, at least in part (and not permanently), of the reality of both violence and sex. Contrary to what he suggests, we may ourselves resist his implication that because she is 'dipped in blood' as his accomplice she should not talk of sexual modesty (l. 126). Even so, there is a compelling element in his harsh logic, and Beatrice fails to answer it both because there *is* no effective answer and because she is part of his world anyway. We should connect what happens in III. iv to what had occurred earlier in the play. Even if Beatrice's sexual feeling had been only for Alsemero, the fact that she is prepared to engage in murder to satisfy it makes her like De Flores, who kills Alonzo because he believes in his turn that it will enable him to satisfy his lust for her. But it is not only this similarity of sentiment which is important: De Flores and Beatrice have become obvious partners because, unconsciously, Beatrice reciprocated his feeling for her when she threw down her glove. If we insist on misreading the play as though Beatrice is conscious of what she does on such an occasion, her later surrender to De Flores will continue to strike us as 'unrealistic', in the negative sense of the word. But III. iv, where it occurs, makes perfect sense if we understand that De Flores brings into action here a deep current of feeling for him of which Beatrice had not been aware. Her sexual enjoyment at the end of this scene is obvious when De Flores comments: ''Las, how the turtle pants!' This is not an emotion produced by bullying, leave alone something like rape, as is so often claimed. I do not mean, of course, that there is no bullying – only that it cannot by itself explain Beatrice's positive sexual response.

Beatrice's surrender should not be taken to mean that she has now reached an adequate understanding of herself. In fact, it is part of her tragedy that she is largely incapable of doing so. Sexual enjoyment, the dramatists imply, does not guarantee greater consciousness of one's psychological make-up. To protect her position, Beatrice thinks up the absurd scheme of letting her maid Diaphanta substitute for her on her wedding night. Diaphanta's own sexual urge, of which, unlike Beatrice, she is at all times conscious, is nonetheless dangerous and ultimately proves her undoing. But more important than the potency of Diaphanta's sexuality is the state of Beatrice's mind. When she thought up the scheme, she did not want Alsemero to detect that she had lost her virginity. In her conscious mind, she continues yet more emphatically to do what she thinks society demands, even now that she has followed the true inclination of her 'blood' (chiefly, her sexual urge). She is still not willing to admit that inclination to herself. She manages to persuade herself that she is an honest, respectable person, and this comes particularly to the fore at the beginning of Act V:

> One struck, and yet she lies by 't! – O my fears!
> This strumpet serves her own ends, 'tis apparent now,
> Devours the pleasure with a greedy appetite,
> And never minds my honour or my peace,
> Makes havoc of my right. But she pays dearly for't:
> No trusting of her life with such a secret,
> That cannot rule her blood to keep her promise.
> Beside, I have some suspicion of her faith to me,
> Because I was suspected of my lord,
> And it must come from her.   (ll. 1–10)

The measure of Beatrice's insanity here lies in the extent to which she deludes herself about feelings and actions which she imputes to Diaphanta (i.e., she 'projects' them), when she should recognize them as her own. Diaphanta can hardly be called a 'strumpet', but

Beatrice had shown herself a whore in her affection, as De Flores puts it (III. iv. 142), by switching from Alonzo to Alsemero. Now that she has a sexual relationship with De Flores, begun even before her wedding to Alsemero, there can be no doubt that the word 'strumpet' is more applicable to her than to Diaphanta. She accuses Diaphanta of a 'greedy appetite' because that is what she has herself, though significantly she will not admit that to her conscious mind. Her talk about Diaphanta not minding her 'honour' shows just how confused she is about what she is doing. A normal person might try to keep up appearances while aware of her own sin; Beatrice, by contrast, has persuaded herself that it is Diaphanta who is sinning. Throughout the speech, Beatrice's staggering ability to avoid seeing the truth about herself can only be explained on the assumption that she is insane. Indeed, she is insane exactly because she cannot see the truth about herself, and thus comes to invent a 'reality' which does not exist.

As I suggested before, De Flores' grasp on reality is not perfect either. The lustful relationship between him and Beatrice has become habitual by V. i, and, to protect what he calls 'Our pleasure and continuance' (l. 50), he proposes to set fire to part of Diaphanta's chamber, in order to wake up the household, including Diaphanta. This mad scheme alarms even Beatrice, who points out that it may 'endanger the whole house' (l. 33). Probably the dramatists want us to see the fire as symbolic of the sexual passions of the lovers, which De Flores is more dominated by than he knows. Although he is conscious of the fact that his relationship with Beatrice gives him 'pleasure', he appears to be unaware that it is clouding his judgement. He now appears to be influenced by Beatrice's psychology, for he counters her fear with the statement: 'You talk of danger when your fame's on fire?'

The reference to her 'fame' (i.e., reputation) immediately and tellingly distracts Beatrice's mind from her consideration of a danger that might well occur in reality, and her reaction is simply: 'That's true; do what thou wilt now'. De Flores explains to her that either the others will think that Diaphanta has escaped from her room because of the fire, or, if she hastens back towards her lodging, he will shoot her. This solicitude for her welfare prompts Beatrice to say:

> I'm forced to love thee now,
> 'Cause thou provid'st so carefully for my honour. (ll. 47–8)

Such a statement, in such a situation, does not proceed from a normal person who is merely lying; it shows the confusion and self-deceit of a sick mind. One of the many interesting implications here is that Beatrice is now beginning to seek a rationalization

for her love for *De Flores* rather than Alsemero. Similarly, when
the fire has been discovered, she exclaims:

> Already! How rare is that man's speed!
> How heartily he serves me! His face loathes one,
> But look upon his care, who would not love him?
> The east is not more beauteous than his service.   (ll. 69–72)

And, in fact, De Flores' plan works, so that for the time being she
can continue to live in her fantasy world. But Jasperino, who in
IV. ii had already informed Alsemero of the illicit relationship
between De Flores and Beatrice, now produces the proof which
had been lacking. Thus V. iii opens with his statement:

> Your confidence, I'm sure, is now of proof.
> The prospect from the garden has showed
> Enough for deep suspicion.   (ll. 1–3)

Obviously De Flores and Beatrice no longer bother even to disguise their liaison carefully. When Alsemero, acting on what he
has seen, accuses Beatrice of being a whore, she replies:

> What a horrid sound it hath!
> It blasts a beauty to deformity;
> Upon what face soever that breath falls,
> It strikes it ugly. O, you have ruined
> What you can ne'er repair again!   (ll.31–5)

Typically, and insanely, Beatrice is preoccupied with the 'sound'
of the word 'whore', not with the content as it applies to her –
indeed, she makes out that it is Alsemero who is doing her harm by
using such an ugly word, and her words are those of a person who
is lying to herself rather than to him. She tries to evade the reality
which lies behind the word, as though the two can be separated.

 Even when the truth comes closer to her, she still tries to turn it
away and into something different. Amazingly, she comes to boast
of the murder of Alonzo as an act caused by her love for Alsemero;
and she sees similar virtue in her having 'kissed poison for it,
stroked a serpent' (l. 66). Strikingly, she now begins once again to
deny her feelings for De Flores, and it does not take her long to
persuade herself that she has been faithful to Alsemero all along.
In her conception of things, that loyalty is compatible with the
adulterous relationship which she has just confessed to having,
and thus she no doubt believes her own falsehood when she says to
Alsemero:

> Remember I am true unto your bed.   (l. 82)

Shortly afterwards, however, she experiences a rare moment of insight, and then admits:

> Alsemero, I am a stranger to your bed.   (l. 159)

By this time, De Flores has spoken openly about their misdeeds to Alsemero, who has then locked up the pair in his closet. What happens there appears to be hinted at unmistakably in the text. Tomazo, Alonzo's brother, comes to seek recompense for 'murder and adultery' (l. 138). What he refers to, of course, is Alonzo's murder, and the adultery which he feels Alsemero has committed by marrying Beatrice. But exactly as the words 'murder and adultery' are spoken, Beatrice, in the closet, is heard to utter 'O, O, O!', and Alsemero comments 'Hark! 'Tis coming to you!' What he means is that at this very moment Beatrice and De Flores are engaged in adultery,[17] and De Flores in murder as he stabs her. Again, sex and violence are combined. However, this shocking and bizarre episode jolts Beatrice into recognition of reality, and she is thus able to say to her father:

> O come not near me, sir; I shall defile you.
> I am that of your blood was taken from you
> For your better health.   (ll. 149–51)

At last, Beatrice confirms to us what, at a deep level, has been plain throughout the play: that *she* is the most quintessential changeling, not Antonio, to whom that role is assigned in the Dramatis Personae. Antonio is no more than a counterfeit fool; and, as the sub-plot and the main plot are related ironically, this means that the real changeling is a person who is genuinely mad. That person is Beatrice. She turns out to be the ugly child that her father to his distress must accept in lieu of the beautiful daughter he thought he had. As the play makes clear in its language, there are several characters who 'change' and are 'changelings' in that sense, while others are substitutes (notably Diaphanta), and Antonio is a 'changeling' in the sense of 'idiot'. But, as Bawcutt points out, the word in the seventeenth century 'referred in the first place to the ugly or mentally deficient child which the fairies were supposed to leave in place of a normal child which they stole' (p.3); and this meaning, with some variation, can only apply to Beatrice. Her origin is found in the bad blood which would have made her father insane if he had kept it, although this truth comes to light only now.

   The Changeling is usually seen as a play with a tragic main plot and a comic sub-plot. This might suggest that, as the comic plot

---

[17] The incident is approached quite differently by Dorothea Kehler, in 'Middleton and Rowley's *The Changeling*, V. iii. 175–7', *The Explicator* 26 (1968), item 41, but we agree on the question of intercourse. I offer further details in the commentary.

would have a lower status, the play has an unhappy ending. It has been my contention that the importance of the comic plot is generally underrated, and that the play cannot be adequately understood without it. But I think its significance is such that we must also seriously question whether the final view of the play is a tragic one. If we say that a play has an 'unhappy' ending, we must also ask: for whom, and with what effect? The ending certainly is not a happy one for either Beatrice or De Flores. However, many probably do not feel sad about their deaths, as they find it difficult to see these characters as anything but evil. And so they are, in that they clearly cause unhappiness for others. But some of the moral evaluations of them strike me as simplistic or misguided. Much of the moralism is based on the assumption that Beatrice consciously chooses to do evil. I do not wish to suggest that she never does so, but I submit that much of the time the question of a moral judgement does not arise because an insane person cannot be held responsible for actions which spring from the unconscious. This is not to say that the dramatists therefore condone her actions or wish us to see them as excusable – merely that they are more interested in Beatrice's psychology than her morality. In any case, however, it is difficult to experience a sense of grave loss at her parting, though we can come to terms with it more easily as a result of her having at the end some awareness of the evil she has done. De Flores is a different proposition. He is highly conscious of having sinned against conventional morality but shows himself unrepentant. It is again difficult to apply a moral judgement to this. His unorthodox attitude is shocking, but that means that his death is not very tragic either, while his defiance provides a curiously pungent contrast with the rather shallow characters around him and is almost comically entertaining. (He should in more than one sense be compared with the unorthodox sex-obsessed Lollio.) I do not mean that the dramatists are frivolous or do not offer a profound insight into human nature; rather, it seems to me that they try to prevent us from interpreting things in a simplistic or platitudinous fashion.

The deaths of Alonzo and Diaphanta are perhaps less 'deserved' than those of Beatrice and De Flores, but I do not think that we are allowed to identify very closely with either character. Much of *The Changeling* is emotionally very distant from people while it shows a more intimate grasp of what goes on inside them than many plays that enable us to feel more warmly towards at least some of the characters in them. Even Isabella, however commendable or indeed human in a pleasing fashion (as when she rebukes her husband), does not invite the kind of feeling that we may develop for, say, Cordelia: her plight is too 'normal' for that, and she deals with it too toughly and capably. This is not to say we can feel no sympathy, but that a sense of awe or pathos such as is often characteristic of tragedy is not what this play inspires. Of course, Isabella is part of the comic plot, and at the end the two plots merge. We could even argue that the ultimate mood is comic rather than tragic in that the most evil characters are dead, Isabella is triumphant, Alibius will learn (or so he says), and the society of Alicante appears to be quite harmonious. On the other hand, we would deceive ourselves if we believed that this kind of order is characteristic of human affairs, and that people like Beatrice and De Flores could not be amongst us again at any moment.

Laughter is regularly (though not inescapably) associated with comedy, which tends towards a more optimistic view of human affairs than tragedy and offers a happy ending. Much of the sub-plot of *The Changeling* is very witty indeed. I have argued that it has a serious purpose, but that is not incompatible with humour. I do not think that the play offers us the comparative comfort of satire, with its moral perspective and the implication that we could obtain order if only we avoided the vices ridiculed. *The Changeling* does, in its sub-plot as in its main plot, concern itself with a presentation of what is irrational in our conduct. The main plot does this more soberly, as it shows that outside lunatic asylums people like to believe that they are controlled by reason; the sub-plot, however, gives free rein to a highly imaginative and audacious rendering of the irrational part of our nature. It would be wrong to see it as making fun of incurable patients who deserve our sympathy. We get our ideas of folly and madness from the roles played by Antonio and Franciscus; real imbeciles are not presented, and the little we see of the insane makes them frightening and pathetic rather than amusing. Even so, the actions of Antonio and Franciscus do allow us to see folly and madness in mankind as funny – in the sense of bizarre and incongruous.[18]

Imagery in both plots is firmly functional, relatively sparse and generally free of connotation. The creative imagination expresses itself not so much in figurative language as in irony, punning, and

---

[18] For stimulatingly different discussions of the relationship between the 'comic' and the 'tragic' elements in the play, see Mooney (note 10) and Brooke (note 13). The play often permits more than one response to one and the same thing. For example, De Flores' lust is responsible for a good deal of evil, but we can also see how it makes him suffer. Beatrice's self-centredness generally is either insane or morally repugnant but has a touch of pathos in 'I must trust somebody' (V. i. 15).

the imaginative handling of characters and plots.[19] Even images are often treated punningly and ironically. Let us briefly return to the imagery of fingers and holes. By the time De Flores cuts off Alonzo's finger with Beatrice's ring on it we are possibly more aware of the sexual significance of the finger and ring than their mere physical presence. Our sense of irony springs from such awareness. Beatrice and Alonzo were meant to be man and wife: ironically, Alonzo is killed, but, yet more ironically, De Flores, when cutting off the finger, is unconsciously confronted with the fact that the Beatrice-Alonzo union continues. We may further see his violent action as having ironic implications for the course of his own sexual union with Beatrice, the ending of which appears to be anticipated. Puns, or at least double meanings, abound particularly in the sub-plot, though they are also frequent in the main plot. They make us aware of things which we do not normally see. Very often, the characters are not themselves aware of more than one meaning, though Lollio-the-realist is a master-punner. There is thus a close relationship between punning and irony. One of the play's fundamental points is that we very frequently are too stupid – or more often too obsessed – to be aware of a fact outside us which in the end we cannot dodge. A pun enables a dramatist to show the existence of such a fact at the same time as our unawareness of it in our preoccupation with something else, with resultant irony. Nor is it accidental that so many of the puns are sexual. We are tremendously indebted to Christopher Ricks' seminal article 'The Moral and Poetic Structure of *The Changeling*',[20] which first dealt with this matter extensively and illuminatingly and remains essential reading for admirers of the play. Interestingly, Ricks made the point that 'a major connection [between the two plots] still seems lacking' and added 'I must admit that the thesis which I have put forward cannot establish one' (p. 301). This is true, but Ricks' work can help us to see the function of the sexual puns more clearly now that we shall perhaps come to agree that the major connection between the two plots is such as I have argued. If that argument is accepted, a chief significance of the puns is that they

---

[19] My remarks on irony and puns here are general; for details, see the commentary. I also discuss there many of the images, but it may be useful to mention some of the more significant ones here. Images of disguise (and thus change) are associated with, e.g., Antonio and Franciscus, but more gravely with Beatrice. (De Flores dons no disguise inasmuch as his appearance shows his nature.) The madhouse should be compared with the fortress: it is outwardly secure, but 'within are secrets' (I. i. 164). Food and drink are usually associated with sex. De Flores is a serpent in Beatrice's eyes and thus like the Devil, while she seems like Eve to Alsemero. Barley-break is a game involving the exchange of partners, with one couple ending up in a place called Hell.

[20] *Essays in Criticism* 10 (1960), 290–306

reveal on the one hand that our actions are prompted by an insatiable sexual drive while on the other hand we are often not conscious of that fact.

The command of double meanings and irony seems to me absolutely dazzling in this play, as does that of the relationship between the two plots and the inventive presentation of characters like Antonio and Franciscus in the sub-plot. The creative energy displayed shows an imaginative capacity of the first order and is often underrated in a quest for a Shakespearean type of language. That quest seems misguided, as it will not do justice to the very real artistic qualities of the play and applies an irrelevant yardstick to it. It certainly is the case that the language of *The Changeling* lacks such resonance as is often typical of Shakespeare. But that is because the characters are not conceived in the grand manner, and a rather more prosaic view of mankind is adopted; also, because the artistic methods – which are no less exciting and clever when once understood – have a very different emphasis and nature. It would be misleading to put too much emphasis on the more spectacular aspects of the play's art, for its greatest success, I believe, lies in the way in which the sub-plot points towards a profound presentation of madness in the main plot which is based on an extraordinarily subtle and unusual kind of dramatic suggestiveness.

THE PLAY IN PERFORMANCE

Imagining the Play in its Jacobean Theatre

It is possible to derive great enjoyment from *The Changeling* purely by reading it. Indeed, a performance of the play could not proceed without a thorough and appreciative study of its text. But the dramatists wrote for the stage, and the reader who does not at least try to imagine a performance of the play within the Jacobean theatre for which it was intended will inevitably do less than ideal justice to Middleton and Rowley's work. It is in such a theatre, too, that the play should preferably be performed.

The play was licensed to be acted in 1622 at the Phoenix, a small private theatre in Drury lane. Despite attempts at reconstruction[21] and analysis of what the original may have looked like, we can only form an approximate notion. The Cockpit or Phoenix was built by Christopher Beeston in 1616. A plan which was drawn up by Inigo

---

[21] In recent years there has been tremendous interest and progress in this area. A tiny version of something like the Phoenix has been reconstructed by C. Walter Hodges as 'The Plaie House' for the Bear Gardens Museum, London.

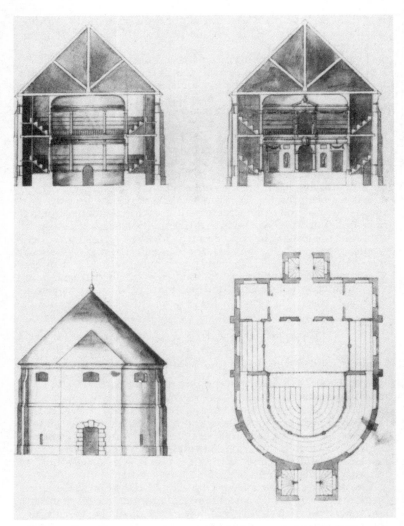

Plans made in about 1616 by Inigo Jones, probably for Beeston's Cockpit playhouse in Drury Lane. A theatre something like this may have been used for the first performance of *The Changeling*. (Photo by courtesy of the Syndics of Cambridge University Library, reproduced by permission of the Provost and Fellows of Worcester College, Oxford)

Jones in 1616–18 survives and may have been intended for this theatre.[22] It should be understood, however, that it has been argued that the plan could never have been acted upon as the basis for a real building, that the Cockpit may well have been quite different from the Inigo Jones plan, and that there is no certainty that Jones' plan was meant for this particular theatre. Furthermore, the Cockpit (so named because it was probably adapted from an old game house) was burned down in a riot in 1617, and the Phoenix – supposedly arising from its ashes – was probably not identical. Even so, both the drawing and what is known of private theatres generally may allow one a plausible guess at what kind of theatre we should envisage.

The theatre was no doubt small enough to give the audience itself, and not only the characters in the play, the sense of being within an enclosed space, which is especially fitting in the case of *The Changeling*. As, moreover, the stage jutted out well into the audience, which largely sat around it, it would have been natural for all involved to feel that they were part of the same action (within a fortress, madhouse, or indeed hell from which no escape was possible), and the many asides and soliloquies so characteristic of the play would have seemed much more normal than on a typical modern stage: it would not look strange, in such a situation, for an actor to address the audience rather than another character on stage. A sense of 'alienation' – of distance from the emotions of the characters, resulting from awareness that one was watching something illusory – would have arisen naturally and is exploited by the dramatists along with the fact that, nevertheless, the audience was allowed to view the inner workings of the characters' minds more readily than can be achieved with a large stage placed well in front of the audience.

But for this play the actual structure of the stage itself is perhaps yet more important for us to consider. Almost certainly, the central division between the audience and the characters on stage on the one hand and the actors in the 'tiring-house' (where they dressed and stayed when not on stage) on the other was formed by what is called the facade, parting the two areas. This would have presented the appearance of two levels, which together could have seemed like a fortress, madhouse, or any other building. The lower level was the more important one. It no doubt looked like a wall which could be either external or internal, so that it was unnecessary to change sets, leave alone to use a lot of properties: the audience was given the basic image of the static facade and

---

[22] See the illustration opposite and Andrew Gurr's comments in his valuable volume *The Shakespearean Stage 1574–1642* (2nd (rev.) ed., 1980), especially on pp. 147–50. Also see Gurr's *Playgoing in Shakespeare's London* (1987).

used its imagination in relation to that. Thus at the beginning of the play we are to imagine that the area (on stage) before the facade is a harbour with the castle in the background, and later scenes must be thought of as taking place, now within one room of the castle, then in another.

The make-up of the lower level of the facade would have been one central opening flanked by two doors, each at some distance from the central opening, which would normally have been used for entrances and exits. Thus at the beginning of II. i, where Beatrice and Jasperino enter 'severally', they appear on stage through separate doors. At the end of what we now somewhat misleadingly call 'scene i' of Act III, De Flores and Alonzo leave through one door and re-enter through the other – that is, they use one of the two doors for their exit at the end of the scene and the other for their entry in the next.

It is likely that the larger opening in the centre also had a door (cf. IV. i. 17–18), but whether it had or not, it often would have been much easier to cover it, when not in use, with a curtain, and that would also allow the audience to hear the madmen 'within', Beatrice's cries in the closet (V. iii) and anything else that might be staged in similar fashion. The area 'within' is traditionally called the 'inner stage', and I think that this word is more useful in the case of *The Changeling* than such modern terms as the 'discovery space', so long as we realize that the 'inner stage' is not separate from the main stage but merely a recessed area at the back of it, so to speak 'beyond' the facade or 'through' it, in which no really separate scenes were acted out, but in which certain parts of the action could nevertheless appropriately take place.

It is this area, I feel, of which the dramatists make superb use in *The Changeling*, not just for mundane theatrical purposes, but especially for symbolic ones. As David Bevington writes in his illuminating work *Action is Eloquence: Shakespeare's Language of Gesture* (1984), to the dramatists of the period the significant element of their stage is 'not scenic verisimilitude but spatial relationship' (p. 108). Thus it was quite usual for the facade to represent a seemingly reassuring fortress, while the world behind it is used to suggest that 'an inner weakness vitiates what appears to our visual sense to be so strong' (p. 102). The apertures in the facade thus 'stress a duality between what is seen and unseen, between what a character supposes to be within and what in fact is to be found there' (p. 109). The world behind the facade is not to be thought of as something separate from the remainder of life, however, for that which is hidden, lying within, 'exists only in contrast to what is visible' (p. 116). At all times there is a relationship between the main action and the hidden world behind the facade inasmuch as that is made part of the play; therefore the action of the 'inner stage' is never something which we should think of as isolated. This is of course particularly true when that recess actually gets used, but it is also true by extension of the whole inner world that we may be called on to imagine as lying behind the facade.

In the case of *The Changeling*, the unseen world of which the characters are normally unaware – as indeed are we – is of course especially important, and the stage is brilliantly exploited to match the language. Such a fusion is one which we should try to recover in our age, which too often presents visual communication as something totally separate from the verbal language which we have come to associate with books. The reader may of course experience the total effect of a play imaginatively but if that does not happen might not understand the significance of the words that are placed in Vermandero's mouth: 'our citadels / Are placed conspicuous to outward view / On promonts' tops, but within are secrets' (I. i. 162–4). I admit there is no guarantee that a spectator would grasp all the implications at once, but proper connections are more likely to establish themselves in the mind, at least gradually, if one actually *sees* the fortress as Vermandero speaks.

Some of the things which happen behind the facade are hidden from sight in a rather obvious way: a significant theatrical effect would be lost if in V. iii Beatrice and De Flores were presented as copulating in full view instead of behind a curtain (or door), and De Flores' stabbing of Beatrice, too, must come as a surprise to most of the characters on stage as well as the audience. Even here, however, the action has more significance than at first appears, as the more general point of the play is reinforced that the libido and violence are usually related psychologically and unseen for that reason rather than because sexual and violent actions are often kept secret from others. The hidden world behind the facade thus not only represents one of, for example, illicit sex or murder, but, far more meaningfully and unusually, an inner world of 'secrets' which is totally unknown to superficial people like Vermandero, especially the world of the unconscious. It is thus no accident if the fortress contains within it a world of madness which is *not* public knowledge, unlike that of Alibius' madhouse. Thus any sympathetic staging of the play which makes use of some such facade as that used in Jacobean times would almost inevitably bring out the essential connections between the superficial security of our 'outer' world which we like to think of as a fortress, another 'outer' world of recognized madness which we try to keep from view (it is an 'inner' world in that we do not usually see the madmen in Alibius' hospital), and yet another world of madness which we normally do not see at all, and which throughout the play is suggested rather than actually shown. The upper level of the facade, containing what I prefer to call the 'upper stage', on one occasion presents Alibius' madmen visually: in III. iii, where they make Isabella aware of sexual promptings which she can deal with, unlike Beatrice who is not conscious of them, so that the workings of her inner world erupt into that of the fortress only at the end of the play.

Brief Outline of Performances

The Changeling was licensed to be acted at the Phoenix in 1622, but the earliest recorded performance took place on 4 January 1624, at Court. However, there is nothing remarkable about this situation, and it is the association with the Phoenix which is important. The company then acting there was called the Lady Elizabeth's Servants, but when this disbanded during the plague of 1625, the acting rights of the play remained with Christopher Beeston, the owner of the Phoenix. Subsequently Queen Henrietta's Company produced the play in the Phoenix until 1636, when it faced another outbreak of the plague and moved to the Salisbury Court Theatre in Whitefriars. It performed *The Changeling* there, until the Lord Chamberlain intervened and assigned the rights to Beeston's son William for performance by the King and Queen's Young Company, who were then playing at the Phoenix. In 1642 the Phoenix was closed, like the other theatres, and was perhaps inhabited by one John Rhodes, a former actor, who in 1659 – just before the Restoration – assembled another company at the Phoenix which included the play in its repertoire. This company (the Duke of York's) played at the Salisbury Court Theatre for a while until it moved to its new theatre in Lincoln's Inn Fields in 1661. Before this move, Samuel Pepys had seen the play on 23 February and reported that 'it takes exceedingly'. On the whole, the popular part in these early performances turned out to be that of Antonio. However, a performance at Court on 30 November 1668 is the last before the twentieth century (the play's revival amongst readers dates from the nineteenth century).

Modern interest in the play as a script for performance is extensive and dates back to about 1930. There have been numerous performances in countries as far apart as Britain, the United States and New Zealand, not only in a variety of theatres and theatrical modes, but also on the radio and on television. Modern technology should not necessarily be seen as incompatible with the play's nature. It was a pity that a performance on BBC radio in 1950 omitted the sub-plot, but in principle radio drama can do justice to the 'enclosed' world of *The Changeling* and the vigour of its language. A 1974 BBC television version was generally considered successful, not only because of the superb acting (with Stanley Baker as De Flores and Helen Mirren as Beatrice), but also as a result of the fact that 'the close proximity and intensity of the work was achieved because of the dictates of the small screen'.[23]

As far as Britain is concerned, a useful tool for finding one's bearings concerning modern theatrical performances is provided by Lisa Cronin's *Professional Productions in the British Isles since 1880 of Plays by Tudor and Early Stuart Dramatists (Excluding Shakespeare)*, commendably published in 1987 by the University of Warwick (edited from the Graduate School of Renaissance Studies, which also produces an informative *Renaissance Drama Newsletter*). Cronin lists 42 different productions from 1950 to 1984 (of which 26 date from 1978 and after) and also mentions reviews. No doubt Cronin's survey will be updated and thus come to include, for example, a production by the National Theatre in 1988.

The first performance listed by Cronin is an amateur one by the First Folio Theatre Club in London in 1950. The first professional production (one of considerable importance) was directed by Tony Richardson for the English Stage Company at the Royal Court in February–March 1961. The play was set in the period of Goya's Spain. Richardson liked the Royal Court as 'an intimate theatre and therefore one which suits the intimate style of *The Changeling*'.[24] He saw the relating of the sub-plot to the main plot as a special difficulty, which he tried to help 'by introducing certain of the minor characters into the main plot at points where they were not originally written and in putting in the discovery of the two counterfeit madmen during the Masque of the fools and madmen.'

Of the many performances that have taken place since Richardson's, two in 1978 drew considerable attention, one directed by Peter Gill at the Riverside Studios, Hammersmith, and another directed by Terry Hands for the Royal Shakespeare Company at the Aldwych. In Gill's performance, the lunatics were interestingly allowed to roam below the audience, which was placed on raked seating formed on scaffolding. The use of lighting was significant in this production, especially as the intrinsic disadvantage of a large stage could at appropiate moments be counteracted by constricting it, while at other times full lights were not unsuitable. By comparison with Gill's, Hands' production was often seen as unnecessarily gross, with, for example, its presentation of a cardboard Beatrice getting married to Alsemero during the dumb show while the 'real' Beatrice and De Flores copulated at the back of the stage. Yet, although this presentation does not show the restraint of the text, one can say in Hands' defence, against his

[23] Michael Scott, *Renaissance Drama and a Modern Audience* (1982), p. 88
[24] *Plays and Players*, April 1961, 5

detractors, that he certainly presented, in visual language, a duality in Beatrice which the text wishes us to imagine. In a case like this, I would suggest that the point is not so much whether it is legitimate for the director to show the fornication on stage, but whether he manages to suggest that it serves the purpose which the dramatists imply: in other words, I would see such explicit sex as inappropriate if it was merely sensationalist or used to imply conscious hypocrisy on Beatrice's part, but not necessarily if it is offered as a visual sign of what we know she actually does and wishes to do in her unconscious. Hands' production emphasized the importance of sexual puns in the play (which seems to me proper), and his use of red and black as the dominant colours of the production, suggesting particularly sex and death, was commented on by reviewers; these colours are defensible.

Recent events make plain that there is considerable controversy about the question as to how the play should be staged: a controversy which at the very least suggests a lively involvement on the part of those engaged in it. Richard Eyre's production for the National Theatre in 1988 was very widely reviewed, but what was in question was not so much the intrinsic quality of the play (or even whether it *could* be a theatrical success), but whether Eyre's production was of the right kind. One reviewer stated his concern as prompted by 'the sense that the play's meaning is being imparted visually rather than verbally'. I am not sure that there is anything wrong in emphasizing visual effects, but I would agree that such an emphasis is wrong if it obscures the sense of the words of the text or goes against them. In the case of Eyre's production, this indeed appears to have happened: there is no reason, for example, why De Flores should be presented in such a way that (in the words of another reviewer) 'the livid marks on the face of . . . De Flores – a man of primitive drives which, once released, cannot be stopped – are tribal scarifications'. This kind of approach tells us more about the director than the play and is in no sense justified by it.

Ultimately, there is the real risk that some of the costly and exuberant modern productions do more harm to the play than more elementary non-professional ones, of which there have been plenty, and which we are always in some danger of ignoring. There is, however, more than one way in which the play can legitimately be performed, and the success of the performance, of whatever kind and in whatever mode, will depend less on the question of cost or technology or flamboyance of effect than on whether an honest and intelligent attempt is made to do justice to what the play seems to say. It will thus always be necessary for us to weigh our own individual reactions to the text as written against the interpretations of others, whether critics or performers.

(1993) During 1992 and 1993 the Royal Shakespeare Company offered a noteworthy production of the play, directed by Michael Attenborough. It commenced at the Swan in Stratford and afterwards moved to the Pit in London's Barbican. In both cases the small theatre was generally found to be congenial to the spirit of the play. The audience felt involved as it was seated close to the action. Staging was simple and economical. There were very few properties, the largest being Beatrice's bride-bed. In the Swan, the fools and mad people were kept under the stage, entering and leaving through the trap-door. In the Pit, there was a set which served throughout as the exterior of a castle. Emerging from slits in this wall were numerous clawing, grasping, beseeching hands. Overall, in both theatres, there was a feeling of intimacy and claustrophobia, of a closed world and hidden secrets.

I asked two spectators who both admire the play to give me their accounts of this production. One, a man well aware of the interpretation of the play advanced in this edition, was a little disappointed. To him, the production—which he saw in Stratford—came across as too 'safe'. The best scene in the play, he found, was the fools' and mad people's masque, which was presented as a terrifying, grotesque parody of the action so far; he considered that more could have been done to present the nature of madness, particularly in the case of Beatrice. 'Her initial loathing of De Flores gave no suggestion of sublimated attraction. Even when De Flores had subdued her to his will—during his "dove-panting" speech, as he held her tightly to his chest—there was only the faintest, momentary indication of sexual interest on her part. It was so brief you wondered if the actress intended it as such. In this portrayal of her, Beatrice-Joanna was simply a wilful thoughtless woman who was beguiled by a villain. Interestingly, this made her seem a faintly absurd figure. Deprived of any motive beyond that of which she herself was conscious, the character seemed curiously less alive, more of a mere stage-figure.'

This spectator felt that De Flores, also, was rather too one-dimensional and that there should have been a richer evocation of that man's soul. The other spectator, however, a woman who saw the play (which she did not know) later, in London, felt that Malcolm Storry's De Flores was extraordinarily dynamic. She at once sensed hidden (and potentially evil) depths. De Flores' vivid purple birthmark did not make him repellent or hideous; rather, it set him apart from others, perhaps in part explaining Beatrice's initial aversion, while his raw sexuality was bound to disturb her. 'When Beatrice dropped her glove it was hard to decide whether she did it deliberately, and in their early scenes together you were never quite sure whether she truly loathed him as much as she kept protesting. But I think this ambiguity should be there—it certainly is in the text. The *suggestion* of unrecognised or unacknowledged lust was certainly present in Cheryl Campbell's Beatrice, and it became stronger at the end of III.iv, when De Flores takes her in his arms. Her love scenes with Alsemero never approached the intensity of passion that *every* scene with De Flores achieved.'

Whatever the reasons for these two very dissimilar reactions, it is clear that the two performances (which may have differed from each other) provoked a good deal of interesting thought in these two theatre-goers. The future of *The Changeling* on stage looks assured.

Unfortunately the most recent TV performance known to me, broadcast on BBC2 (11 December 1993), appears to have been far from successful. Despite the presence of Bob Hoskins as a powerful De Flores, the *Times* reviewer (13/12/93) complained that the words were whispered inaudibly rather than spoken. Amazingly, the sub-plot was removed. Yet the play provides an excellent script for a TV or film production.

NOTE ON THE TEXT

The only seventeenth-century text of the play is a printed one produced a long time after it was written (1622) and after Middleton and Rowley died. *The Changeling* had appeared on stage many times before its publication rights were acquired in 1652 by Humphrey Moseley, who had it printed by Thomas Newcomb so as to appear late in 1652 or early in 1653. Two title pages exist: the one of which a facsimile reproduction appears on page 1 below and one which omits the reference to Moseley, simply stating 'LONDON, Printed in the Year, 1653'. These title pages do not refer to different editions but appear due to the fact that Moseley chose a bad time for publication of his Quarto: the Puritans had been responsible for the closing of the theatres in 1642, and by 1653 even the printing of a play could get one into trouble, which presumably Moseley's new title page was intended to avoid. There is a third title page accompanying a reissue of the play by Moseley's widow in 1668; again, this version is not a different edition, as the sheets used for the play were those of the 1653 version. Thus, despite the variation in title pages, there is only one seventeenth-century edition of the play.

There is therefore no point in, for example, comparing a 1668 copy of the play with one produced in 1653 in the hope of finding significant differences. Differences between individual copies do occur, but they are not related to the question of title pages; instead, they are due to the fact that some corrections were made to the sheets while printing was in progress. (Indeed, uncorrected sheets were used in 1668.) The corrections were not carried out systematically. Nevertheless, where they occur they are generally an improvement and have on the whole been accepted as such by editors on the basis of good sense, although nothing is known about their authority.

Like other editors, I have compared a number of copies to study the variants which occur. All copies which are held by the British Library and by the Bodleian Library in Oxford have been collated for this purpose, but I have discovered nothing new. One or two trivial variants appear according to the reports of other scholars in copies examined by them which I have not seen.[25] There is general agreement that for the purposes of a modernized edition only three variants need to be noted as substantial. In II. i. 149 uncorrected 'we are' was changed into 'w'are', as the metre demands; in II. ii. 131 the nonsensical 'my selfe that' became 'myself of that'; and in IV. ii. 88 'tho' was turned into 'thou'. As this last change was wrong (the earlier 'tho' correctly represented 'though', while 'thou' makes no sense), it can be assumed that the proofreader responsible for it was guessing rather than basing his judgement on a manuscript, although it remains possible that he did so in other instances.

It is not easy to decide how reliable Q is. It is unlikely that the printed text was based directly on work done by the dramatists, although there are a few traces of their linguistic habits which have survived the process of transmission. It is more probable that the source for Q was a transcript of a promptbook, and it has been suggested that Moseley had such a transcript of the play prepared before he sent it to the printer.[26] But in any case the text as it has come down to us is probably some stages removed from the work of the dramatists. Opinions differ as to how much faith we should put in what we do have. There appears to be more evidence for the belief that one compositor set the type than that more were involved, but we do not know how accurate that compositor was. The earliest editors of the play, notably Dilke and Dyce (but also many of their successors), were inclined to emend the text of Q fairly readily where they considered it deficient in sense or metre.

---

[25] See especially R. G. Lawrence, 'A Bibliographical Study of Middleton and Rowley's *The Changeling*', *The Library*, March 1961, 37–43; see also Richard Proudfoot, in *NQ*, April 1968, 154, where he discusses Black's edition.

[26] Williams (p. xi) believes that the text has been set not from authorial foul papers or from a promptbook, but probably from a fair scribal transcript (written in secretary hand) of the authors' foul papers. Bawcutt thinks that Q's source was 'probably a transcript from theatrical prompt-copy' (p. xvi), either a private transcript made some years before 1653 or one specially commissioned by Moseley. Certainly Q's spelling is typically that of c. 1650.

Earlier this century such an approach was rejected, and editors perhaps veered towards the other extreme, defending Q readings as though Q were sacrosanct. In the present edition I have tried to steer a middle course, but I do believe that Dyce, in particular, was far more often likely to be correct than those whose confidence in Q seems close to dogmatic. It is surprising to see such confidence expressed and acted on given the fact that we know so little about Q's authority and that there are so many errors which appear to have been conceded by all editors. Even so, where I could persuade myself that Q could possibly be correct (whether I liked what I saw or not) I have tended to follow it, and I have in any case indicated all substantial departures. (As in many editions, only very obvious errors like misprints have been silently emended.)

Unless otherwise specified, the version of Q which I refer to is the copy in the British Library (London) which has the press-mark 162.k.10 and which was used by N. W. Bawcutt in his facsimile edition of the play.[27] The copy is a good, clear one. I think it is a major advantage that anyone who wishes to see what I have done can compare my text with a facsimile of the copy which I have used, even though the facsimile is far from ideal. It is true that 162.k.10 contains a few trivial misprints which are known to have been corrected in other copies, but these are really of no concern for the present edition, and the copy contains several more pages on which corrections are known to occur, including the substantial alterations discussed above. I have moreover very thoroughly inspected the other Q copies to which I had direct access and have equally carefully collated my own edited text with all other editions. Collation of the original quartos has been as direct as I could make it (unfortunately one cannot take a copy from one library to another!). Eye-contact with an original copy is always better than reliance on photographic reproduction, including microfilms, as certain details – for example, faint letters – will often only be visible in the original, and may vary from one copy to another.

I have drastically modernized the text, retaining original features only where they served a genuine purpose. I see no point in, for example, retaining *burthen* instead of *burden*. On the other hand, I have retained contracted forms like *y'are*, not only for metrical reasons but also because they are clear and inoffensive enough in a modern text. It so happens that some of these forms are helpful in determining the matter of authorship, but I have not been concerned to preserve them for that reason. Someone who wishes to carry out serious research into such a matter should not use my edition anyway, but the original quartos. Thus, although

[27] Published by Scolar Press in 1973

'um is Rowley's form rather than Middleton's, I have, in keeping with the policy for 'New Mermaids', adopted *'em* throughout. To most modern readers, *'um* would seem peculiar if not unintelligible; there is no difference in meaning; and there is no loss in artistic effect if *'em* is used. I have no doubt that Middleton and Rowley, who wrote as collaborators for the stage, would not object to the consistent use of *'em* if they were alive today.

That criterion – 'What would the dramatists want one to do?' – has in fact guided my thought in the whole process of modernization. Some modern editors have modernized the words of the text but been coy about changing its punctuation. The fact is, though, that seventeenth-century punctuation on the whole served a rhetorical function rather than the grammatical one that modern punctuation does. Furthermore, I agree with those who believe that the Q punctuation is singularly bad (misleading rather than helpful in any respect) and cannot be regarded as authoritative (Middleton's own practice in the holograph of *A Game at Chess* differs radically from that used in Q). I have therefore punctuated the text in a modern way which I hope will be natural and useful in bringing out syntactical connections and divisions. However, I have not refrained from retaining Q punctuation (or equivalent modern marks) where I believed that it might be truly significant; I have also commented on some such instances even where I departed from Q.

The 1653 quarto divided the play into acts but not into scenes. This was first done by Dyce, whose arrangement has become the accepted one. Indications of scene, like expanded speech prefixes ('Jasperino' for 'Jasp.' etc.) and a number of stage directions which do not occur in Q, are a feature of modern editions, including this one. Added material (apart from expanded speech prefixes) is enclosed in square brackets. The stage directions were in general first suggested by Dilke and Dyce and have been adopted (sometimes adapted) by their successors, but I have given more liberal guidance than many of my predecessors and added directions where I felt they were needed. As such material is kept apart from that which is part of Q, the additions can hardly harm, whether offered within the body of the text or in notes. I have borne in mind not only the needs of those staging the play but also those of readers, who are often at a loss as to what they should imagine is happening unless this is clearly indicated. On the other hand, I have tried to provide essential directions rather than merely fanciful ones.

I have paid more attention than is customary to the question as to how the lines should be pronounced. This is a controversial matter, and one's answers depend on one's sense of English pronunciation in the 1620s as well as one's view of the likely prosodic

intentions of the authors. As usual I have given the facts of Q but
have not refrained from showing my hand by suggesting
alterations. Prosody is dealt with in the Appendix, and I here
indicate only what practices have been adopted within the text.
The lineation, largely based on that of Dilke and Dyce, has been
drastically revised from that found in Q. (See the Appendix for a
list of the departures.) The general result has been to produce
iambic verse where Q does so imperfectly even though its presence
seems to be implied and to turn into prose some of the 'verse' given
to some of the 'low' speakers, notably Lollio. Accent marks are
employed where I believe a word is stressed in an unexpected way,
e.g. 'survéy' (noun). The diaeresis is used to suggest the presence
of an extra syllable (e.g., 'deceivëd' as trisyllabic). The following
line shows the function of both marks (I. i. 211):

> A courtiër and a gallánt, enriched

Here 'courtiër', is trisyllabic (and as it happens also has *metrical*
stress on its last syllable), while 'gallánt' is disyllabic but stressed
on its second syllable. (I have provided these marks wherever the
modern reader could be in any doubt, and probably have been
modest even so.)

Q is highly consistent in differentiating between verbal forms
with suffix -*ed* spelled in full and those ending instead with a mere
'*d* or *t*. Those with -*ed* may be like 'discarded', where the -*ed* is
sounded as it is now, while the shorter forms (Q 'stretcht', etc.)
indicate that the suffix is not sounded (as in modern 'stretched').
As the modern reader will not confuse these two categories
anyway, -*ed* has been used throughout. Where, however, the -*ed* is
used in Q to indicate that the syllable is sounded for *metrical* purposes (something the reader could not otherwise automatically
infer), I have used the diaeresis to indicate the fact – thus
'deceivëd' as in I. i. 15. (See the Appendix for more detailed comments.) Verbal forms like 'stretcht' are exceptional in having been
expanded; thus I have preserved monosyllabic 'that's' instead of
using 'that is', etc.

FURTHER READING

There is a good deal of worthwhile writing on *The Changeling*. Some of it is mentioned in the course of the Introduction. Recent bibliographies should be consulted, and a useful start is provided by Dorothy Wolff, *Thomas Middleton: An Annotated Bibliography* (1985), which offers full listings and pertinent comments. Previous editions like those by Bawcutt and Williams contain valuable material. For stimulating discussions see:

T. S. Eliot, 'Thomas Middleton' (*Times Literary Supplement* 30 June 1927; repr. in, e.g., *Elizabethan Dramatists*, 1963)

William Empson, *Some Versions of Pastoral* (1935)

M. C. Bradbrook, *Themes and Conventions of Elizabethan Tragedy* (1935)

Una Ellis-Fermor, *The Jacobean Drama* (1936; rev. 1953 and 1958)

Samuel Schoenbaum, *Middleton's Tragedies: A Critical Study* (1955)

G. R. Hibbard, 'The Tragedies of Thomas Middleton and the Decadence of the Drama', *University of Nottingham Renaissance and Modern Studies* 1 (1957), 35–64

R. H. Barker, *Thomas Middleton* (1958)

Christopher Ricks, 'The Moral and Poetic Structure of *The Changeling*', *Essays in Criticism* 10 (1960), 290–306

Richard Levin, *The Multiple Plot in English Renaissance Drama* (1971)

C. L. Cherry, *The Most Unvaluedst Purchase: Women in the Plays of Thomas Middleton* (1973)

B. J. Baines, *The Lust Motif in The Plays of Thomas Middleton* (1973)

J. M. Duffy, 'Madhouse Optics: *The Changeling*', *Comparative Drama* 8 (1974), 184–98

M. E. Mooney, ' "Framing" as Collaborative Technique: Two Middleton-Rowley Plays', *Comparative Drama* 13 (1979), 127–41

Nicholas Brooke, *Horrid Laughter in Jacobean Tragedy* (1979)

Margot Heinemann, *Puritanism and Theatre: Thomas Middleton and Opposition Drama under the Early Stuarts* (1980)

Peter Morrison, 'A Cangoun in Zombieland: Middleton's Teratological *Changeling*', in Kenneth Friedenreich, ed., *'Accompaninge the players': Essays Celebrating Thomas Middleton, 1580–1980* (1983)

1 FURTHER READING

A. P. Slater, 'Hypallage, Barley-break, and *The Changeling*', *The Review of English Studies* n.s. 34 (1983), 429-40

T. McAlindon, *English Renaissance Tragedy* (1986; rev. repr. 1988)

Joost Daalder, 'Folly and Madness in *The Changeling*', *Essays in Criticism* 38 (1988), 1-21

A. A. Bronham and Zara Bruzzi, *'The Changeling' and the Years of Crisis, 1619-1624* (1990)

Cristina Malcolmson, ' "As Tame as the Ladies": Politics and Gender in *The Changeling*', *English Literary Renaissance* 20 (1990), 320-39

Sara Eaton, 'Beatrice-Joanna and the Rhetoric of Love', in David Scott Kastan and Peter Stallybrass, eds, *Staging the Renaissance* (1991)

Michael Neill, ' "Hidden Malady": Death, Discovery, and Indistinction in *The Changeling*', *Renaissance Drama* (1991), 95-121

Joost Daalder, 'The Role of Diaphanta in *The Changeling*', *AUMLA* 76 (1991), 13-21

Joost Daalder, 'The Role of Isabella in *The Changeling*', *English Studies* 73, 1 (1992), 22-29

Arthur L. Little Jr, ' "Transshaped" Women: Virginity and Hysteria in *The Changeling*', in James Redmond, ed., *Madness in Drama* (1993)

Marjorie Garber, 'The Insanity of Women', in Valeria Finucci and Regina Schwartz, eds, *Desire in the Renaissance: Psychoanalysis and Literature* (1994)

Deborah G. Burks, ' "I'll want my will else": *The Changeling* and Women's Complicity with Their Rapists', *ELH* 62, 4 (1995), 759-90

Marjorie Garber, 'The Insincerity of Women', in Margreta de Grazia, Maureen Quilligan and Peter Stallybrass, eds, *Subject and Object in Renaissance Culture* (1996)

THE
CHANGELING:

As it was Acted (with great Applause)
at the Privat house in D R U R Y : L A N E,
and *Salisbury Court.*

Written by ⟨ *THOMAS MIDLETON,*
and
WILLIAM ROWLEY. ⟩ Gent°.

Never Printed before.

L O N D O N,
Printed for H U M P H R E Y M O S E L E Y, and are to
be sold at his shop at the sign of the *Princes-Arms*
in St. *Pauls* Church-yard, 1 6 5 3.

DRAMATIS PERSONAE

VERMANDERO, *father to Beatrice*
TOMAZO DE PIRACQUO, *a noble lord*
ALONZO DE PIRACQUO, *his brother, suitor to Beatrice*
ALSEMERO, *a nobleman, afterwards married to Beatrice*
JASPERINO, *his friend*
ALIBIUS, *a jealous doctor*
LOLLIO, *his man*
PEDRO, *friend to Antonio*
ANTONIO, *the changeling*
FRANCISCUS, *the counterfeit madman*
DE FLORES, *servant to Vermandero*
MADMEN
SERVANTS
BEATRICE [also called JOANNA or BEATRICE JOANNA], *daughter to Vermandero*
DIAPHANTA, *her waiting-woman*
ISABELLA, *wife to Alibius*

The scene: Alicant

Source of names All but Lollio, Pedro, Antonio and Franciscus can fairly confidently be traced to Reynolds' *God's Revenge* (cf. R. V. Holdsworth, 'John Reynolds as a Source for Two Names in *The Changeling*', *NQ*, Dec. 1988, 491).

Meaning of names (See William Power, 'Middleton's Way with Names', *NQ* 205 [1960], 26–9, 56–60, 95–8, 136–40 and 175–9.) The meaning of a name often gives some – but not a rigid – idea of a character's nature. The following senses seem reasonably clear: TOMAZO – cf. the notion of a 'doubting Thomas', derived from the apostle in the Bible (John 20:25); ALIBIUS – 'he who is elsewhere'; FRANCISCUS – (= 'Frenchman') 'a free – and thus licentious – man'; DE FLORES – (spelled 'Deflores' in Q) 'deflowerer' (homonymically; technically and ironically = 'of the flowers'); BEA-TRICE – 'she who makes happy' (ironic); JOANNA – 'the Lord's grace' (ironic); DIA-PHANTA – (1) 'the diaphanous one' (pretty, but flimsy and transparent); (2) 'the red hot one' (as in a fire – sexually); ISABELLA 'God has sworn' (as in the equivalent 'Elizabeth'), and *bella* indicates beauty – also = 'yellowish white'.

The scene Alicant, or Alicante, is a seaport on the east coast of Spain, about 75 miles south of Valencia.

THE CHANGELING

Act I [, Scene i]

Enter ALSEMERO

[ALSEMERO]
'Twas in the temple where I first beheld her,
And now again the same. What omen yet
Follows of that? None but imaginary:
Why should my hopes of fate be timorous?
The place is holy, so is my intent: 5
I love her beauties to the holy purpose,
And that, methinks, admits comparison
With man's first creation, the place blest,
And is his right home back, if he achieve it.
The church hath first begun our interview,   10
And that's the place must join us into one;
So there's beginning, and perfection too.

Enter JASPERINO

JASPERINO
O sir, are you here? Come, the wind's fair with you;
Y'are like to have a swift and pleasant passage.

The Changeling (1) one given to change, inconstant person; (2) a person (surrepti-
tiously) put in exchange for another; (3) a child secretly substituted for another in
infancy – especially a child (usually stupid or ugly) supposed to have been left by
fairies in exchange for one stolen (also applied to the stolen child); (4) idiot,
imbecile; (5) (cf. Slater) also with reference to such reversal as indicated by 'the
rhetorical figure *Hypallage*' (*OED*, 5)

Act I, Scene i Q merely 'Actus Primus', later 'Actus Secundus', etc.; Dilke 'Act I',
etc.; division in scenes by Dyce

Scene i author: Rowley; place: near the harbour of Alicante (cf. Dramatis Personae)

  1–2 *'Twas ... same* In Reynolds (the source) Alsemero is a 'cavalier' who, originally
from Valencia, comes to Alicante in order to travel on to Malta (l. 16), to gain
military glory in the cause of Christendom. However, he falls in love when he sees
Beatrice in a church and returns the next day to meet her. The action of the play
also implies a second visit.

  4 *of* Bawcutt conj. (or Q); cf. l. 110.

  6 *the holy purpose* marriage

  7–9 He compares marriage to Paradise, man's true home which Adam lost and to
which he (any man, including Alsemero) may return through marriage.

  10 *interview* mutual view; meeting

  12 The church offers the *beginning* of the relationship but also its *perfection* – the
completing of a circle (often symbolic of perfection and eternity) – when it brings
the couple together in wedlock (cf. also the circular movement of ll. 7–9).

ALSEMERO
  Sure y'are deceivëd, friend; 'tis contrary   15
  In my best judgement.
JASPERINO   What, for Malta?
  If you could buy a gale amongst the witches
  They could not serve you such a lucky pennyworth
  As comes a' God's name.
ALSEMERO   Even now I observed
  The temple's vane to turn full in my face;   20
  I know it is against me.
JASPERINO   Against you?
  Then you know not where you are.
ALSEMERO   Not well, indeed.
JASPERINO
  Are you not well, sir?
ALSEMERO   Yes, Jasperino;
  Unless there be some hidden malady
  Within me that I understand not.
JASPERINO   And that   25
  I begin to doubt, sir. I never knew
  Your inclinations to travels at a pause,
  With any cause to hinder it, till now.
  Ashore you were wont to call your servants up,
  And help to trap your horses for the speed;   30
  At sea I have seen you weigh the anchor with 'em,
  Hoist sails for fear to lose the foremost breath,
  Be in continual prayers for fair winds:
  And have you changed your orisons?

17 *If ... witches* reference to the common superstitious belief that witches could sell winds (cf., e.g., *Macbeth* I. iii. 11)

18 *pennyworth* bargain

19 *a' God's name* in God's name – therefore 'in the course of nature', 'for free' (contrast between God's gift and the seeming bargain offered by the devil's agents)

20 *vane* the wind-vane on the top of the church which ironically turns in a circle *against* him as a symbol of change, though in fact the wind is 'fair' (l. 13), as it would remove him from disaster

21 *it is* Dyce ('tis Q); fits metre.

22–3 *Not well ... not well* example of R's 'cue-catching', in which 'one character repeats a word or phrase of the previous speaker in such a way as to alter the meaning' (cf. Bawcutt, xl)

26 *doubt* fear

27 *inclinations* So Q, probably correctly despite *it* in l. 28, for cf. II. i. 84–5.

30 *to ... speed* to provide your horses with trappings so as to speed things up

31 *'em* the servants

34 *orisons* prayers

ALSEMERO   No, friend,
  I keep the same church, same devotiön.   35
JASPERINO
  Lover I'm sure y'are none, the stoic was
  Found in you long ago; your mother nor
  Best friends, who have set snares of beauty (ay,
  And choice ones, too), could never trap you that way.
  What might be the cause?
ALSEMERO   Lord, how violent   40
  Thou art! I was but meditating of
  Somewhat I heard within the temple.
JASPERINO   Is this
  Violence? 'Tis but idleness compared
  With your haste yesterday.
ALSEMERO
  I'm all this while a-going, man.   45

Enter SERVANTS

JASPERINO
  Backwards, I think, sir. Look, your servants.
1 SERVANT
  The seamen call; shall we board your trunks?
ALSEMERO
  No, not today.
JASPERINO   'Tis the critical day,
  It seems, and the sign in Aquarius.
2 SERVANT [*Aside*]
  We must not to sea today; this smoke will bring forth   50
  fire!
ALSEMERO
  Keep all on shore; I do not know the end,
  Which needs I must do, of an affair in hand
  Ere I can go to sea.
1 SERVANT
  Well, your pleasure.   55

---

35 This is a veiled reference to Beatrice rather than 'prayers for fair winds' (l. 33).
36 *stoic* (here) person repressing emotion
47 *board* put on board
48 *critical* crucial (astrologically – and as in a disease)
49 *the . . . Aquarius* i.e., the sign of the zodiac which the sun has entered is the Water-
   carrier – a good time for a sea voyage
50 *smoke* Presumably of Alsemero's sexual passion (*fire* – cf. *PSB*), with allusion to
   the proverb 'No smoke without some fire' (*ODEP*, p. 573) – note the real fire at
   end of play (the seaman's land is less safe than *sea* = pun for 'see').

2 SERVANT [*Aside*]
Let him e'en take his leisure too; we are safer on land.
Exeunt SERVANTS

Enter BEATRICE, DIAPHANTA, *and* SERVANTS
[ALSEMERO *greets* BEATRICE *and kisses her*]

JASPERINO [*Aside*]
How now! The laws of the Medes are changed, sure!
Salute a woman? He kisses too. Wonderful! Where learnt
he this? And does it perfectly too; in my conscience, he
ne'er rehearsed it before. Nay, go on; this will be stranger   60
and better news at Valencia than if he had ransomed half
Greece from the Turk.
BEATRICE
You are a scholar, sir?
ALSEMERO   A weak one, lady.
BEATRICE
Which of the sciences is this love you speak of?
ALSEMERO
From your tongue I take it to be music.   65
BEATRICE
You are skilful in't, can sing at first sight.
ALSEMERO
And I have showed you all my skill at once.
I want more words to express me further,
And must be forced to repetitïon:
I love you dearly.
BEATRICE   Be better advised, sir.   70
Our eyes are sentinels unto our judgements,
And should give certain judgement what they see;
But they are rash sometimes, and tell us wonders
Of common things, which when our judgements find,

56 sd Q adds 'Joanna' after 'Servants', probably unaware of the combination 'Beatrice Joanna'.
57 *laws of the Medes* These were supposedly unalterable (cf. Daniel 6 : 8).
58 *Salute* greet with a kiss (*OED*, 2.e; cf. *sb.*¹, 2)
59 *in my conscience* upon my word; perhaps also 'to my knowledge'
61 *Valencia* Alsemero's hometown
61–2 *if . . . Turk* Malta was 'the terror of Turkey' (Reynolds); if Alsemero did manage what Jasperino refers to he would be outstandingly successful, as Greece had been under Turkish rule from 1460.
64 *the sciences* any of the branches of learning, including arts and crafts. Beatrice flirtatiously – but typically – confuses sex and use of reason.
66 *can . . . sight* can sight-read music/make love at first sight. R associates eyesight with sensual impulse.
68 *want* lack
74 *Of* about

They can then check the eyes, and call them blind.   75
ALSEMERO
But I am further, lady: yesterday
Was mine eyes' employment, and hither now
They brought my judgement, where are both agreed.
Both houses then consenting, 'tis agreed;
Only there wants the confirmatïon   80
By the hand royal – that is your part, lady.
BEATRICE
O there's one above me, sir. [*Aside*] For five days past
To be recalled! Sure, mine eyes were mistaken:
This was the man was meant me. That he should come
So near his time and miss it!   85
JASPERINO [*Aside*]
We might have come by the carriers from Valencia, I see,
and saved all our sea-provision; we are at farthest, sure.
Methinks I should do something too – I meant to be a
venturer in this voyage. Yonder's another vessel; I'll
board her. If she be lawful prize, down goes her   90
top-sail.   [*Greets* DIAPHANTA]

Enter DE FLORES

DE FLORES
Lady, your father –
BEATRICE   Is in health, I hope.

75 *check* curb and rebuke
76 *further* i.e., more advanced than those who are misled by their eyes and do not use
   their judgement, having used my eyes yesterday and my judgement today
77 *employment* also: copulation (ironic pun). Cf. H and Ricks.
79–81 *Both ... lady* 'The metaphor is legislative; both houses of parliament (the
   senses and the intellect) have approved the bill; it now needs only the queen's
   signature to make it law' (Williams); *consenting* also = 'being in harmony'.
81 *that is* Dyce (that's Q); fits metre.
82 *one* her father, who wants Alonzo as his son in law, and whose status resembles
   that of God above the queen
   five days i.e., the period of her engagement to Alonzo. She now believes her eyes
   were mistaken when she fell in love with him and that her 'judgement' is leading
   her towards Alsemero.
85 *his time* the moment which might/should have been his (Alsemero's)
86 *the carriers* land transport
87 *at farthest* the furthest point in our journey, and from what we should be doing
89 *venturer* sharer of (commercial) risk or gain
   voyage A sea-voyage was regarded as sexually exciting (H).
   another vessel a metaphor for Diaphanta, perhaps with play on the Biblical phrase
   'the weaker vessel' and sexual symbolism
90 *board* come alongside and get aboard to attack sexually; accost
90–1 *If ... top-sail* if I am legally allowed to capture her, sexually, she'll lower her sail
   as a sign of surrender

DE FLORES
>Your eye shall instantly instruct you, lady.
>He's coming hitherward.

BEATRICE   What needed then
>Your duteous preface? I had rather   95
>He had come unexpected: you must stall
>A good presence with unnecessary blabbing,
>And how welcome for your part you are
>I'm sure you know.

DE FLORES [*Aside*]   Will't never mend, this scorn,
>One side nor other? Must I be enjoined   100
>To follow still whilst she flies from me? Well,
>Fates, do your worst; I'll please myself with sight
>Of her, at all opportunities,
>If but to spite her anger. I know she had
>Rather see me dead than living – and yet   105
>She knows no cause for't but a peevish will.

ALSEMERO
>You seemed displeased, lady, on the sudden.

BEATRICE
>Your pardon, sir; 'tis my infirmity.
>Nor can I other reason render you
>Than his or hers, of some particular thing   110
>They must abandon as a deadly poison
>Which to a thousand other tastes were wholesome.

94 *What needed* what need was there for
96 *stall* forestall
97 *A good presence* i.e., the impressive demeanour of her father
   blabbing inept babbling
99 *Will't* Dilke (Wilt Q)
100 *One . . . other* on the one side or the other (probably: because either she stops
    scorning me or I stop creating that attitude in her)
    enjoined i.e., commanded by the *Fates* of l. 102 (in effect his lust)
101 *still* all the time
104 *to . . . anger* i.e., in compensation for frustrated lust
106 *peevish* wide range of senses other than just 'childishly fretful', 'ill-tempered':
    e.g., 'senseless', 'spiteful', 'perverse', 'headstrong', 'coy' (see *OED*)
    will modern sense but also 'inclination', 'desire' – including 'sexual desire' (which
    ironically she does *not* know, especially in relation to De Flores)
107 *displeased* Dyce: 'displeasèd' – perhaps correctly, but Q's 'displeas'd' results in an
    acceptable line of two iambs followed by three trochees, or perhaps the caesura
    before 'lady' indicates a pause substituted for a weak syllable.
110 *his or hers* i.e., any other person's
    of Dilke (or Q, cf. l. 4); concerning
    particular individual (i.e., idiosyncratically disliked)
111 *abandon* reject
110–12 *some . . . wholesome* clearly an allusion to the proverb 'One man's meat [i.e.,
    food] is another man's poison' (*ODEP*, p. 522). 'Meat'/'food' often implies sex.

   Such to mine eyes is that same fellow there,
   The same that report speaks of, the basilisk.
ALSEMERO
   This is a frequent frailty in our nature.   115
   There's scarce a man amongst a thousand found
   But hath his imperfection: one distastes
   The scent of roses, which to infinites
   Most pleasing is, and odoriferous;
   One oil, the enemy of poïson;   120
   Another wine, the cheerer of the heart
   And lively refresher of the countenance.
   Indeed this fault, if so it be, is general:
   There's scarce a thing but is both loved and loathed.
   Myself, I must confess, have the same frailty.   125
BEATRICE
   And what may be your poison, sir? I am bold with you.
ALSEMERO
   What might be your desire perhaps: a cherry.

113–14 'Such (i.e., like a deadly poison) is that same fellow here, the very same as
   rumour speaks of, namely the basilisk.' Q (though followed by eds) is surely
   wrong in printing 'of the', not 'of, the'.

114 *the basilisk* a fabulous reptile, supposedly hatched by a serpent from a cock's egg,
   whose breath and even mere glance were fatal. Cf. proverb 'The basilisk's eye is
   fatal' (*ODEP*, p. 31) – frequent in Shakespeare, as in *Cymbeline* II. iv. 107–8: 'It is
   a basilisk unto mine eye, / Kills me to look on't'.

116 *found* Dilke (sound Q). Bawcutt defends Q and interprets: 'There's hardly a man
   in a thousand people who has not some imperfection'. But Williams (with eds
   generally) rejects Q as 'it provides an unconvincing reading: "Almost every man
   in a thousand healthy people is unhealthy." The thousand thus cannot be sound.'
   And in copying an *f* could easily have been confused with a long *s*, which is found
   in Q. Alsemero appears to utter a platitude to the effect that no one is perfect or
   that everyone has a weak spot.

117 *distastes* has a distaste for

118 *infinites* an unlimited number of people

120 *oil* probably thought of as a laxative to remove poison rather than that it is an
   antidote; or perhaps a volatile oil (with smell); or an ointment

121 *wine* Perhaps R here remembered Psalm 104:15, 'And wine that maketh glad the
   heart of man, and oil to make his face to shine . . .'

122 *lively* i.e., imparting life

127 Alsemero dislikes the very thing which perhaps Beatrice likes – a cherry, his
   particular 'poison'. Interestingly (and ironically, in Beatrice's company) he
   expresses distaste for something generally viewed as trivial ('not worth a cherry'),
   but also sexy (cf. the mouth seen as a cherry; 'A woman and a cherry are painted
   for [i.e., paint themselves for] their own harm', *ODEP*, p. 907; the sense of
   'hymen' is probably not yet present). Beatrice takes no offence (and none is
   intended), yet Alsemero's remark may strike us as not very tactful. R may imply
   that *she* is his 'cherry'; she will certainly prove his poison.
   What Dilke (And what Q; 'And' no doubt repeated from previous line)

BEATRICE
I am no enemy to any creature
My memory has but yon gentleman.
ALSEMERO
He does ill to tempt your sight, if he knew it.   130
BEATRICE
He cannot be ignorant of that, sir:
I have not spared to tell him so; and I want
To help myself, since he's a gentleman
In good respect with my father, and follows him.
ALSEMERO
He's out of his place then now.   [*They talk apart*]   135
JASPERINO
I am a mad wag, wench.
DIAPHANTA
So methinks; but for your comfort I can tell you we have a
doctor in the city that undertakes the cure of such.
JASPERINO
Tush, I know what physic is best for the state of mine own
body.   140
DIAPHANTA
'Tis scarce a well-governed state, I believe.
JASPERINO
I could show thee such a thing with an ingredient that we
two would compound together, and if it did not tame the
maddest blood i' th' town for two hours after, I'll ne'er

130 Alsemero means by *tempt* 'make trial of, in a way that involves risk'; R implies that
De Flores tries to attract Beatrice sexually and so *does ill* in a different way, with *if
he knew it* carrying the sense that he himself does not know what evil he is causing.
131 Perhaps decasyllabic, but *cannot* may be pronounced 'can't', as elsewhere.
132 *want* lack means
134 *respect* repute
follows him is one of his retainers
135 Alsemero means: 'He shouldn't be here'.
136 *mad* 'uncontrolled by reason', and specifically 'sexually infatuated'
wag (naughty and humorous) fellow
137–8 *a doctor* Alibius
139 *physic* medicine (here, as he thinks, sex)
139–41 *state* (1) condition; (2) body politic (which ought to be governed rationally)
142 *such a thing* his envisaged remedy and 'a well-governed state'; also *thing* =
copulation (H)
ingredient (also) intermixture of semen and ovaries (*PSB*)
143 *compound* make up as in a mortar (with a phallic pestle). The pounding motion is
sexually suggestive. Obviously *compound*, though derived from Lat. *componere*, is
thought of as *com* (with, together) + *pound* (cf. *pounded*, III. iii. 10). Cf. also H;
PSB.
144 *blood* also 'passion' and 'sexual desire'

profess physic again.   145
DIAPHANTA
A little poppy, sir, were good to cause you sleep.
JASPERINO
Poppy? I'll give thee a pop i' th' lips for that first, and
begin there [*Kisses her*]: poppy is one simple indeed, and
cuckoo what-you-call't another. I'll discover no more
now; another time I'll show thee all.   150
BEATRICE
My father, sir.

Enter VERMANDERO *and* SERVANTS

VERMANDERO   O Joanna, I came to meet thee.
Your devotion's ended?
BEATRICE   For this time, sir.
[*Aside*] I shall change my saint, I fear me; I find
A giddy turning in me. [*To* VERMANDERO] Sir, this while
I am beholding to this gentleman   155
Who left his own way to keep me company,
And in discourse I find him much desirous
To see your castle. He hath deserved it, sir,
If ye please to grant it.
VERMANDERO   With all my heart, sir.
Yet there's an article between: I must know   160

145 *physic* medical science
146 *poppy* opiate prepared from poppy seeds. But cf. pun in Jasperino's answer.
     sleep (also) copulate
147 *pop* probably a 'thrust', hence a kiss, though with bawdy play on *lips* as those of the
     vagina. He does not want an opiate (*poppy*) but sexual intercourse.
148 *begin there* He will start at one pair of lips in anticipation of a greater *pop i'* later (*for
     that* = towards that purpose, i.e., to 'sleep').
     simple (unmixed) medicinal herb; fool(ish thing)
149 *cuckoo what-you-call't* (1) the wild arum, called cuckoo-pintle – i.e., 'cuckoo-
     penis' – after its appearance; (2) another form of cuckoo flower, lady's smock,
     traditionally used as a cure for madness (Williams); (3) *cuckoo* = fool(ish thing).
     Jasperino pretends to agree with Diaphanta about herbs but hints that he prefers
     sex as a cure for his madness; yet – in R's view if not in his – the activity is foolish.
     discover lay bare (literally)
152 *devotion* act of worship
153 *I . . . saint* i.e., change from religious to secular worship, and thus pray to a differ-
     ent saint (Alsemero). *Saint* could mean 'lover' (Sampson) – fittingly, here.
154 *giddy* (1) dizzying, whirling; (2) insane (a common early meaning – here used with
     grave irony)
     turning (1) vertigo; (2) conversion – with negative senses of 'perversion' and
     'desertion' implied
155 *beholding* beholden
158 *your castle* In Reynolds, Vermandero is the captain of the castle of Alicante.
160 *article between* a stipulation which intervenes

Your country. We use not to give survéy
Of our chief strengths to strangers: our citadels
Are placed conspicuous to outward view
On promonts' tops, but within are secrets.

ALSEMERO
A Válencían, sir.

VERMANDERO   A Válencían?   165
That's native, sir. Of what name, I beseech you?

ALSEMERO
Alsemero, sir.

VERMANDERO   Alsemero? Not the son
Of John de Alsemero?

ALSEMERO   The same, sir.

VERMANDERO
My best love bids you welcome.

BEATRICE [*Aside*]   He was wont
To call me so, and then he speaks a most   170
Unfeignëd truth.

VERMANDERO   O sir, I knew your father;
We two were in acquaintance long ago
Before our chins were worth iülan down,
And so continued till the stamp of time
Had coined us into silver. Well, he's gone;   175
A good soldier went with him.

ALSEMERO
You went together in that, sir.

VERMANDERO
No, by Saint Jaques; I came behind him.
Yet I have done somewhat too. An unhappy day

161 *use* are accustomed
162 *strengths* strongholds
164 *promonts* promontories
166 *native* i.e., to this region
169–71 *He . . . truth* Beatrice means that Vermandero used to call her his 'best love';
        but ironically she – as his 'best love' – does indeed welcome Alsemero, and with
        the greatest love possible.
173 *iülan* referring to the first growth of the beard; an adjective derived from Iulus
        Ascanius, the young son of Aeneas in Virgil's *Aeneid*. Some learned members of
        the audience perhaps realized that in its turn the name 'Iulus' was held to have
        been adapted from a Greek word for 'down' (thus in Servius' commentary, cf.
        Aeneid I, 267). To most, *iulan* can have meant no more than 'youthful, like that of
        Iulus (Ascanius)', with *down* alone conveying the notion of hair. R and his audi-
        ence may also have known *iulus* = catkin, although *OED* does not cite that for this
        date. No other instance of *iulan* appears to have survived.
177 *went together* i.e., were his equal
178 *Saint Jaques* (*Jaques* perhaps disyllabic) patron saint of Spain, St James of
        Compostella

Swallowed him at last at Gíbraltár   180
In fight with those rebellious Hollanders,
Was it not so?
ALSEMERO   Whose death I had revenged,
Or followed him in fate, had not the late league
Prevented me.
VERMANDERO   Ay, ay, 'twas time to breathe. –
O Joanna, I should ha' told thee news: 185
I saw Piracquo lately.
BEATRICE [*Aside*]   That's ill news.
VERMANDERO
He's hot preparing for his day of triumph:
Thou must be a bride within this sevennight.
ALSEMERO [*Aside*]   Ha!
BEATRICE
Nay, good sir, be not so violent; with speed
I cannot render satisfactiön   190
Unto the dear companion of my soul,
Virginity, whom I thus long have lived with,
And part with it so rude and suddenly.
Can such friends divide, never to meet again,
Without a solemn farewell?
VERMANDERO   Tush, tush, there's a toy.   195
ALSEMERO [*Aside*]
I must now part, and never meet again
With any joy on earth. [*To* VERMANDERO] Sir, your
      pardon;
My affairs call on me.
VERMANDERO   How, sir? By no means;
Not changed so soon, I hope. You must see my castle,

---

180 *Gíbraltár* The Dutch defeated a Spanish fleet here on 25 April 1607; from a
    Spanish point of view they were 'rebellious' because they were under the political
    control of Spain but rose against that country to fight the War of Independence
    (1568–1648).
183 *the late league* the truce which was signed in 1609 and lasted until 1621
184 *Prevented* forestalled
    'twas . . . breathe a claim unlikely to impress an English audience which was anti-
    Spanish in any case, and knew that Spain was in difficulty when it accepted the
    armistice
187 *hot* (sexually) ardent
    his Dyce conj. (this Q; no doubt anticipating *this* in next line)
    triumph joyful celebration (not necessarily of a conquest)
188 *sevennight* week
    farewell perhaps stressed 'fárewell'
    toy whimsical fancy; play on 'copulation' (*PSB*)

And her best entertainment, ere we part;   200
I shall think myself unkindly us'd else.
Come, come, let's on. I had good hope your stay
Had been a while with us in Alicant:
I might have bid you to my daughter's wedding.
ALSEMERO [*Aside*]
He means to feast me, and poisons me beforehand.   205
[*To* VERMANDERO] I should be dearly glad to be there,
     sir,
Did my occasions suit as I could wish.
BEATRICE
I shall be sorry if you be not there
When it is done, sir; – but not so suddenly.
VERMANDERO
I tell you, sir, the gentleman's complete,   210
A courtïer and a gallánt, enriched
With many fair and noble ornaments.
I would not change him, for a son-in-law,
For any he in Spain, the proudest he;
And we have great ones, that you know.
ALSEMERO   He's much   215
Bound to you, sir.
VERMANDERO   He shall be bound to me
As fast as this tie can hold him; I'll want
My will else.
BEATRICE [*Aside*] I shall want mine if you do it.
VERMANDERO
But come, by the way I'll tell you more of him.
ALSEMERO [*Aside*]
How shall I dare to venture in his castle,   220
When he discharges murderers at the gate?

201 *us'd* Q; Dyce: usèd
204 This is an ironic statement, in view of the wedding which actually follows and feelings already present.
205 *poisons me beforehand* as Alonzo is the intended groom
206 *dearly* very
208 *I . . there* Of course Beatrice does wish to see Alsemero at her wedding, and as a husband – but the utterance is probably not calculated.
210 *complete* perfect
211 *gallánt* polished lover
214 *he* common for 'man'
216 *Bound . . . bound* (1) indebted; (2) tied
217–18 *want* / *My will* lack what I desire – sexually in Beatrice's case (l. 218), though she may simply mean 'volition'
221 *murderers* i.e., small cannons. Alsemero refers to Vermandero's killing him by talking about Alonzo, while R may ironically allude to the real murderers, Beatrice and De Flores.

But I must on, for back I cannot go.

BEATRICE [*Aside*]

Not this serpent gone yet?   [*Drops a glove*]

VERMANDERO   Look, girl, thy glove's fall'n.
Stay, stay. – De Flores, help a little.

[*Exeunt* VERMANDERO, ALSEMERO, JASPERINO,
and SERVANTS]

DE FLORES   Here lady. [*Offers the glove*]

BEATRICE

Mischief on your officious forwardness!   225
Who bade you stoop? They touch my hand no more:
There, for t'other's sake I part with this –

[*Takes off and throws down the other glove*]

Take 'em and draw thine own skin off with 'em.

Exeunt [BEATRICE, DIAPHANTA, *and* SERVANTS]

DE FLORES

Here's a favour come, with a mischief! Now I know
She had rather wear my pelt tanned in a pair   230
Of dancing pumps than I should thrust my fingers
Into her sockets here. I know she hates me,
Yet cannot choose but love her.
No matter: if but to vex her I'll haunt her still;
Though I get nothing else, I'll have my will.   *Exit*   235

---

223 *this serpent* i.e., De Flores. Beatrice probably means 'this venomous reptile', while
R refers to the Devil, the serpent in the Garden, tempter of Eve (with whom
Alsemero associated Beatrice in his first speech). Cf. *scurvy*, II. ii. 77.

sd All editors accept that Beatrice drops a glove. Some suggest she does it consciously, as a challenge and invitation to Alsemero. More probably the action is
unconscious, prompted by her response to De Flores at a deep sexual level. De
Flores almost reveals the sexual symbolism of finger and glove in his soliloquy. In
dropping a glove Beatrice makes herself sexually available to him, although he
understands that point little better than she. Beatrice's aroused sexuality appears
to have moved from Alonzo to Alsemero and is now almost uncontrollable in De
Flores' presence.

Look . . . fall'n Beatrice is presumably in a trance-like state from which this remark
recalls her; then, her consciously shown aggression (ll. 225–8) matches, in confusion and vehemence, the libido underneath.

224 *Stay* to Beatrice as she moves to pick up the glove

228 *Take . . . 'em* (1) a reference to De Flores' ugly skin, which she wants to see
removed; (2) 'vitalize yourself, like a snake with its new skin'. Probably much of
the meaning is beyond her own grasp though strongly felt (thus *forwardness*,
l. 225, perhaps = 'lust', cf. Ricks; and *touch*, l. 226, could mean 'caress sexually').

229 *favour* token worn by a knight for his lady; sexual favour

232 *sockets* Superficially the 'fingers' of her gloves, but *socket* could mean vagina (see
OED and *PDS*) and De Flores is no doubt alluding to that sense.

234 *if . . . vex her* i.e., if his lust (his *will*, l. 235) cannot find a sexual outlet, he will
satisfy it by harassing her

[Act I, Scene ii]

Enter ALIBIUS *and* LOLLIO

ALIBIUS

  Lollio, I must trust thee with a secret,

  But thou must keep it.

LOLLIO

  I was ever close to a secret, sir.

ALIBIUS

  The diligence that I have found in thee,

  The care and industry already past,   5

  Assures me of thy good continuance.

  Lollio, I have a wife.

LOLLIO

  Fie, sir, 'tis too late to keep her secret; she's known to be

  married all the town and country over.

ALIBIUS

  Thou goest too fast, my Lollio. That knowledge   10

  I allow no man can be barrëd it;

  But there is a knowledge which is nearer,

  Deeper and sweeter, Lollio.

LOLLIO

  Well, sir, let us handle that between you and I.

ALIBIUS

  'Tis that I go about, man. Lollio,   15

  My wife is young.

LOLLIO

  So much the worse to be kept secret, sir.

ALIBIUS

  Why, now thou meet'st the substance of the point:

  I am old, Lollio.

LOLLIO

  No, sir, 'tis I am old Lollio.   20

Scene ii   author: Rowley; place: Alibius' madhouse

   3 *close to a secret* (1) secretive about a secret; (2) close to a private part (i.e., lustful).
     Alibius generally fails to grasp Lollio's puns.

   8 *keep her secret* (1) keep her status as wife concealed; (2) preserve her private part

  11 *barrëd* bar'd Q; Dyce: barrèd – probably correctly unless Q's *r* is 'syllabic'
     anyway. Cf. *fea̐r* in l.26.

  12 *knowledge* i.e., carnal knowledge, sexual intimacy

  14 *let ... I* 'let us manage that as men between us' – with implied bawdy sense

  18 *now ... point* He takes Lollio to mean that it is difficult to keep a young wife
     concealed, whereas Lollio implied that she should not be.

ALIBIUS

> Yet why may not this concórd and sympathize?
> Old trees and young plants often grow together,
> Well enough agreeing.

LOLLIO

> Ay, sir, but the old trees raise themselves higher and
> broader than the young plants. 25

ALIBIUS

> Shrewd application! There's the feaï, man.
> I would wear my ring on my own finger;
> Whilst it is borrowed it is none of mine,
> But his that useth it.

LOLLIO

> You must keep it on still then; if it but lie by, one or other 30
> will be thrusting into't.

ALIBIUS

> Thou conceiv'st me, Lollio; here thy watchful eye
> Must have employment. I cannot always be
> At home.

LOLLIO

> I dare swear you cannot. 35

ALIBIUS

> I must look out.

LOLLIO

> I know't, you must look out; 'tis every man's case.

ALIBIUS

> Here I do say must thy employment be:
> To watch her treadings, and in my absence
> Supply my place. 40

---

21 *this* i.e., an apparently incongruous marriage; or *this* = these (our different ages)

24–5 *Ay ... plants* Alibius might be cuckolded, so that his horns would raise him above his wife.

26 *feaï* The *r* is syllabic here; see Appendix, p. 121.

27 *ring* not just 'the token of my marriage' but also implying 'vagina' (cf. the refer- ence to *sockets* and *fingers* in I. i. 231–2); see *PDS* and *PSB*. Isabella gave him a ring in a double sense when she married him.

32 *conceiv'st me* catchest my meaning

33 *employment* (also) copulation

34 *At home* (also) in my wife's vagina. Cf. III. iii. 216.

36 *look out* (1) be vigilant; (2) go on brief excursions (to do business)

37 *case* 'plight' but also 'vagina', and probably 'brothel' (cf. *PDS*). Lollio agrees that Alibius must be vigilant – it's every man's plight; also, Alibius, like every man, is bound to go on brief sexual excursions (to 'Dryadës'; cf. III. iii. 51).

39 *treadings* (1) comings and goings; (2) acts of copulation

40 *Supply my place* (1) supervise her for me (Alibius' sense); (2) have intercourse with her (R's ironic sense, consistent with Lollio's later attempt)

LOLLIO

I'll do my best, sir; yet surely I cannot see who you should
have cause to be jealous of.

ALIBIUS

Thy reason for that, Lollio? 'Tis a comfortable question.

LOLLIO

We have but two sorts of people in the house, and both
under the whip: that's fools and madmen. The one has not   45
wit enough to be knaves, and the other not knavery
enough to be fools.

ALIBIUS

Ay, those are all my patients, Lollio.
I do profess the cure of either sort;
My trade, my living 'tis, I thrive by it.   50
But here's the care that mixes with my thrift:
The daily visitants, that come to see
My brainsick patiënts, I would not have
To see my wife. Gallánts I do observe
Of quick enticing eyes, rich in habits,   55
Of stature and proportion very comely:
These are most shrewd temptations, Lollio.

LOLLIO

They may be easily answered, sir. If they come to see the
fools and madmen, you and I may serve the turn, and let
my mistress alone; she's of neither sort.   60

ALIBIUS

'Tis a good ward; indeed, come they to see
Our madmen or our fools, let 'em see no more
Than what they come for. By that consequent

---

42 *jealous* suspicious
43 *comfortable* seeking reassurance
45 *fools* imbeciles
51 *care* worry
   thrift profit
52 *daily visitants* not just bona fide visitors but also people who came to view the
   inmates for amusement, as at Bethlehem Hospital ('Bedlam') in London, which R
   probably has in mind
52 ff. *see* often used with innuendo – 'for sexual purposes'
54 *Gallánts* fashionably dressed ladies' men
55 *habits* clothes
57 *shrewd* wicked; cunning; difficult to resist
59 *serve the turn* (1) be sufficient; (2) offer the copulation they seek
61 *ward* guard (in fencing)
63 *consequent* logical sequence

They must not see her: I'm sure she's no fool.

LOLLIO

And I'm sure she's no madman.   65

ALIBIUS

Hold that buckler fast, Lollio; my trust
Is on thee, and I account it firm and strong.
What hour is't, Lollio?

LOLLIO

Towards belly-hour, sir.

ALIBIUS

Dinner time? Thou mean'st twelve o'clock?   70

LOLLIO

Yes, sir, for every part has his hour. We wake at six and
look about us, that's eye-hour; at seven we should pray,
that's knee-hour; at eight walk, that's leg-hour; at nine
gather flowers and pluck a rose, that's nose-hour; at ten we
drink, that's mouth-hour; at eleven lay about us for vic-   75
tuals, that's hand-hour; at twelve go to dinner, that's
belly-hour.

ALIBIUS

Profoundly, Lollio! It will be long
Ere all thy scholars learn this lesson, and
I did look to have a new one ent'rëd; – stay,   80
I think my expectation is come home.

Enter PEDRO, *and* ANTONIO *like an idiot*

PEDRO

Save you, sir. My business speaks itself:
This sight takes off the labour of my tongue.

---

64 *I'm . . . fool* Alibius is no authority on fools, as he is in charge of the lunatics. The
reverse is true of Lollio. This crossing over (hypallage), while humorous, also
indicates how confused the characters are.

65 *no madman* (1) not mad; (2) not a mad *man*

66 *buckler* shield

71 *his* its

74 *pluck a rose* a vernacular term for urinate (in the garden-privy)

75 *lay about* look around

76 *dinner* It was common to have only two meals, dinner and supper.

81 sd *like an idiot* Antonio may have worn a long-skirted coat and a high pointed cap,
with a child's primer dangling from his wrist (as in the frontispiece to F. Kirk-
man's *The Wits*, 1672; cf. ed. J. J. Elson, 1932). But the question of his acting
matters more. It appears to be superficially persuasive, but probably not good
enough for Lollio, who suspects him of being a gentleman. If Lollio is allowed
such insight, then presumably so is the audience. Some of the characters are taken
in by Antonio, but he is not apparently capable of deluding many other than
himself; and it can only help our understanding of the play (and our excitement) if
we know from the start that he is acting a role.

ALIBIUS
Ay, ay, sir,
'Tis plain enough; you mean him for my patient.   85
PEDRO
And if your pains prove but commodious, to give but
some little strength to the sick and weak part of nature in
him, these are [*Gives money*] but patterns to show you of
the whole pieces that will follow to you, beside the charge
of diet, washing, and other necessaries fully defrayed.   90
ALIBIUS
Believe it, sir, there shall no care be wanting.
LOLLIO
Sir, an officer in this place may deserve something: the
trouble will pass through my hands.
PEDRO
'Tis fit something should come to your hands then,
sir.   [*Gives him money*]   95
LOLLIO
Yes, sir, 'tis I must keep him sweet and read to him. What
is his name?
PEDRO
His name is Antonio. Marry, we use but half to him, only
Tony.
LOLLIO
Tony, Tony; 'tis enough, and a very good name for a fool.   100
– What's your name, Tony?
ANTONIO
He, he, he! Well, I thank you, cousin! He, he, he!
LOLLIO
Good boy! Hold up your head. – He can laugh: I perceive
by that he is no beast.
PEDRO
Well, sir,   105
If you can raise him but to any height,

86 *commodious* beneficial
87 *the* Dilke (his Q; probably influenced by *sick* and *him*)
88 *patterns* samples (i.e., 'small change')
96 *sweet* pleasant; clean
98 *Marry* by Mary
99 *Tony* common for 'fool', with a hint of *to tony* = befool or swindle (cf. *PDS*)
101 *What's . . . Tony* Antonio responds with a foolish giggle ('He, he, he!') and the deliberately illogical 'Well', as though Lollio had asked him 'How are you?'
104 *no beast* reference to the belief (found in, e.g., Aristotle) that the ability to laugh sets humans apart from beasts
105–14 *Well . . . gentleman* Pedro is pretending, like Antonio, but perhaps expresses the genuine concerns of any friend. He hopes that Lollio will be able to raise the

Any degree of wit – might he attain
(As I might say) to creep but on all four
Towards the chair of wit, or walk on crutches,
'Twould add an honour to your worthy pains,   110
And a great family might pray for you,
To which he should be heir, had he discretion
To claim and guide his own; assure you, sir,
He is a gentleman.

LOLLIO

Nay, there's nobody doubted that; at first sight I knew   115
him for a gentleman – he looks no other yet.

PEDRO

Let him have good attendance and sweet lodging.

LOLLIO

As good as my mistress lies in, sir; and, as you allow us
time and means, we can raise him to the higher degree of
discretion.   120

PEDRO

Nay, there shall no cost want, sir.

LOLLIO

He will hardly be stretched up to the wit of a magnifico.

PEDRO

O no, that's not to be expected – far shorter will be
enough.

LOLLIO

I warrant you [I'll] make him fit to bear office in five   125
weeks; I'll undertake to wind him up to the wit of constable.

---

level of Antonio's understanding ('wit'), which would result in financial reward.
The irony (both comic and tragic) is that a fool cannot be made more intelligent, so
that Antonio will never have the 'discretion' (faculty of judgement) needed to
'guide his own' (manage his estate), leave alone satisfy the greed of his keepers,
who benefit from his presence anyway. Cf. also IV. iii. 211–12: perhaps we should
suspect any such attitude as Pedro espouses.

116 *he ... yet* (1) I can clearly see through his disguise and acting; (2) he is not a true
fool yet. Lollio's judgement 'at first sight' (l. 115) is sharper than that of, e.g.,
Alsemero in the main plot.

117 *sweet* (1) clean; (2) sexually sweet if Antonio succeeds in seducing Isabella

118 *As ... in* Lollio presumably guesses what Antonio is after, interpreting *lodging*
(l. 117) as 'bedroom' (cf. *OED*, 4).

121 *there ... want* all of your expenses will be repaid

122 *hardly* with difficulty
magnifico person of high judicial authority

125 *I ... I'll* Williams (Ile warrant you Q; probably arising from anticipation – Dyce:
I'll warrant you I'll)

126–7 *constable* proverbially stupid and satirized in plays (e.g., *Much Ado About Nothing*). Cf. 'You might be a constable for your wit' (*ODEP*, p. 140).

PEDRO

If it be lower than that it might serve turn.

LOLLIO

No, fie, to level him with a headborough, beadle, or
watchman were but little better than he is; constable I'll   130
able him. If he do come to be a justice afterwards, let him
thank the keeper. Or I'll go further with you – say I do
bring him up to my own pitch, say I make him as wise as
myself.

PEDRO

Why, there I would have it.   135

LOLLIO

Well, go to; either I'll be as arrant a fool as he, or he shall
be as wise as I, and then I think 'twill serve his turn.

PEDRO

Nay, I do like thy wit passing well.

LOLLIO

Yes, you may. Yet if I had not been a fool, I had had more
wit than I have too: remember what state you find me in.   140

PEDRO

I will, and so leave you. Your best cares, I beseech
you.   *Exit* PEDRO

ALIBIUS

Take you none with you; leave 'em all with us.

ANTONIO

O my cousin's gone! Cousin, cousin, O!

LOLLIO

Peace, peace, Tony! You must not cry, child – you must be   145
whipped if you do. Your cousin is here still: I am your
cousin, Tony.

ANTONIO

He, he! Then I'll not cry, if thou be'st my cousin! He, he,
he!

129 *headborough* petty constable
    beadle parish constable
130 *watchman* constable of the watch
131 *able him* make him fit for
    justice often seen as stupid (cf. 2 *Henry IV*)
133 *pitch* height
136 *arrant* unmitigated; wandering (lit. and fig.)
137 *wise* (also) clever
    serve his turn be sufficient for him
138 *passing* surpassingly
140 *state* as a keeper of fools – a job an intelligent person would not choose, and which
    reduces one's 'wit' (so he claims, seeking sympathy and money)
144 *cousin* kinsman; friend; with play on sense of 'strumpet' or 'lover' in l. 148

LOLLIO

I were best try his wit a little, that I may know what form   150
to place him in.

ALIBIUS

Ay, do, Lollio, do.

LOLLIO

I must ask him easy questions at first. – Tony, how many
true fingers has a tailor on his right hand?

ANTONIO

As many as on his left, cousin.   155

LOLLIO

Good. And how many on both?

ANTONIO

Two less than a deuce, cousin.

LOLLIO

Very well answered. I come to you again, cousin Tony.
How many fools goes to a wise man?

ANTONIO

Forty in a day sometimes, cousin.   160

LOLLIO

Forty in a day? How prove you that?

ANTONIO

All that fall out amongst themselves, and go to a lawyer to
be made friends.

LOLLIO

A parlous fool! He must sit in the fourth form at least, I
perceive that. – I come again, Tony. How many knaves   165
make an honest man?

ANTONIO

I know not that, cousin.

150 *try* test
    form school class
154 *true* honest
    tailor Cf., e.g., 'There is knavery in all trades, but most in tailors' (*ODEP*, p. 431).
155 That is, (1) five; (2) none.
157 That is, two less than two – none (possibly 'a deuce' also = a devil).
158 *Very well answered* i.e., if you had said 'ten' you would have lacked wit. (Lollio
    approves of Antonio's cynical view of evil and his verbal games.)
159 *goes to* (1) make up (Lollio); (2) visit (Antonio); common occurrence of singular
    verb with plural subject (cf. Abbott, §333 ff.)
162 *a lawyer* visited by fools, in the observation of the dramatists (M's mother was for
    long involved in lawsuits against his stepfather) and others. Cf. 'Lawyers' houses
    are built on the heads of fools' (*ODEP*, p. 447, which contains several proverbs
    showing lawyers, and not just their clients, in a bad light).
164 *parlous* i.e., perilous – dangerously cunning
166 *make* (1) create; (2) make up (cf. 'goes to', l. 159) – unanswerable in both senses
    this time

LOLLIO

No, the question is too hard for you. I'll tell you, cousin:
there's three knaves may make an honest man – a sergeant,
a jailor, and a beadle. The sergeant catches him, the jailor   170
holds him, and the beadle lashes him. And if he be not
honest then, the hangman must cure him.

ANTONIO

Ha, ha, ha! That's fine sport, cousin!

ALIBIUS

This was too deep a question for the fool, Lollio.

LOLLIO

Yes, this might have served yourself, though I say't. –   175
Once more, and you shall go play, Tony.

ANTONIO

Ay, play at push-pin, cousin, ha, he!

LOLLIO

So thou shalt. Say how many fools are here.

ANTONIO

Two, cousin: thou and I.

LOLLIO

Nay, y'are too forward there, Tony. Mark my question: 180
how many fools and knaves are here? A fool before a
knave, a fool behind a knave, between every two fools a
knave: how many fools, how many knaves?

ANTONIO

I never learnt so far, cousin.

ALIBIUS

Thou putt'st too hard questions to him, Lollio.   185

LOLLIO

I'll make him understand it easily. – Cousin, stand there.

ANTONIO

Ay, cousin.

---

173 *sport* theatrical performance (also 'jest' and 'pastime') provided by Lollio himself
as well as the sergeant, etc.

175 *this ... yourself* this would have done for you (as questioner or pupil), because it
concerns knaves and is 'deep' in the sense of 'crafty' (not just 'difficult' or 'profound')

177 *push-pin* (1) child's game; (2) copulation (common; in the game one pushed a pin –
a frequent bawdy term for 'penis')

180 *y'are ... there* i.e., you are a bit too rash and cheeky ('forward') this time because
your answer includes me but excludes Alibius. Hence Lollio asks a different question, presented as though it were the same.

181–3 *A fool before ... knaves* The actors must be in the order Lollio, Alibius,
Antonio, as Lollio's question could make no sense if Alibius were not in the
middle.

185 Perhaps Alibius senses what Lollio is aiming at.

LOLLIO
Master, stand you next the fool.
ALIBIUS
Well, Lollio?
LOLLIO
Here's my place. Mark now, Tony, there['s] a fool before a   190
knave.
ANTONIO
That's I, cousin.
LOLLIO
Here's a fool behind a knave, that's I; and between us two
fools there is a knave, that's my master. 'Tis but we three,
that's all.   195
ANTONIO
We three, we three, cousin!   MADMEN *within*
1 [MADMAN] *within*
Put's head i' th' pillory, the bread's too little.
2 [MADMAN] *within*
Fly, fly, and he catches the swallow.

190 *there's* Dilke's emendation
192 *That's I* Antonio co-operates because (1) he supposedly *is* a fool and (2) the
arrangement turns Alibius into a knave, not him. Viewed differently, he and
Lollio 'are really the knaves who are trying to make a fool of Alibius' (Bawcutt),
who thus ends up doubly humiliated and exposed.
194 *we three* 'A stock joke was a picture of two fools, entitled "We Three", the third of
course being the spectator' (Spencer); the basic idea is that two 'fools' make a fool
of an unsuspecting third person (cf. *Twelfth Night* II. iii. 16–17). R may intend
that Antonio and Lollio are perceptive and clever yet ironically foolish in wasting
their intelligence.
196 sd *within* i.e., possibly, within the 'inner stage', a space behind the main platform
normally closed off by a door or curtain; or else the expression refers more generally to the concealed area behind the façade at the back of the stage. (See
Introduction, 'The Play in Performance'.)
197 The first speaker is obviously hungry ('the bread's too little'), hence suggesting
that Alibius' (or perhaps Lollio's) head be put 'i' th' pillory'.
198 'The Madman imagines he has seen fulfilled the ironic proverb "Fly and you will
catch the swallow" (Tilley, S 1024)' – Frost. Thus the madness would consist of
the character's imagining that something is possible which is not, and such a
misunderstanding of reality is indeed characteristic of madness in the play (con-
trasted with the folly – i.e., lack of intelligence – which we have just seen demon-
strated). However, *swallow* no doubt also puns on 'swallow' *OED sb.*², 4.b,
'appetite for food and drink', showing that a genuine and immediate reality under-
lies the speaker's supposed (and partly real) insanity.

3 [MADMAN] *within*

Give her more onion, or the devil put the rope about her
crag.   200

LOLLIO

You may hear what time of day it is: the chimes of Bedlam
goes.

ALIBIUS

Peace, peace, or the wire comes!

3 [MADMAN] *within*

Cat-whore, cat-whore, her permasant, her permasant!

ALIBIUS

Peace, I say! – Their hour's come; they must be fed, 205
Lollio.

LOLLIO

There's no hope of recovery of that Welsh madman was
undone by a mouse that spoiled him a permasant; lost his
wits for't.

ALIBIUS

Go [you] to your charge, Lollio; I'll to mine.   210

LOLLIO

Go you to your madmen's ward; let me alone with your
fools.

ALIBIUS

And remember my last charge, Lollio.   *Exit*

LOLLIO

Of which your patients do you think I am? – Come, Tony,

199–200 This speaker, like the others, wants his hunger satisfied, although again the
point is made in language which is not immediately intelligible, and his mind's
contact with reality is tenuous. He asks for more onion (*her* = me – use of stage-
Welsh), which is a proverbially meagre food (cf. 'If thou hast not a capon feed on
an onion', *ODEP*, p. 102), or else let the devil strangle him (*crag* = neck) with a
rope (of onions, or the hangman's). His obsession with food is further illustrated
in subsequent speeches.

201 *chimes of Bedlam* the peculiarly expressed requests for food, at noon, from these
inmates of a madhouse reminiscent of Bethlehem Hospital

203 *wire* whip of wire

204 The Welshman complains about a cat who has behaved like a whore in disloyally
allowing a mouse to steal his (*her* = my) Parmesan (*permasant*) cheese (see Lollio's
next speech). Obviously his present hunger revives in him the memory of an
earlier trauma.

207–9 *There's . . . for't* Recovery might ironically be possible if only the patient were
given cheese, of which the Welsh were considered very fond (cf. 'Welsh rabbit';
examples in Bawcutt). His appetite seems innocuous compared with the greed of
his keepers or the lust of, e.g., Beatrice.

210 *you* Craik (perhaps superfluously, but cf. 'you' – 'I', and l. 211)

213 *my last charge* i.e., to spy on Isabella

214 *Of . . . am* i.e., a madman or a fool

you must amongst your school-fellows now. There's 215
pretty scholars amongst 'em, I can tell you; there's some of
'em at *stultus, stulta, stultum*.

ANTONIO
I would see the madmen, cousin, if they would not bite
me.

LOLLIO
No, they shall not bite thee, Tony.   220

ANTONIO
They bite when they are at dinner, do they not, coz?

LOLLIO
They bite at dinner indeed, Tony. Well, I hope to get
credit by thee; I like thee the best of all the scholars that
ever I brought up, and thou shalt prove a wise man, or I'll
prove a fool myself.   *Exeunt* 225

Act II [, Scene i]

Enter BEATRICE *and* JASPERINO *severally*

BEATRICE
O sir, I am ready now for that fair service
Which makes the name of friend sit glorious on you!
Good angels and this conduct be your guide;
                              [*Gives a paper*]
Fitness of time and place is there set down, sir.

JASPERINO
The joy I shall return rewards my service.   *Exit*   5

BEATRICE
How wise is Alsemero in his friend!
It is a sign he makes his choice with judgement.

216 *pretty* (also) clever
217 *stultus ... stultum* i.e., some can use the Latin word for 'stupid' in the nominative
   (referring to themselves), in the masculine form, or feminine, or neuter
222 *bite* perhaps = steal. Probably *bite at dinner* has a sexual innuendo, the appetites
   being often associated.
Act II, Scene i   author: Middleton; place: Vermandero's castle
   sd *severally* from different directions
   1 *that fair service* Ostensibly as performed by Jasperino, but, inasmuch as the pos-
     itioning of the word may allude to *her* service, M introduces perhaps already the
     sense of 'sexual service' (copulation) which the word comes to acquire in so many
     places (cf. Ricks, pp. 296 ff.) – often without the conscious awareness of the
     speakers.
   3 *conduct* sheet with directions
   5 *return* take back to Alsemero

Then I appear in nothing more approved
Than making choice of him;
For 'tis a principle, he that can choose   10
That bosom well who of his thoughts partakes,
Proves most discreet in every choice he makes.
Methinks I love now with the eyes of judgement,
And see the way to merit, clearly see it.
A true deserver like a diamond sparkles;   15
In darkness you may see him, that's in absence,
Which is the greatest darkness falls on love:
Yet is he best discerned then,
With intellectual eyesight. What's Piracquo
My father spends his breath for? And his blessing   20
Is only mine as I regard his name;
Else it goes from me, and turns head against me,
Transformed into a curse. Some speedy way
Must be rememb'rëd – he's so forward too,
So urgent that way, scarce allows me breath   25
To speak to my new comforts.

                    Enter DE FLORES

DE FLORES [*Aside*]   Yonder's she.
    Whatever ails me, now a-late especially
    I can as well be hanged as refrain seeing her.
    Some twenty times a day, nay not so little,
    Do I force errands, frame ways and excuses   30
    To come into her sight – and I have small reason for't,
    And less encouragement: for she baits me still
    Every time worse than other, does profess herself
    The cruellest enemy to my face in town,
    At no hand can abide the sight of me,   35
    As if danger or ill luck hung in my looks.

   8 *approved* justified
  11 *bosom* bosom friend
  14 *to merit* i.e., towards recognizing merit
  15 Diamonds were supposed to be luminous and magical.
  17 *falls* i.e., that falls
  20–1 *And . . . name* his blessing is given only if I respect his name by marrying well
      (*his* = Vermandero)
  22 *turns head* directs its power
  23–4 *Some . . . rememb'rëd* I must think of a quick way of solving this problem
  24 *he* the impatient and one-sided Vermandero (cf. I. i. 187)
  26 *my new comforts* as derived from Alsemero. But note De Flores' entrance.
  27 *a-late* of late
  32 *baits* (1) taunts like a bull (cf. l. 80); (2) tempts
  35 *At no hand* on no account
  36 *As . . . looks* Cf. V. iii. 154–5 (and ll. 89–90 here).

I must confess my face is bad enough,
But I know far worse has better fortune,
And not endured alone, but doted on:
And yet such pick-haired faces, chins like witches', 40
Here and there five hairs, whispering in a corner
As if they grew in fear one of another,
Wrinkles like troughs, where swine-deformity swills
The tears of perjury that lie there like wash
Fallen from the slimy and dishonest eye – 45
Yet such a one plucks sweets without restraint,
And has the grace of beauty to his sweet.
Though my hard fate has thrust me out to servitude,
I tumbled into th' world a gentleman.
She turns her blessèd eye upon me now, 50
And I'll endure all storms before I part with't.

BEATRICE [*Aside*]
Again!
This ominous, ill-faced fellow more disturbs me
Than all my other passions.

DE FLORES [*Aside*]   Now't begins again;
I'll stand this storm of hail though the stones pelt me. 55

BEATRICE
Thy business? What's thy business?

DE FLORES [*Aside*]   Soft and fair;
I cannot part so soon now.

BEATRICE [*Aside*]   The villain's fixed. –
[*To* DE FLORES] Thou standing toad-pool!

DE FLORES [*Aside*]   The shower falls amain now.

BEATRICE
Who sent thee? What's thy errand? Leave my sight!

---

40 *pick-haired* i.e., with a beard consisting of a few hairs like picks (sharp points –
    often seen as phallic; cf. H)
    chins i.e., with chins
44 *wash* watery discharge
46 *plucks* Dilke (pluckt Q)
47 *to his sweet* (1) in his sweetheart's eyes; (2) as his sweetheart; (3) for his dessert
    (with 'grace'= thanksgiving) – linking devotion, food, and sex ('grace' also =
    sexual favour)
53 *ominous* Cf. I. i. 2.
54 *passions* (1) sufferings; (2) vehement emotions; (3) sexual desires (ironic)
56 *Soft and fair* proverbial: 'Fair and softly goes far' (*ODEP*, p. 238)
58 *standing toad-pool* stagnant and foul water which exudes toads, etc.; reference to
    De Flores' skin (cf. *scurvy*, II. ii. 77)
    shower Dilke (showre Q; perhaps a monosyllable)
    amain with full force

DE FLORES
  My Lord your father charged me to deliver   60
  A message to you.
BEATRICE   What, another since?
  Do't and be hanged then; let me be rid of thee.
DE FLORES
  True service merits mercy.
BEATRICE   What's thy message?
DE FLORES
  Let beauty settle but in patiënce,
  You shall hear all.
BEATRICE   A dallying, trifling torment!   65
DE FLORES
  Signor Alonzo de Piracquo, lady,
  Sole brother to Tomazo de Piracquo –
BEATRICE
  Slave, when wilt make an end?
DE FLORES [*Aside*]   Too soon I shall.
BEATRICE
  What all this while of him?
DE FLORES   The said Alonzo,
  With the foresaid Tomazo –
BEATRICE   Yet again?   70
DE FLORES
  Is new alighted.
BEATRICE   Vengeance strike the news!
  Thou thing most loathed, what cause was there in this
  To bring thee to my sight?
DE FLORES   My lord your father
  Charged me to seek you out.
BEATRICE   Is there no other
  To send his errand by?
DE FLORES   It seems 'tis my luck   75
  To be i' th' way still.
BEATRICE   Get thee from me!
DE FLORES [*Aside*]   So! –
  Why, am not I an ass to dévise ways
  Thus to be railed at? I must see her still;
  I shall have a mad qualm within this hour again,

61 *since* Cf. I. i. 92.
65 *dallying* (1) chatting idly (main sense); (2) playing amorously
   trifling time-wasting and frivolous
   torment a reference to his speech
68 *wilt* Dilke (wil't Q)
78 *still* all the time
79 *qualm* an attack of illness – here of lust

I know't, and, like a common Garden-bull,   80
I do but take breath to be lugged again.
What this may bode I know not. I'll despair the less
Because there's daily precedents of bad faces
Beloved beyond all reason. These foul chops
May come into favour one day 'mongst his fellows.   85
Wrangling has proved the mistress of good pastime;
As children cry themselves asleep, I ha' seen
Women have chid themselves a-bed to men.

                                            Exit DE FLORES

BEATRICE
I never see this fellow but I think
Of some harm towards me: danger's in my mind still,   90
I scarce leave trembling of an houȑ after.
The next good mood I find my father in,
I'll get him quite discarded. – O, I was
Lost in this small disturbance and forgot
Affliction's fiercer torrent that now comes   95
To bear down all my comforts!

                Enter VERMANDERO, ALONZO, TOMAZO

VERMANDERO   Y'are both welcome,
But an especial one belongs to you, sir,
To whose most noble name our love presents
The addition of a son, our son Alonzo.
ALONZO
The treasury of honour cannot bring forth   100
A title I should more rejoice in, sir.
VERMANDERO
You have improved it well. – Daughter, prepare:
The day will steal upon thee suddenly.
BEATRICE [*Aside*]
Howe'er, I will be sure to keep the night,

80 *a common Garden-bull* an ordinary bull at Paris Garden (on the Bankside near the
    Globe Theatre), an arena in which bulls and bears were baited
81 *lugged* pulled by the ear or hair (when baited by dogs)
84 *chops* his jaws/mouth; thus his cheeks or even the whole face
85 *his* = 'its', or 'theirs', referring to the ugly *chops*
88 *have* i.e., who have; common omission of relative (cf. Abbott, §244)
91 *of* for
    houȑ perhaps a monosyllable, if *after* is trochaic
97 *one* i.e., welcome (antecedent implied)
99 *addition* i.e., the additional title
100 *treasury of honour* 'the whole compendium of honorific titles' (Frost). The lan-
    guage is formal here – cf. Vermandero's royal plural in l. 98.
102 *improved* either 'enhanced' or (cf. *OED* improve *v.*³, 1) 'proved correct'
104 *keep the night* 'avoid that day, not see it dawn' (Gomme); or perhaps rather 'keep

If it should come so near me.

[BEATRICE *and* VERMANDERO *talk apart*]

TOMAZO   Alonzo.
ALONZO   Brother?   105
TOMAZO
In troth I see small welcome in her eye.
ALONZO
Fie, you are too severe a censurer
Of love in all points; there's no bringing on you
If lovers should mark everything a fault
Affection would be like an ill-set book   110
Whose faults might prove as big as half the volume.
BEATRICE
That's all I do entreat.
VERMANDERO   It is but reasonable.
I'll see what my son says to 't. – Son Alonzo,
Here's a motion made but to reprieve
A maidenhead three days longer. The request   115
Is not far out of reason, for indeed
The former time is pinching.
ALONZO   Though my joys
Be set back so much time as I could wish
They had been forward, yet, since she desires it,
The time is set as pleasing as before;   120
I find no gladness wanting.
VERMANDERO   May I ever
Meet it in that point still. Y'are nobly welcome, sirs.

Exeunt VERMANDERO *and* BEATRICE

TOMAZO
So. Did you mark the dulness of her parting now?

---

    the night of the wedding to myself – deny myself to Alonzo' (ironic in that she
    proceeds to deny herself to Alsemero)

107 *censurer* judge, critic

108 *points* i.e., 'respects'; also 'punctuation marks'
    bringing on you Dilke inserted a semi-colon here, perhaps correctly, with
    phrase = 'making you see sense' and 'exciting you sexually' (*PDS*). But Q is
    intelligible: 'one cannot get you to see that if . . .'

110 *ill-set* badly typeset

111 *faults* (list of) misprints

114 *motion* simply 'proposal', or a formal application made to a court or judge (so used
    by R in *A Fair Quarrel*, ed. R. V. Holdsworth, 1974, I. i. 225)

117 *the former time* Cf. I. i. 188.
    joys with implication 'of sexual intimacy' (*PSB*)

121 *wanting* lacking

121–2 *May . . . still* may I for ever satisfy your gladness in just this way

ALONZO

What dulness? Thou art so exceptious still!

TOMAZO

Why, let it go then. I am but a fool   125
To mark your harms so heedfully.

ALONZO   Where's the oversight?

TOMAZO

Come, your faith's cozened in her, strongly cozened:
Unsettle your affection with all speed
Wisdom can bring it to; your peace is ruined else.
Think what a torment 'tis to marry one   130
Whose heart is leapt into another's bosom:
If ever pleasure she receive from thee,
It comes not in thy name, or of thy gift –
She lies but with another in thine arms,
He the half father unto all thy children   135
In the conception; if he get 'em not,
She helps to get 'em for him, in his passions;
And how dangerous
And shameful her restraint may go in time to
It is not to be thought on without sufferings.   140

ALONZO

You speak as if she loved some other then.

TOMAZO

Do you apprehend so slowly?

ALONZO   Nay, and that
Be your fear only, I am safe enough.
Preserve your friendship and your counsel, brother,
For times of more distress; I should depart   145
An enemy, a dangerous, deadly one
To any but thyself that should but think

124 *exceptious* given to making objections
126 *the* i.e., my
127 *cozened* deceived
132 *pleasure* sexual enjoyment
134 'Although physically she sleeps with you, her imagination actually makes her lie
    with her lover.'
135–7 Beatrice would experience her lover's passions even when physically in her
    husband's arms, the imagined sexual union with her lover being of greater impor-
    tance, and making the lover half-father.
138–40 'And, if she attempted to restrain herself under these conditions, it is painful
    to consider how dangerous and shameful her behaviour may eventually become.'
    Presumably Tomazo means that Beatrice would make a conscious effort not to act
    on her feelings for her lover, but would fail. Alternatively, *her restraint* = 'if you
    attempted to restrain her'.
142 *and* if

She knew the meaning of inconstancy,
Much less the use and practice. Yet w'are friends:
Pray let no more be urged – I can endure   150
Much, till I meet an injury to her,
Then I am not myself. Farewell, sweet brother;
How much w'are bound to heaven to depart lovingly!
                                                        Exit

TOMAZO
Why, here is love's tame madness: thus a man
Quickly steals into his vexatïon.   *Exit*   155

[Act II, Scene ii]

Enter DIAPHANTA *and* ALSEMERO

DIAPHANTA
The place is my charge; you have kept your hour,
And the reward of a just meeting bless you!
I hear my lady coming. Cómplete gentleman,
I dare not be too busy with my praises;
Th'are dangerous things to deal with.   *Exit*
ALSEMERO   This goes well.   5
These women are the ladies' cabinets;
Things of most precious trust are lock[ed] into 'em.

Enter BEATRICE

BEATRICE
I have within mine eye all my desires;
Requests that holy prayers ascend heaven for,

---

149 *use* also 'sexual enjoyment' (*PSB*; *OED*, 3.b)
          Yet as yet, still
153 'How indebted we are to heaven for parting as friends' (ironic in view of III. ii).
154 *madness* This has the same rather simple sense as *mad* in I. i. 136 – but Alonzo also
          confuses his image of Beatrice with the reality as perceived by Tomazo.
155 *steals . . . vexatïon* i.e., slides into his suffering without noticing it
Scene ii   author: Middleton; place: Vermandero's castle
   1 *my charge* my responsibility
   3 *Cómplete* perfect
   4 *praises* i.e., of you
   5 *dangerous* as Beatrice might hear them
          to deal with to have dealings with; with a play on sense of 'copulate' (*OED*, 11.b) –
          things perhaps = sexual organs (cf. H). Diaphanta's punning may be intentional.
   6 *cabinets* secret receptacles
   7 *locked* Dilke: lock'd (lock Q)

And brings 'em down to furnish our deféts,   10
Come not more sweet to our necessities
Than thou unto my wishes.

ALSEMERO   W'are so like
In our expressions, lady, that unless I borrow
The same words, I shall never find their equals.

                                              [*Kisses her*]
BEATRICE
How happy were this meeting, this embrace,   15
If it were free from envy! This poor kiss,
It has an enemy, a hateful one,
That wishes poison to't. How well were I now
If there were none such name known as Piracquo,
Nor no such tie as the command of parents!   20
I should be but too much blessëd.

ALSEMERO   One good service
Would strike off both your fears, and I'll go near it too,
Since you are so distressed. Remove the cause,
The command ceases; so there's two fears blown out
With one and the same blast.

BEATRICE   Pray let me find you, sir;   25
What might that service be, so strangely happy?

ALSEMERO
The honourablest piece about man, valour.
I'll send a challenge to Piracquo instantly.

BEATRICE
How? Call you that extinguishing of fear
When 'tis the only way to keep it flaming?   30
Are not you ventured in the actiön,
That's all my joys and comforts? Pray, no more, sir.

---

10 *brings* The subject is *holy prayers* (l. 9) although the verb is singular (cf. Abbott, §333 ff.), and *'em* is in effect superfluous: 'Requests which holy prayers ascend to heaven for and which they bring down – once granted – to supply what we lack ...'

16 *envy* enmity

17 *an enemy* Alonzo, who would wish the kiss to be poisonous if he knew of it

22 *strike off* the way fetters are struck off, or items on a list of debts
   I'll ... it i.e., I'll come near to spelling it out

23–4 *Remove ... ceases* i.e., if you get rid of Alonzo ('the cause'), you also eliminate your father's command (cf. 'Take away the cause and the effect must cease', *ODEP*, p. 112)

25 *the same blast* The image is of blowing out two lights at once (Sampson), and continued by Beatrice in ll. 29–30; *blast* = puff of air.
   find i.e., understand

26 *happy* fortunate in its results

27 *about* Dilke ('bout Q – resulting in a final trochee and a jerky rhythm, but not necessarily incorrect); *piece about* = part of

Say you prevailed, you're danger's and not mine then:
The law would claim you from me, or obscurity
Be made the grave to bury you alive.   35
I'm glad these thoughts come forth; O keep not one
Of this condition, sir! Here was a course
Found to bring sorrow on her way to death:
The tears would ne'er ha' dried till dust had choked
    'em.
Blood-guiltiness becomes a fouler visage;   40
[*Aside*] – And now I think on one: I was too blame
I ha' marred so good a market with my scorn.
'T had been done questionless: the ugliest creature
Creation framed for some use! Yet to see
I could not mark so much where it should be!   45
ALSEMERO
Lady –
BEATRICE [*Aside*] Why, men of art make much of poison,
Keep one to expel another. Where was my art?
ALSEMERO
Lady, you hear not me.
BEATRICE   I do especially, sir.
The present times are not so sure of our side
As those hereafter may be; we must use 'em then   50
As thrifty folks their wealth, sparingly now,
Till the time opens.

33 *you're* Dyce (your Q)
34 *The law* i.e., against duelling
    obscurity as, at best, he would be a fugitive from justice
37 *condition* quality
38 *on . . . death* by giving birth to sorrow, as the start of its long life, only extinguished
    once Beatrice herself dies
41 *one* i.e., a fouler face, that of De Flores
    too blame so Q – i.e., 'too blameworthy'. The phrase is a misconstruction of 'to
    blame' (cf. Williams).
42 She means 'in that, through my contempt for him, I have spoiled the good market
    (De Flores) where I might have bought a murder'; cf. 'The market is marred'
    (*ODEP*, p. 512).
43 *'T had . . . questionless* 'He'd have done it without question' (Black).
44 *for some use* a reference to the common belief that everything in nature has been
    created for *some* useful purpose
45 *where . . . be* what use might be found for De Flores
46 *art* science; cunning
47 *Keep . . . another* Cf. 'One poison drives out another' (*ODEP*, p. 597).
48 *I do especially* Beatrice doubtless means 'I interpret your meaning in a special way'
    – referring back to Alsemero's earlier suggestion that Alonzo might be removed
    (l. 23).
49 *sure of* securely on   52 *opens* becomes favourable

ALSEMERO   You teach wisdom, lady.
BEATRICE
  Within there! Diaphanta!

                    Enter DIAPHANTA

DIAPHANTA   Do you call, madam?
BEATRICE
  Perfect your service, and conduct this gentleman
  The private way you brought him.
DIAPHANTA   I shall, madam.   55
ALSEMERO
  My love's as firm as love e'er built upon.
                    Exeunt DIAPHANTA *and* ALSEMERO

                    Enter DE FLORES

DE FLORES [*Aside*]
  I have watched this meeting, and do wonder much
  What shall become of t'other; I'm sure both
  Cannot be served unless she transgress. Happily
  Then I'll put in for one; for if a woman   60
  Fly from one point, from him she makes a husband,
  She spreads and mounts then, like arithmetic,
  One, ten, a hundred, a thousand, ten thousand –
  Proves in time sutler to an army royal.
  Now do I look to be most richly railed at,   65
  Yet I must see her.
BEATRICE [*Aside*]   Why, put case I loathed him
  As much as youth and beauty hates a sepulchre,
  Must I needs show it? Cannot I keep that secret,
  And serve my turn upon him? See, he's here.

54–5 *Perfect . . . him* Ricks points out that indeed Diaphanta will come to perfect
  (perhaps stressed 'pérfect') her service (i.e., copulation) with Alsemero (in a way
  that Beatrice does not suspect), and suggests a sexual implication in 'private way'.
56 Presumably M indicates that no love can be firmly built upon, and least of all
  Alsemero's. De Flores' entry is ironic.
58 *t'other* Alonzo
59 *Happily* (read 'hap'ly') perhaps; with luck
60 *I'll . . . one* apply for a share, with innuendo of a share of Beatrice's sexual favour.
  For the sexual sense of *put in* see also IV.iii.36.
61 *point* (also) penis
62 *spreads; mounts* The metaphor alludes to birds; there are obvious bawdy innu-
  endoes.
64 *sutler* (1) camp-follower selling supplies to soldiers; (2) whore (H)
66 *put case* suppose
69 *serve . . . him* (chiefly, and as she intends) use him for my own purpose – but cf.
  I.ii.59, and for *secret* (l. 68) cf. I.ii.3. The audience has just heard De Flores'
  'served' (l. 59) and other sexual puns.

    [*To him*] De Flores.
DE FLORES [*Aside*]   Ha, I shall run mad with joy!   70
  She called me fairly by my name, De Flores,
  And neither rogue nor rascal.
BEATRICE   What ha' you done
  To your face a-late? Y'have met with some good
    physician;
  Y'have pruned yourself methinks: you were not wont
  To look so amorously.
DE FLORES [*Aside*]   Not I; –   75
  'Tis the same physnomy, to a hair and pimple,
  Which she called scurvy scarce an hour ago.
  How is this?
BEATRICE   Come hither, nearer, man!
DE FLORES [*Aside*]
  I'm up to the chin in heaven.
BEATRICE   Turn, let me see.
  Faugh, 'tis but the heat of the liver, I perceive't;   80
  I thought it had been worse.
DE FLORES [*Aside*]   Her fingers touched me!
  She smells all amber.
BEATRICE
  I'll make a water for you shall cleanse this
  Within a fortnight.
DE FLORES   With your own hands, lady?
BEATRICE
  Yes, mine own, sir; in a work of cure   85
  I'll trust no other.
DE FLORES [*Aside*]   'Tis half an act of pleasure
  To hear her talk thus to me.
BEATRICE   When w'are used
  To a hard face, it is not so unpleasing;

---

74 *pruned* preened, adorned (used of a bird and its feathers)
75 *amorously* (1) lovable; (2) (ironically) lustful
76 *physnomy* physiognomy (i.e., the face)
77 *scurvy* adjective. See *OED, scurf*, 'A morbid condition of the skin, esp. of the head,
    characterized by the separation of branny scales, without inflammation' (*sb.*¹, 1);
    or just 'scabby', without specification of the disease – perhaps mange.
80 *the liver* traditionally the seat of love and violent passions; an ironically appro-
    priate speech (Williams)
82 *amber* i.e., ambergris, used in perfume
83 *a water* 'The preparation of household remedies was an Elizabethan feminine
    accomplishment' (Sampson); here = 'a lotion'.
86 *pleasure* with subsidiary sense of sexual enjoyment; *act* often = copulation (*PSB*)
88 *hard* ugly
    it is Dilke ('tis Q – metrically awkward)

    It mends still in opinion, hourly mends,
    I see it by experience.
DE FLORES [*Aside*]   I was blest   90
    To light upon this minute; I'll make use on't.
BEATRICE
    Hardness becomes the visage of a man well:
    It argues service, resolution, manhood,
    If cause were of employment.
DE FLORES   'Twould be soon seen,
    If e'er your ladyship had cause to use it.   95
    I would but wish the honour of a service
    So happy as that mounts to.
BEATRICE
    We shall try you. – O my De Flores!
DE FLORES [*Aside*]   How's that?
    She calls me hers already, 'my' De Flores!
    [*To* BEATRICE] You were about to sigh out somewhat,
        madam?   100
BEATRICE
    No, was I? I forgot. – O!
DE FLORES   There 'tis again,
    The very fellow on't.
BEATRICE   You are too quick, sir.
DE FLORES
    There's no excuse for't now; I heard it twice, madam.
    That sigh would fain have utterance; take pity on't,
    And lend it a free word. 'Las, how it labours   105
    For liberty! I hear the murmur yet
    Beat at your bosom.
BEATRICE   Would creatiön –
DE FLORES
    Ay, well said, that's it.

---

90 *I . . . experience* 'Ironically, Beatrice traps herself here by a pretended change'
    (Harrier).
94 *employment* (also) copulation. M (more so than his characters, even De Flores)
    incorporates an abundance of sexual puns in these speeches, playing on such
    senses as 'service' = sexual attention, 'honour' = pudendum, 'mount' and 'use'
    = copulate with – all as elsewhere in the play.
98 *try* (also) take the sexual measure of (cf. Ricks and H)
    O with a sigh
102 *on't* i.e., of your previous sigh
    quick (also) sexually vigorous (H). De Flores obviously interprets the sighs as
    signs of sexual ardour – correctly so in view of Beatrice's play-acting and (ironi-
    cally) her unconscious libido.
103 *for't now; I* Dilke (for't, now I Q)
107 *creatiön* taken as 'procreation' by De Flores

BEATRICE   Had formed me man.
DE FLORES
  Nay, that's not it.
BEATRICE   O, 'tis the soul of freedom!
  I should not then be forced to marry one   110
  I hate beyond all depths; I should have power
  Then to oppose my loathings, nay, remove 'em
  For ever from my sight.
DE FLORES   O blest occasion! –
  Without change to your sex you have your wishes.
  Claim so much man in me.
BEATRICE   In thee, De Flores?   115
  There's small cause for that.
DE FLORES   Put it not from me,
  It's a service that I kneel for to you.   [Kneels]
BEATRICE
  You are too violent to mean faithfully.
  There's horror in my service, blood and danger;
  Can those be things to sue for?
DE FLORES   If you knew   120
  How sweet it were to me to be employed
  In any act of yours, you would say then
  I failed, and used not reverence enough
  When I receive[d] the charge on't.
BEATRICE [Aside]   This is much,
    methinks;
  Belike his wants are greedy, and to such   125
  Gold tastes like angels' food. [To DE FLORES] Rise.
DE FLORES
  I'll have the work first.
BEATRICE [Aside]   Possible his need
  Is strong upon him. [Gives him money] – There's to
    encourage thee;
  As thou art forward and thy service dangerous,
  Thy reward shall be precious.
DE FLORES   That I have thought on.   130

112 *remove* Cf. Alsemero in l. 23.
113 *occasion* opportunity
118 *to mean faithfully* to intend truthfully what you say
122–4 *you . . . on't* then – in that imaginary situation – you would say that I failed to use
     enough reverence at the time you gave me my instructions
124 *received* Dilke: receiv'd (receive Q)
125 *Belike . . . greedy* perhaps his needs are those of a hungry man
126 *angels' food* the biblical 'manna', food from heaven (Psalm 78:25)
127 *Possible* possibly; typically an adverb with adjectival form (cf. Abbott, §1)
129 'To the degree that you are courageous and your service is dangerous . . .'
130 *Thy reward* She means 'financially', but De Flores takes her to say 'sexually'.

I have assured myself of that beforehand,
And know it will be precious; the thought ravishes!
BEATRICE
  Then take him to thy fury.
DE FLORES   I thirst for him.
BEATRICE
  Alonzo de Piracquo.
DE FLORES   His end's upon him,
  He shall be seen no more.   [*Rises*]
BEATRICE   How lovely now   135
  Dost thou appear to me! Never was man
  Dearlier rewarded.
DE FLORES   I do think of that.
BEATRICE
  Be wondrous careful in the execution.
DE FLORES
  Why, are not both our lives upon the cast?
BEATRICE
  Then I throw all my fears upon thy service.   140
DE FLORES
  They ne'er shall rise to hurt you.
BEATRICE   When the deed's done,
  I'll furnish thee with all things for thy flight;
  Thou may'st live bravely in another country.
DE FLORES
  Ay, ay, we'll talk of that hereafter.
BEATRICE [*Aside*]   I shall rid myself
  Of two inveterate loathings at one time,   145
  Piracquo, and his dog-face.   *Exit*
DE FLORES   O my blood!
  Methinks I feel her in mine arms already,

---

131 De Flores presumably means that he is joyfully aware that he will deflower a
    virgin (cf. his later comment, III.iv. 116–17); the audience would believe that he is
    convinced of her virginity because that has been more than once referred to (the
    first time in his presence, I.i. 192). Hence the thought of his reward *ravishes*
    (l. 132) – 'enraptures' and 'rapes' (a sense clearly not obvious to Beatrice).
133 *I . . . him* The image of intense appetite unites De Flores' violence and his longing
    for Beatrice; cf. III. iv. 107–8.
135 *lovely* kind; worthy of love; attractive; amorous
137 *rewarded* than you shall be
139 *cast* throw of the dice (so in l. 140 *throw* = stake)
141 *deed* (1) the murder; (2) (unconscious pun) copulation
143 *bravely* splendidly
146 *his dog-face* an ironical title for De Flores (Bawcutt), or simply 'De Flores' face,
    which looks like that of a dog' (cf. 'dog-faced baboon')
    blood (especially, here) sexual desire; violence seems implied. Cf. *deed*, l. 141.

Her wanton fingers combing out this beard,
And, being pleasëd, praising this bad face.
Hunger and pleasure, they'll commend sometimes   150
Slovenly dishes, and feed heartily on 'em,
Nay, which is stranger, refuse daintier for 'em.
Some women are odd feeders. – I'm too loud:
Here comes the man goes supperless to bed,
Yet shall not rise tomorrow to his dinner.   155

Enter ALONZO

ALONZO
    De Flores.
DE FLORES   My kind, honourable lord?
ALONZO
    I am glad I ha' met with thee.
DE FLORES   Sir.
ALONZO   Thou canst show me
    The full strength of the castle?
DE FLORES   That I can, sir.
ALONZO
    I much desire it.
DE FLORES   And if the ways and straits
    Of some of the passages be not too tedious for you,   160
    I will assure you, worth your time and sight, my lord.
ALONZO
    Puh, that shall be no hindrance.
DE FLORES   I'm your servant, then.
    'Tis now near dinner-time; 'gainst your lordship's rising
    I'll have the keys about me.
ALONZO   Thanks, kind De Flores.
DE FLORES [*Aside*]
    He's safely thrust upon me beyond hopes.   *Exeunt*   165

150 *pleasure* sexual desire, often linked with appetite for food ('hunger')
151 *Slovenly* base; lewd
        dishes (also) men seen as sexual food (H)
        feed often = devour sexually, copulate (*PSB*)
154–5 Alonzo will be killed before supper that day, and thus will go 'to bed' for ever
        without sexual gratification (cf. also I. ii. 76, *dinner*).
158 *That . . . sir* in a way unintended by Alonzo
159 *ways* pathways left between walls; *straits* narrow pathways
160 *tedious* troublesome
161 *I will assure* Read 'I'll 'sure you'.
        worth This relates back to *strength*.
163 *'gainst . . . rising* by the time your lordship rises from the table
165 *safely* in that the murder and the body can be kept from view; ironic otherwise

Act III [, Scene i]

Enter ALONZO *and* DE FLORES
(*In the act-time* DE FLORES *hides a naked rapier*)

DE FLORES
    Yes, here are all the keys. I was afraid, my lord,
    I'd wanted for the postern; this is it.
    I've all, I've all, my lord; this for the sconce.
ALONZO
    'Tis a most spacious and impregnable fort.
DE FLORES
    You'll tell me more, my lořd. This descent   5
    Is somewhat narrow, we shall never pass
    Well with our weapons, they'll but trouble us.
                                    [*Takes off his sword*]
ALONZO
    Thou sayest true.
DE FLORES   Pray let me help your lordship.
                                    [*Takes* ALONZO's *sword*]
ALONZO
    'Tis done. Thanks, kind De Flores.
DE FLORES   Here are hooks, my lord,
    To hang such things on purpose.   [*Hangs up the swords*]
ALONZO   Lead, I'll follow thee.   10
                Exeunt at one door and enter at the other

[Act III, Scene ii]

DE FLORES
    All this is nothing; you shall see anon

Act III, Scene i   author: Middleton; place: Vermandero's castle
        sd The *act-time* is the interval between Acts II and III. De Flores hides his rapier
        in a convenient place near the casement where he will kill Alonzo (cf. ii. 6). How-
        ever, to deceive Alonzo he wears a sword which is left, with Alonzo's, when they
        come to the descent (l. 5) which De Flores describes as narrow. Apparently the
        entrance to this passage is through one stage door (see sd at end of scene), so that
        their entry through the other door suggests that they have made their descent and
        are now at a different level.
    2 *I'd . . . postern* that I had lacked the key for the back door
    3 *sconce* small, separate fortification
    5 *You'll . . . lořd* i.e., when once you've seen more
    8 *sayest* Dyce (sayst Q; cf. metre)
        help i.e., by taking off your sword-belt
Scene ii   author: Middleton; place: Vermandero's castle

    A place you little dream on.

ALONZO   I am glad
    I have this leisure; all your master's house
    Imagine I ha' taken a gondola.

DE FLORES

    All but myself, sir, – [*Aside*] which makes up my safety.   5
    [*To* ALONZO] My lord, I'll place you at a casement here
    Will show you the full strength of all the castle.
    Look, spend your eye a while upon that object.

ALONZO

    Here's rich variety, De Flores.

DE FLORES   Yes, sir.

ALONZO

    Goodly munition.

DE FLORES   Ay, there's ordnance, sir –   10
    No bastard metal – will ring you a peal like bells
    At great men's funerals. Keep your eye straight, my
        lord,
    Take special notice of that sconce before you:
    There you may dwell awhile.   [*Takes up the rapier*]

ALONZO   I am upon't.

DE FLORES

    And so am I.   [*Stabs him*]

ALONZO   De Flores! O, De Flores!   15
    Whose malice hast thou put on?

DE FLORES   Do you question
    A work of secrecy? I must silence you.   [*Stabs him*]

ALONZO

    O, O, O!

DE FLORES I must silence you.   [*Stabs him; he dies*]
    So, here's an undertaking well accomplished.
    This vault serves to good use now. – Ha! What's that   20

---

  2 *A place* De Flores now takes Alonzo to a vault (l.20) with its casement (l.6). The
    situation is clearer in Reynolds, where the vault is that of a 'casemate' (a vaulted
    chamber in a fortress-wall) and has a 'port-hole' through which Alonzo looks. In
    the theatre the vault could well be the 'inner stage'.
    you . . . on i.e., a wonderful place – and your grave
  6 *casement* a recessed aperture (cf. *OED*), through which the fortifications can be
    viewed – within the vault (the inner stage)
  7 *Will* i.e., which will (cf. ll.11, 21)
 10 *munition* fortifications
 11 *bastard* i.e., impure; also = species of cannon (*OED*, 7)
    peal also = discharge of guns
 13 *sconce* Cf. III. i. 3.
 14 *dwell* (1) linger (mentally); (2) stay (when dead)
 16 *malice* evil; hatred

Threw sparkles in my eye? – O, 'tis a diamond
He wears upon his finger. It was well found:
This will approve the work. What, so fast on?
Not part in death? I'll take a speedy course then:
Finger and all shall off. [*Cuts off the finger*] So, now I'll clear   25
The passages from all suspéct or fear.   *Exit with body*

[Act III, Scene iii]

Enter ISABELLA *and* LOLLIO

ISABELLA

Why, sirrah? Whence have you commissiön
To fetter the doors against me? If you
Keep me in a cage, pray whistle to me,
Let me be doing something.

LOLLIO

You shall be doing, if it please you; I'll whistle to you if   5
you'll pipe after.

ISABELLA

Is it your master's pleasure or your own
To keep me in this pinfold?

LOLLIO

'Tis for my master's pleasure; lest, being taken in another
man's corn, you might be pounded in another place.   10

ISABELLA

'Tis very well, and he'll prove very wise.

---

21 *diamond* Cf. II. i. 15; the vault is obviously semi-dark.

23 *approve* give proof of

24 *Not . . . death* The reference to the marriage ceremony, crude in De Flores' mouth,
makes the serious point that the betrothal contract between Beatrice and Alonzo
was binding; the union also was intended to make them one flesh in that the finger
(Alonzo's) and the ring (Beatrice's) stay together. See *ring*, I. ii. 27, and
cf. III. iv. 37–8.

26 *suspéct* cause of suspicion

Scene iii   author: Rowley; place: Alibius' madhouse

  1 *sirrah* a form of 'sir' used to address inferiors

  5 *doing* i.e., copulating (*PSB*; H)

     please i.e., please sexually

5–6 *I'll . . . after* Isabella had innocuously thought of a bird responding to a whistle.
Lollio alludes to the tag 'To dance after a person's pipe' (*ODEP*, p. 166), and the
bawdy sense of 'dance' = copulate, exploiting the common use of *pipe* = penis.

  8 *pinfold* i.e., pound for stray cattle, but with play on *pin* = penis

10 *pounded* (1) placed in a pound; (2) thumped, as with a pestle – i.e., copulated with
(cf. *compound*, I. i. 143); *another place*: innuendo of vagina (common, cf. H)

LOLLIO

He says you have company enough in the house, if you
please to be sociable, of all sorts of people.

ISABELLA

Of all sorts? Why, here's none but fools and madmen.

LOLLIO

Very well: and where will you find any other, if you should   15
go abroad? There's my master and I to boot too.

ISABELLA

Of either sort one, a madman and a fool.

LOLLIO

I would ev'n participate of both then, if I were as you: I
know y'are half mad already, be half foolish too.

ISABELLA

Y'are a brave, saucy rascal. Come on, sir,   20
Afford me then the pleasure of your bedlam;
You were commending once today to me
Your last-come lunatic: what a proper
Body there was without brains to guide it,
And what a pitiful delight appeared   25
In that deféct, as if your wisdom had found
A mirth in madness. Pray sir, let me partake,
If there be such a pleasure.

LOLLIO

If I do not show you the handsomest, discreetest madman,
one that I may call the understanding madman, then say I   30
am a fool.

ISABELLA

Well, a match: I will say so.

LOLLIO

When you have [had] a taste of the madman, you shall, if
you please, see Fools' College, o' th' [other] side. I seldom

---

18 *participate* i.e., sexually

19 *be . . . too* i.e., have a relationship with me as well as Alibius

20 *brave* fine; bold
   saucy impertinent; wanton

23 *proper* handsome. Isabella professes to be interested in the sexual *pleasure* (l. 21)
   the madhouse might offer, and hence in a handsome body without brains.

29 *discreetest* Lollio appears to hint that Franciscus ought to show such qualities as he
   ostensibly praises him for, and thus that his 'madness' is assumed.

32 *a match* i.e., it's a deal
   I . . . so an easy promise, no matter what Franciscus is like, as she refers merely to
   what she will *say* – about Lollio

33 *had* Dilke

34 *other* Dyce; for the division of wards cf. I. ii. 211–12.

lock there; 'tis but shooting a bolt or two, and you are   35
amongst 'em.   *Exit. Enter presently.*
– Come on, sir, let me see how handsomely you'll behave
yourself now.

Enter FRANCISCUS

FRANCISCUS

How sweetly she looks! O, but there's a wrinkle in her
brow as deep as philosophy. – Anacreon, drink to my mis-   40
tress' health, I'll pledge it. Stay, stay, there's a spider in
the cup! No, 'tis but a grape-stone; swallow it, fear nothing, poet. So, so; lift higher.

ISABELLA

Alack, alack, it is too full of pity
To be laughed at. How fell he mad? Canst thou tell?   45

LOLLIO

For love, mistress. He was a pretty poet too, and that set
him forwards first. The Muses then forsook him; he ran
mad for a chambermaid, yet she was but a dwarf neither.

FRANCISCUS

Hail, bright Titania!
Why stand'st thou idle on these flow'ry banks?   50

35 *shooting a bolt* pulling back a bolt; with allusion to 'A fool's bolt is soon shot' (i.e.,
his/her endeavour is soon made) – *ODEP*, p. 276
37 *handsomely* (1) attractively; (2) cleverly
38 sd Q has 'Enter Loll: Franciscus', but Lollio obviously re-enters at once
(*presently*) at l. 36, calling out to Franciscus as he reappears.
39–40 *How . . . philosophy* This sounds like a 'normal' observation, and is no doubt
meant to alert the audience to the fact that Franciscus is a counterfeit.
40 *Anacreon* (Franciscus addresses Lollio, so as to seem confused) a Greek poet who
according to legend (as narrated in, e.g., Pliny, *Natural History* VII, 7) choked to
death on a grapestone. Thus ' 'tis but a grape-stone' (l. 42) is no greater comfort
than the reference to the spider (l. 41), which was thought to be poisonous.
44–5 *Alack . . . at* Isabella appears indignant at Lollio's mirth (typical of many contemporaries, cf. I. ii. 52), which, however, is doubtless a response to Franciscus'
performance – not his 'madness'.
44 *it is* Dyce ('tis Q; cf. metre)
46 *For love* R plays on the notion that 'The lunatic, the lover, and the poet, / Are of
imagination all compact' (*A Midsummer Night's Dream* (*MND*) V. i. 7–8) – Lollio
sees all three as out of touch with reality, or at least inasmuch as both love and
poetry may cause madness.
    pretty artful; (with irony) fine
46–7 *set . . . forwards* started him off
48 *chambermaid* Cf. IV. iii. 8–11.
    yet . . . neither although she was only a dwarf at that
49 *Titania* (to Isabella) queen of the fairies in *MND*. Oberon (l. 51) is their king.

Oberon is dancing with his Dryadës;
I'll gather daisies, primrose, violets,
And bind them in a verse of poesy. [*Approaches Isabella*]

LOLLIO
Not too near! You see your danger.   [*Holds up a whip*]

FRANCISCUS
O hold thy hand, great Diomed!   55
Thou feed'st thy horses well, they shall obey thee.
Get up, Bucephalus kneels.   [*Kneels*]

LOLLIO
You see how I awe my flock. A shepherd has not his dog at
more obedience.

ISABELLA
His conscience is unquiet; sure that was   60
The cause of this. A proper gentleman.

FRANCISCUS
Come hither, Aesculapius. Hide the poison.

LOLLIO
Well, 'tis hid.   [*Hides the whip*]

FRANCISCUS [*Rising*]
Didst thou never hear of one Tiresias,
A famous poet?   65

LOLLIO
Yes, that kept tame wild-geese.

FRANCISCUS
That's he; I am the man.

51 *Dryadës* wood-nymphs in Greek mythology. Franciscus suggests that Isabella
   may be too inactive while Alibius (Oberon) is copulating (*dancing*) with other
   women.
52 The flowers are symbols of praise, with connotations of freshness (*daisies*), the
   finest and best (*primrose*, with plural sense; cf. Abbott, §471), and chastity
   (*violets*). Isabella is a contrast to her husband – and indeed to Titania in *MND*
   with her changeling boy (cf. *MND* II. i. 23 ff.). Franciscus' talk as a seducer is less
   sex-obsessed than his subsequent conduct.
53 *poesy* (1) poetry; (2) bunch of flowers (= *posy*)
55 *Diomed* king of the Bistones in Thrace, who fed his horses with human flesh
57 *Bucephalus* the charger of Alexander the Great, which only he could ride; *Get
   up* = 'mount' (Franciscus kneels on all fours, lampooning Lollio)
60 *conscience* i.e., 'internal recognition' of external facts. She thinks his approach is
   caused by failure to comprehend reality.
62 *Aesculapius* the Greek god of medicine
64 *Tiresias* the blind prophet of Thebes, who changed into a woman, and then back
   to a man seven years later. From experience, he judged that women derived more
   pleasure from sex than men. For revealing that fact Juno struck him blind.
65 *poet* perhaps a madman's error. Dyce emends to 'prophet'.
66 *wild-geese* licentious prostitutes (H; *PSB*). Cf. also 'To run the wild goose chase'
   (be engaged in a fruitless quest), *ODEP*, p. 889.

LOLLIO
  No!
FRANCISCUS
  Yes. But make no words on't: I was a man
  Seven years ago –   70
LOLLIO
  A stripling, I think, you might –
FRANCISCUS
  Now I'm a woman, all feminine.
LOLLIO
  I would I might see that.
FRANCISCUS
  Juno struck me blind.
LOLLIO
  I'll ne'er believe that; for a woman, they say, has an eye   75
  more than a man.
FRANCISCUS
  I say she struck me blind.
LOLLIO
  And Luna made you mad: you have two trades to beg
  with.
FRANCISCUS
  Luna is now big-bellied, and there's room   80
  For both of us to ride with Hecatë;
  I'll drag thee up into her silver sphere,
  And there we'll kick the dog – and beat the bush –
  That barks against the witches of the night;

---

75 *an eye* with a subsidiary allusion to the vagina (cf. *PSB*; H). The proverb may be
   R's invention (this is the only example in *ODEP*).
78 *Luna* Lunatics are made by Luna, the moon, especially when full.
   two trades blindness and madness (both pretended; Edgar acts the role of a begging 'madman' in *King Lear*)
80 *big-bellied* (1) full; (2) big with child
81 *ride* (1) move; (2) copulate
   Hecatë Greek goddess of witchcraft, frequently associated with night and thus
   seen as goddess of the moon within its *sphere*; she is also identified with Artemis
   (Diana), and hence here represents Isabella (cf. IV.iii.160), viewed as a
   bewitching and chaste goddess.
83 Seemingly confused talk (Dilke emended to 'And there we'll beat the bush, and
   kick the dog'). The dog and bush belonged traditionally to the (Man in the) Moon
   (cf. *MND* V.i.134). Thus they may threaten the moon goddess/witch Hecate =
   Isabella. But Franciscus' violence is that of a sex-starved and unrealistic madman.
   (Ironically *beat the bush* = waste time.)

The swift lycanthropi that walks the round,   85
We'll tear their wolvish skins, and save the sheep.
                   [*Tries to seize* LOLLIO]

LOLLIO

Is't come to this? Nay, then my poison comes forth again
[*Shows the whip*]: mad slave indeed – abuse your keeper!

ISABELLA

I prithee, hence with him, now he grows dangerous.

FRANCISCUS *Sing[s]*
    Sweet love, pity me;   90
    Give me leave to lie with thee.

LOLLIO

No, I'll see you wiser first. To your own kennel!

FRANCISCUS

No noise, she sleeps; draw all the curtains round,
Let no soft sound molest the pretty soul
But love, and love creeps in at a mouse-hole.   95

LOLLIO

I would you would get into your hole!   *Exit* FRANCISCUS
Now, mistress, I will bring you another sort: you shall be
fooled another while. – Tony, come hither, Tony! Look
who's yonder, Tony.

           Enter ANTONIO

ANTONIO

Cousin, is it not my aunt?   100

LOLLIO

Yes, 'tis one of 'em, Tony.

ANTONIO

He, he! How do you, uncle?

---

85 *lycanthropi* sufferers from lycanthropia, a disease in which the patient considers himself a wolf and acts accordingly. R no doubt has in mind Ferdinand in Webster's *Duchess of Malfi*, who develops this form of insanity as a result of his unfulfilled desire for his sister, and thus is the kind of madman who both resembles Franciscus and arouses his aggression.

88 *slave* rascal

90 sd *Sings* Dilke's emendation

91 *lie with* i.e., copulate

92 *kennel* Ironically Franciscus' fury makes him like the dog he meant to attack (l. 83), and he is not to share Isabella's bed.

95 *creeps* innuendo of sexual entry (H)
    mouse-hole punning on the term *mouse* = beloved woman (*PSB*) and *hole* = vagina

96 *hole* i.e., 'cell'

100 *aunt* also = whore

102 *uncle* perhaps also = procurer (cf. H)

LOLLIO

Fear him not, mistress, 'tis a gentle nigget; you may play
with him, as safely with him as with his bauble.

ISABELLA

How long hast thou been a fool? 105

ANTONIO

Ever since I came hither, cousin.

ISABELLA

Cousin? I'm none of thy cousins, fool.

LOLLIO

O mistress, fools have always so much wit as to claim their
kindred.

MADMAN *within*

Bounce, bounce! He falls, he falls! 110

ISABELLA

Hark you, your scholars in the upper room
Are out of order.

LOLLIO

Must I come amongst you there? – Keep you the fool,
mistress; I'll go up and play left-handed Orlando amongst
the madmen. *Exit* 115

ISABELLA

Well, sir.

ANTONIO

'Tis opportuneful now, sweet lady! Nay,
Cast no amazing eye upon this change.

ISABELLA

Ha!

---

103 *nigget* or *nidget*, contraction of 'an idiot' = fool
    play with subsidiary sense of fondle, copulate
104 *bauble* (1) fool's (jester's) baton; (2) penis
107 Isabella interprets Antonio's 'cousin' as 'strumpet', 'lover'; it was often used to
    cover illicit relationships. She probably suspects him (cf. also l. 105).
110 *Bounce . . . falls* vaguely used by the speaker, but so as to suggest a sexual event
111 *in the upper room* Strictly, the madman calls from 'within', i.e., the inner stage;
    however, Lollio will before long appear 'above', i.e., on the upper stage, and as
    that was placed above the inner stage, it makes good sense to act as though the two
    spaces are one and the same.
114 *left-handed Orlando* Orlando is the furious fighter in Ariosto's *Orlando Furioso*;
    Williams suggests that *left-handed* implies that Lollio will be but a poor imitation,
    and this is the more likely because Lollio normally looks after the fools, not the
    madmen, and more than once complains about his new responsibility (cf. l. 167
    ff.). He may also imply that, however furious, he will be inept amongst real
    lunatics.
117 *opportuneful* seasonable
118 *amazing* i.e., amazed
    this change not of clothes, but of acting

ANTONIO

  This shape of folly shrouds your dearest love,   120

  The truest servant to your powerful beauties,

  Whose magic had this force thus to transform me.

ISABELLA

  You are a fine fool indeed.

ANTONIO   O, 'tis not strange!

  Love has an intellect that runs through all

  The scrutinous sciences, and, like a cunning poet,   125

  Catches a quantity of every knowledge,

  Yet brings all home into one mystery,

  Into one secret, that he proceeds in.

ISABELLA

  Y'are a parlous fool.

ANTONIO

  No danger in me; I bring nought but love   130

  And his soft-wounding shafts to strike you with.

  Try but one arrow; if it hurt you, I

  Will stand you twenty back in recompense.   [*Kisses her*]

ISABELLA

  A forward fool too!

ANTONIO   This was love's teaching:

  A thousand ways he fashioned out my way,   135

  And this I found the safest and [the] nearest

  To tread the Galaxía to my star.

120 *shape* guise
    shrouds covers, protects
125 *scrutinous* searching
    cunning clever and artful
127 *one mystery* one superior form of knowledge and skill; secret
128 *secret* also = secret part
    proceeds i.e., mentally and sexually
129 *parlous* (i.e., *perilous*) dangerously cunning
131 *shafts* i.e., of Cupid (with sexual senses implied)
    strike with an innuendo of 'copulate' (*PSB*)
132–3 *I/Will* so Dyce (I'le Q, at beginning of l. 133 – cf. metre)
133 *stand* i.e., provide as payment; with implied sense of 'give you another twenty kisses'; and of 'copulate twenty times' (cf. *PSB* and H)
134 *forward* 'lustful' as well as 'boldly presumptuous'. Cf. Ricks, pp.298 ff.
    love's possibly disyllabic
135 *he* Dyce (she Q; 'he' = Cupid)
    fashioned out formed and contrived, with reference to Antonio's disguise as a counterfeit (see *OED*); ironically: perverted
    my way i.e., towards you
136 *the nearest* Dilke added 'the' (overlooked in copying? – cf. metre)
137 *Galaxía* Milky Way

ISABELLA

Profound withal! Certain you dreamed of this;
Love never taught it waking.

ANTONIO   Take no acquaintance

Of these outward follies. There is within   140
A gentleman that loves you.

ISABELLA   When I see him

I'll speak with him; so in the meantime keep
Your habit, it becomes you well enough.
As you are a gentleman, I'll not discover you;
That's all the favour that you must expect.   145
When you are weary, you may leave the school,
For all this while you have but played the fool.

Enter LOLLIO

ANTONIO

And must again. – He, he! I thank you, cousin;
I'll be your valentine tomorrow morning.

LOLLIO

How do you like the fool, mistress?   150

ISABELLA

Passing well, sir.

LOLLIO

Is he not witty, pretty well, for a fool?

ISABELLA

If he hold on as he begins, he is like
To come to something.

LOLLIO

Ay, thank a good tutor. You may put him to't; he begins to   155
answer pretty hard questions. – Tony, how many is five
times six?

138 *withal* as well
139 *Take no acquaintance* i.e., disregard (Black)
143 *habit* (fool's) dress
144 *discover* betray by revealing
145 *favour* i.e., instead of a sexual favour
147 Two senses: (1) you have not been a serious pupil here; (2) you have been merely foolish, in acting your role.
149 Cf. *cousin* in l. 107; the bawdy sense in l. 148 prompts the use of *valentine*. The phrase 'tomorrow morning' probably derives from 'Tomorrow is Saint Valentine's day', sung by Ophelia in *Hamlet* IV. v. 46, and so explains Antonio's choice of time (Bawcutt).
151 *Passing* surpassingly
153–4 *If . . . something* ostensibly (1) if he persists, he may achieve some level of learning; but (2) *come* and *something* also signify 'have an orgasm'; while (3) he is likely to come to nothing worthwhile
155 *put . . . to't* test him – though R may imply copulation (cf. *PSB*, *put to*; H). It is difficult to know how conscious the characters are of the puns here.

56 MIDDLETON AND ROWLEY [ACT III

ANTONIO
Five times six is six times five.
LOLLIO
What arithmetician could have answered better? How
many is one hundred and seven? 160
ANTONIO
One hundred and seven is seven hundred and one,
cousin.
LOLLIO
This is no wit to speak on! – Will you be rid of the fool
now?
ISABELLA
By no means; let him stay a little. 165
MADMAN *within*
Catch there, catch the last couple in hell!
LOLLIO
Again! Must I come amongst you? Would my master were
come home! I am not able to govern both these wards
together. *Exit*
ANTONIO
Why should a minute of love's hour be lost? 170
ISABELLA
Fie, out again! I had rather you kept
Your other posture; you become not your tongue
When you speak from your clothes.
ANTONIO   How can he freeze
Lives near so sweet a warmth? Shall I alone
Walk through the orchard of the Hesperides 175
And cowardly not dare to pull an apple?
This with the red cheeks I must venture for. [*Kisses her*]

---

159 *What . . . better* a gibe at mathematicians rather than praise of the pupil
166 An allusion to 'barley-break', an old country game traditionally played by six
people – three of each sex – forming couples. One couple, holding hands in the
middle den called 'hell', tried to intercept the other players, who attempted to
rush past them and to change partners (to 'break'). If caught, players had to take
their turn in 'hell', until eventually one last couple remained there. (Cf. Slater,
and *OED*.) The madman's cry thus symbolically serves as a warning to Antonio
and especially Isabella. Cf. V. iii. 162–3.
171 *out* i.e., out of your role as fool
172 *posture* pose
173 *from* i.e., out of keeping with
174 *Lives* i.e., who lives
175 *the Hesperides* guardians of golden apples which grew on a tree protected by the
dragon Ladon, offspring of the giant Tython (cf. l. 178)
176 *pull* pluck

Enter LOLLIO *above*

ISABELLA
Take heed, there's giants keep 'em.
LOLLIO [*Aside*]
How now, fool, are you good at that? Have you read Lip-
sius? He's past *Ars Amandi*; I believe I must put harder   180
questions to him, I perceive that –
ISABELLA
You are bold without fear too.
ANTONIO   What should I fear,
Having all joys about me? Do you [but] smile,
And love shall play the wanton on your lip,
Meet and retire, retire and meet again;   185
Look you but cheerfully, and in your eyes
I shall behold mine own deformity,
And dress myself up fairer. I know this shape
Becomes me not, but in those bright mirrors
I shall array me handsomely.   190
LOLLIO [*Aside*]
Cuckoo, cuckoo –   *Exit*

[*Enter*] MADMEN *above, some as birds, others as beasts*

ANTONIO
What are these?
ISABELLA   Of fear enough to part us,
Yet are they but our schools of lunatics,
That act their fantasies in any shapes

178 *giants* Isabella has obviously caught sight of Lollio.
    'em the apples and her cheeks
179–80 *Lipsius* a famous Renaissance scholar. The allusion plays on 'lips' but also
    raises images of sexual and intellectual inconstancy – cf. Sidney Gottlieb, *NQ*,
    March 1985, 63–5.
180 *Ars Amandi* a treatise by Ovid, *The Art of Loving*, and particularly seduction,
    which Antonio appears to have mastered
183 *Do ... smile* imperative mood
    but Ellis; fits metre, and cf. l. 229.
184 *the wanton* i.e., lasciviously, in kissing
188 *shape* guise (as fool)
189 *mirrors* i.e., Isabella's eyes
191 *Cuckoo* The cry of the bird suggested the word 'cuckold', here used of Alibius.
    Cuckoo often = cuckold (*PSB*). The madmen in their appearance as birds and
    beasts underline the nature of what seems to be happening, as elsewhere. Probably
    they disappear after l. 199 as a result of Isabella's analysis of madness – her control
    is obvious from ll. 213–18. Meanwhile there is irony in their entry *above*, seem-
    ingly superior to Isabella and especially Antonio.
192 *Of fear* i.e., frightening
194 *fantasies* things that they imagine, especially in their delusion

Suiting their present thoughts: if sad, they cry;   195
If mirth be their conceit they laugh again;
Sometimes they imitate the beasts and birds,
Singing or howling, braying, barking – all
As their wild fancies prompt 'em.

> [*Exeunt* MADMEN *above*]

Enter LOLLIO

ANTONIO   These are no fears.
ISABELLA
But here's a large one – my man.   200
ANTONIO
Ha, he! That's fine sport indeed, cousin!
LOLLIO
I would my master were come home! 'Tis too much for
one shepherd to govern two of these flocks. Nor can I
believe that one churchman can instruct two benefices at
once: there will be some incurable mad of the one side, and   205
very fools on the other. – Come, Tony.
ANTONIO
Prithee, cousin, let me stay here still.
LOLLIO
No, you must to your book now; you have played suf-
ficiently.
ISABELLA
Your fool is grown wondrous witty.   210
LOLLIO
Well, I'll say nothing, but I do not think but he will put
you down one of these days. *Exeunt* LOLLIO *and* ANTONIO
ISABELLA
Here the restrainèd current might make breach,
Spite of the watchful bankers. Would a woman stray,

195 *present thoughts* i.e., things that come to mind immediately as distinct from
  reasoning, which would prevent them – or lovers – from acting upon their fantasies
200 *my man* Lollio
201 *sport* Cf. I. ii. 173.
204 *benefices* Some ministers, not content with one stipend, derived their living from
  two or more churches – a notorious practice.
205 *of . . . side* i.e., in the one ward (*of* = on)
208 *now; you* now you Q; perhaps correctly if *now* = now that
211–12 *put you down* outwit you – and with a sexual innuendo
214 *bankers* dike-builders – not, surely, Alibius and Lollio (Black), who are not at all
  watchful, but metaphorically used to say that unless extraordinarily strong
  defences are used, sexual assault (normally restrained) would soon succeed. Part
  of Isabella's point is that if *a woman* wished to stray (i.e., sin sexually), the opportunity would arise readily.

She need not gad abroad to seek her sin,   215
It would be brought home one ways or other:
The needle's point will to the fixëd north,
Such drawing arctics women's beauties are.

Enter LOLLIO

LOLLIO
How dost thou, sweet rogue?
ISABELLA
How now?   220
LOLLIO
Come, there are degrees: one fool may be better than
another.
ISABELLA
What's the matter?
LOLLIO
Nay, if thou giv'st thy mind to fool's-flesh, have at
thee!   [*Tries to kiss her*] 225
ISABELLA
You bold slave, you!
LOLLIO
I could follow now as t'other fool did:
'What should I fear,
Having all joys about me? Do you but smile,
And love shall play the wanton on your lip,   230
Meet and retire, retire and meet again;
Look you but cheerfully, and in your eyes
I shall behold my own deformity,
And dress myself up fairer. I know this shape
Becomes me not –'   235
And so as it follows; but is not this the more foolish way?
Come, sweet rogue, kiss me, my little Lacedaemonian.
Let me feel how thy pulses beat. Thou hast a thing about

---

216 *brought home* i.e., delivered – at her own home, but probably with sexual innuendo
      (*home* = deeply, so as to penetrate)
      one ways i.e., in one way (adverbial *ways*, cf. Abbott, §25)
217 *needle's point* i.e., of the compass; and = penis (H)
      will i.e., move
218 *drawing arctics* magnetic poles
233 *my* Lollio's mistake in remembering, or an error in transmission (cf. l. 187)
236 *this* i.e., my way (the more straightforwardly sexual one)
237 *Lacedaemonian* (1) one Laconic of speech; (2) whore – lit. 'a Spartan', with refer-
      ence to the promiscuous Helen of Sparta, and probably with the implication that a
      prostitute does not talk much (cf. H; Frost)
238 *Let . . . beat* with sexual innuendo (cf. H)

thee would do a man pleasure – I'll lay my hand on't.

ISABELLA

Sirrah, no more! I see you have discovered   240
This love's knight-errant, who hath made adventure
For purchase of my love. Be silent, mute,
Mute as a statue, or his injunctiön
For me enjoying shall be to cut thy throat:
I'll do it, though for no other purpose, and   245
Be sure he'll not refuse it.

LOLLIO

My share, that's all! I'll have my fool's part with you.

ISABELLA

No more! Your master.

Enter ALIBIUS

ALIBIUS   Sweet, how dost thou?

ISABELLA

Your bounden servant, sir.

ALIBIUS   Fie, fie, sweetheart,
No more of that.

ISABELLA   You were best lock me up.   250

ALIBIUS

In my arms and bosom, my sweet Isabella,
I'll lock thee up most nearly! – Lollio,
We have employment, we have task in hand.
At noble Vermandero's, our castle-captain,
There is a nuptial to be solemnized –   255
Beatrice Joanna, his fair daughter, bride –
For which the gentleman hath bespoke our pains:
A mixture of our madmen and our fools,
To finish, as it were, and make the fag
Of all the revels, the third night from the first.   260
Only an unexpected passage over,

239 *do* i.e., provide through copulation
     lay (1) place; (2) bet
242 *purchase* i.e., winning the prize
247 *part* (1) share; (2) possibly with bawdy senses (cf. H); (3) role (implication: I
     deserve as much as Antonio, who also is only acting the part of fool)
249 *bounden* (1) duty-bound; (2) imprisoned (spoken sarcastically)
250 *lock* i.e., in a chastity girdle (ironic, in that her imprisonment has not prevented
     sexual approaches). Alibius takes her to mean 'lock me up yet more' without
     catching the extent of the allusion (cf. H and *PSB*).
252 *most nearly* (1) most closely to the action of a real lock; (2) intimately
256 *bride* i.e., being the bride
259 *fag* fag-end, the last and poorest part
261 The madmen and fools are supposed to rush suddenly across the stage. More
     ambitious 'entertainment' of this kind appears in Ford's *The Lover's Melancholy*.

To make a frightful pleasure, that is all –
But not the all I aim at. Could we so act it
To teach it in a wild, distracted measure,
Though out of form and figure, breaking time's head,   265
It were no matter ('twould be healed again
In one age or other, if not in this):
This, this Lollio, there's a good reward begun,
And will beget a bounty, be it known.

LOLLIO
This is easy, sir, I'll warrant you. You have about you   270
fools and madmen that can dance very well; and 'tis no
wonder: your best dancers are not the wisest men – the
reason is, with often jumping they jolt their brains down
into their feet, that their wits lie more in their heels than in
their heads.   275

ALIBIUS
Honest Lollio, thou giv'st me a good reason,
And a comfort in it.

ISABELLA   Y'have a fine trade on't;
Madmen and fools are a staple commodity.

ALIBIUS
O wife, we must eat, wear clothes, and live;
Just at the lawyer's haven we arrive,   280
By madmen and by fools we both do thrive.   *Exeunt*

[Act III, Scene iv]

Enter VERMANDERO, ALSEMERO, JASPERINO, *and* BEATRICE

VERMANDERO
Valencia speaks so nobly of you, sir,
I wish I had a daughter now for you.

262 *a frightful pleasure* i.e., a pleasant fright
263–9 *Could ... known* 'If only we could so perform it as to teach them to do it by
    means of a wild, crazy dance, then that, though not according to proper form and
    pattern, making a cuckold of the musical rhythm, would not be objected to (for it
    would be remedied at some future stage if not now) ... such a thing, Lollio, would
    be the beginning of a good reward and generate bountiful commissions for the
    future, if it became widely known.'
276 *a good reason* i.e., for proceeding with my envisaged 'dance'
280 The notion that fools (and madmen) visited lawyers often was proverbial, cf.
    I. ii. 162–3; but there probably is a reference to the fact that lawyers were needed if
    someone sued for the care of fools or lunatics, to Alibius' benefit (cf.
    IV. iii. 211–12).
Scene iv   author: Middleton; place: Vermandero's castle

ALSEMERO
> The fellow of this creature were a partner
> For a king's love.

VERMANDERO   I had her fellow once, sir,
> But heaven has married her to joys eternal;   5
> 'Twere sin to wish her in this vale again.
> Come, sir, your friend and you shall see the pleasures
> Which my health chiefly joys in.

ALSEMERO
> I hear the beauty of this seat largely.

VERMANDERO
> It falls much short of that.   *Exeunt. Manet* BEATRICE

BEATRICE   So, here's one step   10
> Into my father's favour; time will fix him.
> I have got him now the liberty of the house.
> So wisdom by degrees works out her freedom;
> And if that eye be dark'nëd that offends me
> (I wait but that eclipse), this gentleman   15
> Shall soon shine glorious in my father's liking
> Through the refulgent virtue of my love.

Enter DE FLORES

DE FLORES [*Aside*]
> My thoughts are at a banquet for the deed;
> I feel no weight in't, 'tis but light and cheap
> For the sweet recompense that I set down for't.   20

BEATRICE
> De Flores?

DE FLORES   Lady?

BEATRICE   Thy looks promise cheerfully.

---

6 *vale* i.e., of tears

9 *largely* 'extensively described' or 'wherever I go' – perhaps an incomplete line (Dyce adds 'commended')

10 sd *Manet* remains

11 *fix* make him (Alsemero) a fixture

14 *And... me* Cf. 'And if thine eye offend thee, pluck it out...', Matthew 18:9 (Bawcutt). Beatrice is unaware of M's irony here; she will not achieve anything positive by the death of Alonzo (the shining eye referred to). Frost lists yet other possible biblical allusions, all of them less close.

17 'By the strength of my love, which will reflect him.' The more usual sense of *virtue* (moral virtue, especially chastity) is also present – ironically.

18 *for* on account of. Many eds connect 'for the deed' with the next line, interpreting 'as for ...'. The *banquet* (i.e., sweet dish; cf. l. 20) links food and sex, and *deed* connects 'murder' and 'sexual act'.

20 *For* in exchange for
> *set down* i.e., as in an account

DE FLORES
   All things are answerable: time, circumstance,
   Your wishes, and my service.
BEATRICE   Is it done then?
DE FLORES
   Piracquo is no more.
BEATRICE
   My joys start at mine eyes; our sweet'st delights   25
   Are evermore born weeping.
DE FLORES   I've a token for you.
BEATRICE
   For me?
DE FLORES But it was sent somewhat unwillingly;
   I could not get the ring without the finger.
                           [*Shows her the finger*]
BEATRICE
   Bless me! What hast thou done?
DE FLORES   Why, is that more
   Than killing the whole man? I cut his heart-strings.   30
   A greedy hand thrust in a dish at court
   In a mistake hath had as much as this.
BEATRICE
   'Tis the first token my father made me send him.
DE FLORES
   And I [have] made him send it back again
   For his last token. I was loath to leave it,   35
   And I'm sure dead men have no use of jewels.
   He was as loath to part with't, for it stuck
   As if the flesh and it were both one substance.

---

22 *answerable* fitting

25–6 *My ... weeping* M's characters often express joy through weeping (cf. Bawcutt);
the idea is proverbial, cf. 'To weep for joy is a kind of manna' (*ODEP*, p. 876),
though potently and ironically conveyed here.

26 *token* (1) of the murder; (2) ironically: of love (especially the engagement)

28 Cf. III. ii. 24.

31–2 De Flores means that, as he cut Alonzo's heart-strings, cutting off the finger
was a trifle: the hand of a greedy courtier, stuck into a dish to get a portion, has
accidentally had a finger cut off by another diner's knife.

31 *dish* also: a woman as sexual food (*PSB*). M hints at the phallic aspect of the finger
(cf. *thrust*).

34 *have* Dyce; cf. metre.

36 *jewels* also = signs of virginity and married chastity; but implied is sometimes
'genitals', 'maidenheads' (cf. H; and *ring*, I. ii. 27).

37–8 *it ... substance* M alludes to the biblical notion that a man shall 'cleave to his
wife: and they twain shall be one flesh' (Matthew 19:5). The betrothal was to
establish an indissoluble union.

BEATRICE
  At the stag's fall, the keeper has his fees;
  'Tis soon applied: all dead men's fees are yours, sir.   40
  I pray, bury the finger; but the stone
  You may make use on shortly – the true value,
  Take't of my truth, is near three hundred ducats.
DE FLORES
  'Twill hardly buy a capcase for one's conscience,
    though,
  To keep it from the worm, as fine as 'tis.   45
  Well, being my fees, I'll take it;
  Great men have taught me that, or else my merit
  Would scorn the way on't.
BEATRICE   It might justly, sir.
  Why, thou mistak'st, De Flores: 'tis not given
  In state of recompense.
DE FLORES   No, I hope so, lady;   50
  You should soon witness my contempt to't then.
BEATRICE
  Prithee, thou look'st as if thou wert offended.
DE FLORES
  That were strange, lady; 'tis not possible
  My service should draw such a cause from you.
  Offended? Could you think so? That were much   55
  For one of my performance, and so warm
  Yet in my service.
BEATRICE
  'Twere misery in me to give you cause, sir.

39 'The keeper (warden of a park, etc.) is traditionally given from the dead deer the
   skin, the head, and other parts (cf. 3 *Henry VI*, III. i. 22)' – Williams.
40 De Flores inherits Alonzo's *fee* not just as a dog's share of the game (*OED*, 8.b),
   but also in that he will serve Beatrice as his lady, will be rewarded by her, and will
   die prematurely, without Christian rites. Beatrice means the diamond; pl. *fees*
   usually = wages.
44 *capcase* travelling bag, protective cover
45 *worm* i.e., the gnawings of conscience; the pain of Hell (cf. Mark 9:48)
47–8 *Great . . . on't* Great men have taught De Flores to accept a financial reward for
   his services, but he accepts it reluctantly, as his true merit – he feels – is above such
   a thing; Beatrice mistakenly thinks that he finds the sum too small, while she did
   not intend the diamond to be his reward.
50 *In state of* by way of
54 *cause* blame, reproach
55–7 *That . . . service* M suggests De Flores is unlikely to feel offended in view of the
   magnitude of what he has done for Beatrice, being still *warm* (both 'not yet cold'
   and 'sexually amorous') in his *service* ('performance of duty' and 'sexual
   attention').
58 *'Twere . . . me* (1) I would feel miserable; (2) it would be miserable of me

DE FLORES
    I know so much, it were so: misery
    In her most sharp condition.
BEATRICE   'Tis resolved then;   60
    Look you, sir, here's three thousand golden florins:
    I have not meanly thought upon thy merit.
DE FLORES
    What? Salary? Now you move me.
BEATRICE   How, De Flores?
DE FLORES
    Do you place me in the rank of verminous fellows,
    To destroy things for wages? Offer gold   65
    [For] the life blood of man! Is anything
    Valued too precious for my recompense?
BEATRICE
    I understand thee not.
DE FLORES   I could ha' hired
    A journeyman in murder at this rate,
    And mine own conscience might have [had], and have
        had   70
    The work brought home.
BEATRICE [*Aside*]   I'm in a labyrinth;
    What will content him? I would fain be rid of him.
    [*To* DE FLORES] I'll double the sum, sir.
DE FLORES   You take a course
    To double my vexation, that's the good you do.
BEATRICE [*Aside*]
    Bless me! I am now in worse plight than I was: 75
    I know not what will please him. [*To* DE FLORES] – For
        my fears' sake,

60 *'Tis . . . then* i.e., 'we've solved our misunderstanding'
61 Beatrice probably gives him a promissory note instead of so many coins.
63 *Salary* financial reward
    move i.e., offend, make angry
66 *For* Dilke – offers sense and metre; easily omitted in transmission (cf. 'Of*fer*')
66–7 *Is . . . recompense* De Flores (outraged) means 'In your way of thinking, is there
    anything highly valuable which would be too high a sum for my reward?' and/or
    'Can anything compensate me for such a deed?', while Beatrice probably inter-
    prets: 'Isn't my deed deserving of something like unlimited financial reward?'
68–9 *I . . . rate* 'according to your yardstick, I might have hired myself a professional
    murderer'
70 Q ends the line with 'might have'; Dilke (and most eds) added 'slept at ease'.
    Gomme added 'and have had' from the next line in Q; my additional 'had' would
    help both sense and metre, and could easily have been omitted in transmission by
    anticipation of the second 'had'.
71 *brought home* delivered to me by someone who had already carried it out
76 *fears'* Q fears – which could be singular, but cf. l. 85.

I prithee make away with all speed possible.
And if thou be'st so modest not to name
The sum that will content thee, paper blushes not;
Send thy demand in writing, it shall follow thee.   80
But prithee take thy flight.

DE FLORES   You must fly too then.

BEATRICE
I?

DE FLORES   I'll not stir a foot else.

BEATRICE   What's your meaning?

DE FLORES
Why, are not you as guilty, in, I'm sure,
As deep as I? And we should stick together.
Come, your fears counsel you but ill: my absence   85
Would draw suspéct upon you instantly;
There were no rescue for you.

BEATRICE [*Aside*]   He speaks home.

DE FLORES
Nor is it fit we two, engaged so jointly,
Should part and live asunder.   [*Tries to kiss her*]

BEATRICE   How now, sir?
This shows not well.

DE FLORES   What makes your lip so strange?   90
This must not be 'twixt us.

BEATRICE [*Aside*]   The man talks wildly.

DE FLORES
Come, kiss me with a zeal now.

BEATRICE [*Aside*]   Heaven, I doubt him!

DE FLORES
I will not stand so long to beg 'em shortly.

BEATRICE
Take heed, De Flores, of forgetfulness,
'Twill soon betray us.

---

84 *And . . . together* i.e., as partners in crime, but also like ring and finger. Cf. the use
    of *stuck* in l. 37.

86 *suspéct* suspicion

87 *home* i.e., so as to touch me deeply

88 *engaged* i.e., bound (morally and in the same situation, etc.), but with play on the
    sense of 'betrothed' (like Beatrice and Alonzo before). Cf. the allusion to the
    marriage ceremony in *asunder* (l. 89; see Matthew 19:6).

90 *strange* unfriendly

91 *'twixt* Neilson (betwixt Q); cf. metre and l. 131.

92 *doubt* fear

93 He means 'soon I will refuse to stand for so long begging for your kisses'.

94 *forgetfulness* i.e., of my rank and/or of decorum

DE FLORES   Take you heed first;   95
 Faith, y'are grown much forgetful, y'are too blame in't.
BEATRICE [*Aside*]
 He's bold, and I am blamed for't!
DE FLORES   I have eased you
 Of your trouble; think on't. I'm in pain
 And must be eased of you; 'tis a charity.
 Justice invites your blood to understand me.   100
BEATRICE
 I dare not.
DE FLORES   Quickly!
BEATRICE   O, I never shall!
 Speak it yet further off, that I may lose
 What has been spoken, and no sound remain on't.
 I would not hear so much offence again
 For such another deed.
DE FLORES   Soft, lady, soft!   105
 The last is not yet paid for. O, this act
 Has put me into spirit: I was as greedy on't
 As the parched earth of moisture, when the clouds weep.
 Did you not mark, I wrought myself into't,
 Nay, sued and kneeled for't? Why was all that pains
  took?   110
 You see I have thrown contempt upon your gold:
 Not that I want it [not], for I do piteously –
 In order I will come unto't, and make use on't –
 But 'twas not held so precious to begin with,
 For I place wealth after the heels of pleasure;   115
 And were I not resolved in my belief

96 *forgetful* i.e., of your guilt, and of your obligation to me
 too blame too blameworthy (cf. II. ii. 41)
97 *bold* (sexually) immodest
98 *pain* i.e., of sexual desire (cf. H)
99 *eased* sexually relieved (*of* = by)
 charity (here) a gift to someone sexually deprived
100 'The fact that we are partners in crime and that I have relieved you of your trouble
 – which was sexually inspired – in justice asks your violence/sex to understand my
 feeling, and thus to have intercourse (cf. H, *understandings*) with me.'
105 *Soft* i.e., not so fast
106 *act* i.e., of blood
107 *me . . . spirit* Read 'm'nto spir't'.
 spirit (thought to be produced by blood) animation; sexual desire
109 *into't* perhaps 'intó't'. Cf. also l. 132, and *unto*, ll. 113 and 128.
112 *it not* 'not' (Dilke) was obviously omitted in transmission (cf. sense and metre)
113 *In order* in due course
115 *pleasure* sexual pleasure
116–17 Cf. II. ii. 131; *resolved* = certain.

That thy virginity were perfect in thee,
I should but take my recompense with grudging,
As if I had but half my hopes I agreed for.

BEATRICE
Why, 'tis impossible thou canst be so wicked,   120
Or shelter such a cunning cruelty,
To make his death the murderer of my honour!
Thy language is so bold and viciöus,
I cannot see which way I can forgive it
With any modesty.

DE FLORES   Push, you forget yourself!   125
A woman dipped in blood, and talk of modesty?

BEATRICE
O misery of sin! Would I had been bound
Perpetually unto my living hate
In that Piracquo, than to hear these words!
Think but upon the distance that creation   130
Set 'twixt thy blood and mine, and keep thee there.

DE FLORES
Look but into your conscience, read me there;
'Tis a true book, you'll find me there your equal.
Push, fly not to your birth, but settle you
In what the act has made you; y'are no more now.   135
You must forget your parentage to me:
Y'are the deed's creature; by that name you lost
Your first condition; and I challenge you
As peace and innocency has turned you out
And made you one with me.

BEATRICE   With thee, foul villain?   140

DE FLORES
Yes, my fair murd'ress. Do you urge me,
Though thou writ'st 'maid', thou whore in thy affection?
'Twas changed from thy first love, and that's a kind

122 *honour* (reputation for) chastity
126 'Since you are dipped in blood as a murderer anyway, it is incongruous to complain about losing your virginity, or to lay claim to female "modesty".'
129 *than* rather than
131 *blood* (here) rank
133 *equal* i.e., in violence, and hence in other respects
136 *to* i.e., in favour of. Her kinship is now rather that of De Flores and the murder.
137-8 *by . . . condition* having adopted the name of Murderer, you have lost the original innocence of Eve and your parenthood
138 *challenge* lay claim to
139 *turned you out* i.e., from Paradise and your family
141 *urge* provoke
142 *affection* passionate desire (*PSB*)
143 *changed . . . love* i.e., transferred from Alonzo (cf. play's title)

Of whoredom in thy heart; and he's changed now
To bring thy second on, thy Alsemero,   145
Whom (by all sweets that ever darkness tasted)
If I enjoy thee not, thou ne'er enjoy'st:
I'll blast the hopes and joys of marriäge –
I'll cónfess all; my life I rate at nothing.

BEATRICE
De Flores!

DE FLORES   I shall rest from all plagues then;   150
I live in pain now: that love-shooting eye
Will burn my heart to cinders.

BEATRICE   O sir, hear me!

DE FLORES
She that in life and love refuses me,
In death and shame my partner she shall be.

BEATRICE
Stay, hear me once for all. [*Kneels*] – I make thee master   155
Of all the wealth I have in gold and jewels;
Let me go poor unto my bed with honour,
And I am rich in all things.

DE FLORES   Let this silence thee:
The wealth of all Valencia shall not buy
My pleasure from me.   160
Can you weep fate from its determined purpose?
So soon may [you] weep me.

BEATRICE   Vengeance begins;
Murder I see is followed by more sins.
Was my creation in the womb so curst
It must engender with a viper first?   165

DE FLORES
Come, rise, and shroud your blushes in my bosom.
                                            [*Raises her*]

144 *changed* i.e., from life to death
145 *bring on* introduce and advance, with play on 'excite sexually' (cf. II. i. 108)
146 *sweets* pleasures of sexual intimacy (*PSB*)
150 *all plagues* Dyce conj. (all lovers plagues Q); *plagues* = wounds (*OED*, 1)
151 *love-shooting eye* Dyce conj. (shooting eye Q). The line gives poor sense and metre
    in Q, and *lovers* – instead of *love* – could easily have found its way into l. 150, where
    no such word is wanted. Beatrice's love-shooting eye threatens to make De Flores'
    sexual *pain* (cf. l. 98) all-consuming. Craik: 'fire-shooting' (cf. IV. ii. 106).
157 *honour* Cf. l. 122.
162 *you* Dyce
164–5 'When I was created in my mother's womb, was so great a curse laid upon me
    that I must copulate with a viper before I do so with a man?' Cf. her reference to
    De Flores as a serpent, I. i. 223; M here alludes to a union between Eve and the
    Serpent in the Garden.
166 *shroud* shelter, conceal

Silence is one of pleasure's best receipts:
Thy peace is wrought for ever in this yielding.
'Las, how the turtle pants! Thou'lt love anon
What thou so fear'st and faint'st to venture on.   *Exeunt*   170

Act IV [, Scene i]

[*Dumb show*]

Enter GENTLEMEN, VERMANDERO *meeting them with action of
wonderment at the flight of* PIRACQUO. *Enter* ALSEMERO, *with*
JASPERINO *and* GALLANTS; VERMANDERO *points to him, the*
GENTLEMEN *seeming to applaud the choice.* [*Exeunt in proces-
sion* VERMANDERO], ALSEMERO, JASPERINO *and* GENTLEMEN.
[*Enter*] BEATRICE, *the bride, following in great state, ac-
companied with* DIAPHANTA, ISABELLA, *and other* GENTLE-
WOMEN. [*Enter*] DE FLORES *after all, smiling at the accident.*
ALONZO's *ghost appears to* DE FLORES *in the midst of his smile;
startles him, showing him the hand whose finger he had cut off.
They pass over in great solemnity.*

Enter BEATRICE

BEATRICE
This fellow has undone me endlessly:
Never was bride so fearfully distressed.
The more I think upon th'ensuing night,
And whom I am to cope with in embraces –
One who's ennobled both in blood and mind,   5

167 *receipts* (1) recipes; (2) receptacles
169 *turtle* turtle-dove
     anon at once
Act IV, Scene i   author: Middleton; place: Vermandero's castle
     sd The dumb show 'summarizes a certain part of the plot which, although impor-
     tant as a preliminary for the following complications, would not contribute much
     to the central idea of the play' (Dieter Mehl, *The Elizabethan Dumb Show*, 1965,
     p. 152); *accident* event.
     1 *fellow* 'man of lower rank and no worth'; also and ironically = 'accomplice' and
     'husband'
     undone (1) ruined; (2) had intercourse with. Also perhaps = 'deprived of copula-
     tion' (i.e., ironically, with Alsemero). Cf. *PSB* and H for the contrasting sexual
     senses (both probably M's rather than Beatrice's).
     endlessly no doubt used more loosely by Beatrice than by M
     2 *distressed* also = sexually deprived (H) – which, as a *bride*, she will be
     4 *cope* Beatrice may mean 'meet' (*OED*, 5) and 'contend', but there is a bawdy sense,
     'copulate' (*PSB*).
     5 *who's* Dilke (both Q – no doubt confused by *both* in l. 5 and *whom* in l. 4)

So clear in understanding (that's my plague now),
Before whose judgement will my fault appear
Like malefactors' crimes before tribunals
(There is no hiding on't) – the more I dive
Into my own distress. How a wise man   10
Stands for a great calamity! There's no venturing
Into his bed, what course soe'er I light upon,
Without my shame, which may grow up to danger.
He cannot but in justice strangle me
As I lie by him, as a cheater use me;   15
'Tis a precious craft to play with a false die
Before a cunning gamester. Here's his closet,
The key left in't, and he abroad i' th' park;
Sure 'twas forgot, I'll be so bold as look in't.
                                        [*Opens closet*]
Bless me! A right physician's closet 'tis,   20
Set round with vials, every one her mark too.
Sure he does practise physic for his own use,
Which may be safely called your great man's wisdom.
What manuscript lies here? 'The Book of Experiment,
Called *Secrets in Nature*'; so 'tis, 'tis so   25
'How to know whether a woman be with child or no.'
I hope I am not yet; if he should try though!
Let me see: 'folio forty-five.' Here 'tis;
The leaf tucked down upon't, the place suspicious.

---

9 *the more* correlative with *The more* in l. 3

11 *Stands for* represents ('how the man's cleverness is bound to mean calamity for
   me' – Gomme), or stands open to ('how may even a clever man be struck by a
   calamity like my deceit')

15 *use* (also) copulate with

16 *precious* i.e., obtainable only at great cost – so 'risky' and/or 'difficult'
   die singular of 'dice'

17 *closet* small private room – located within the inner stage as in V. iii

20 *right* true, veritable

21 *vials* small containers holding liquid medicine

22 *physic* medicine

23 Since it protects him against poison.

25 *Secrets in Nature* or *De Arcanis Naturae* by the scholar Antonius Mizaldus
   (1520–78). The tests are not in this work, but similar ones are found in his *Cen-
   turiae IX. Memorabilium*. The manuscript probably contains extracts from both
   works and perhaps others (cf. ll. 44–5), and the title serves as a general indication
   of the subject matter. Alsemero's interest in virginity tests, etc., seems a little
   unhealthy; cf. Alibius' suspicion of his wife.
   'tis so followed in Q by a comma, and perhaps separate from l. 26 in sense (Beatrice
   may be talking rather aimlessly)

26 This is apparently read from a list of contents.

'If you would know whether a woman be with child or   30
not, give her two spoonfuls of the white water in glass C –'
Where's that glass C? O, yonder, I see't now –
'and if she be with child, she sleeps full twelve hours after;
if not, not.'
None of that water comes into my belly: 35
I'll know you from a hundred. I could break you now,
Or turn you into milk, and so beguile
The master of the mystery, but I'll look to you.
Ha! That which is next is ten times worse:
'How to know whether a woman be a maid or not.'   40
If that should be applied, what should become of me?
Belike he has a strong faith of my purity,
That never yet made proof; but this he calls
'A merry sleight, but true experiment, the author
Antonius Mizaldus. Give the party you suspect the quan-   45
tity of a spoonful of the water in the glass M, which upon
her that is a maid makes three several effects: 'twill make
her incontinently gape, then fall into a sudden sneezing,
last into a violent laughing; else dull, heavy, and lumpish.'
Where had I been?   50
I fear it, yet 'tis seven hours to bedtime.

Enter DIAPHANTA

DIAPHANTA
  Cuds, madam, are you here?
BEATRICE [*Aside*]   Seeing that wench now

31 *water* medicinal liquid
     glass i.e., glass container
36 *you* glass C
37 *turn . . . milk* by changing the contents or the 'mark' (l. 21)
38 *mystery* secret
     look to 'watch out for' or 'take care of'
42–3 *Belike . . . proof* perhaps, not having tested my purity, he has strong faith in it
     and will therefore not proceed to do so (ironic in several ways)
44 *sleight* trick (slight Q)
47 *several* different
48 *incontinently* immediately
49 *else* further (in the sequence, cf. l. 115)
50 She means, 'if I had not found out'.
51 *it* i.e., that he will subject me to the experiment (but I still have time)
52 *Cuds* a form of 'God's', used as a mild oath
     wench simply = girl, but also = wanton woman; familiar form of address natural in
     Beatrice's mouth (l. 54)

A trick comes in my mind; 'tis a nice piece
Gold cannot purchase. [To DIAPHANTA] I come hither,
    wench,
To look my lord.
DIAPHANTA [*Aside*] Would I had such a cause   55
    To look him too! [To BEATRICE] Why, he's i' th' park,
    madam.
BEATRICE
    There let him be.
DIAPHANTA   Ay, madam, let him compass
    Whole parks and forests, as great rangers do;
    At roosting time a little lodge can hold 'em.
    Earth-conquering Alexander, that thought the world   60
    Too narrow for him, in the end had but his pit-hole.
BEATRICE
    I fear thou art not modest, Diaphanta.
DIAPHANTA
    Your thoughts are so unwilling to be known, madam;
    'Tis ever the bride's fashion towards bed-time
    To set light by her joys, as if she owed 'em not.   65
BEATRICE
    Her joys? Her fears, thou would'st say.
DIAPHANTA   Fear of what?
BEATRICE
    Art thou a maid, and talk'st so to a maid?
    You leave a blushing business behind,
    Beshrew your heart for't!
DIAPHANTA   Do you mean good sooth,
    madam?

53–4 *'tis . . . purchase* i.e., 'only an exceptionally principled and coy girl cannot be
    bought for money'
55 *look* look for
57–61 *Ay . . . pit-hole Pit-hole* means 'grave', but there is also a definite bawdy innu-
    endo in this context (cf. III.iii.95, *mouse-hole*), so Beatrice's reaction is logical.
    Further bawdy possibilities are *parks* = female bodies, *rangers* = penises, *lodge*
    = vagina, *end* = vagina – cf. esp. H; but the effect is more subtle if the only clear
    pun is at the end, with l. 59 providing a hint.
58 *rangers* (chiefly) gamekeepers; rakes
60 *Alexander* i.e., the Great. Cf. Juvenal *Satire* X, 168–72 and *Hamlet* V. i. 192 ff.
62 *modest* i.e., chaste – in expression/thought, and perhaps action (cf. ll. 68, 78)
63 *Your . . . known* i.e., you say so because your own thoughts are unwilling to make
    themselves known, being themselves far from chaste (cf. ll. 64–5)
65 *owed* owned
67 *maid* virgin
68 'Your words leave me blushing'; but *business* also meant 'sexual intercourse'
    (*PSB*), so Beatrice may imply that Diaphanta is no longer a virgin.
69 *Beshrew* curse   *sooth* truth (so: are you serious?)

BEATRICE
  Well, if I'd thought upon the fear at first,   70
  Man should have been unknown.
DIAPHANTA   Is't possible?
BEATRICE
  I will give a thousand ducats to that woman
  Would try what my fear were, and tell me true
  Tomorrow, when she gets from't; as she likes
  I might perhaps be drawn to't.
DIAPHANTA   Are you in earnest?   75
BEATRICE
  Do you get the woman, then challenge me,
  And see if I'll fly from't. But I must tell you
  This by the way: she must be a true maid,
  Else there's no trial, my fears are not hers else.
DIAPHANTA
  Nay, she that I would put into your hands, madam,   80
  Shall be a maid.
BEATRICE   You know I should be shamed else,
  Because she lies for me.
DIAPHANTA   'Tis a strange humour!
  But are you serious still? Would you resign
  Your first night's pleasure, and give money too?
BEATRICE
  As willingly as live. [*Aside*] – Alas, the gold   85
  Is but a by-bet to wedge in the honour.
DIAPHANTA [*Aside*]
  I do not know how the world goes abroad
  For faith or honesty; there's both required in this. –
  Madam, what say you to me, and stray no further?
  I've a good mind, in troth, to earn your money.   90

70–1 *Well . . . unknown* (1) if I had thought of my fear of losing my virginity, I would
    have chosen to stay a virgin by not marrying; (2) (inwardly) if I had known how
    scared I would be of Alsemero finding out, I would not have lost my virginity to
    De Flores. M appears also to hint that 'Man should have been unknown' if Eve
    had shared Beatrice's professed fear of intercourse.
74 *when . . . from't* when she removes herself from intercourse
76 *challenge me* demand the money from me
82 *lies for* a frequent pun: 'copulates' and 'cheats'
   humour whim
86 The gold is only a side-bet to make secure her honour. In the event, Diaphanta is
   hardly a *nice* girl (cf. l. 53), and the bribe thus almost unnecessary.
87–8 *I . . . honesty* 'I do not know how much faith or honesty can be found in the
   world nowadays' (Bawcutt); she is surprised because Beatrice is neither faithful
   nor honest as a bride. Ironically *honesty* also means chastity.

BEATRICE
   Y'are too quick, I fear, to be a maid.
DIAPHANTA
   How? Not a maid? Nay, then you urge me, madam!
   Your honourable self is not a truer,
   With all your fears upon you –
BEATRICE [*Aside*]   Bad enough then.
DIAPHANTA
   Than I with all my lightsome joys about me.   95
BEATRICE
   I'm glad to hear't. Then you dare put your honesty
   Upon an easy trial?
DIAPHANTA   Easy? – Anything.
BEATRICE
   I'll come to you straight.   [*Goes to the closet*]
DIAPHANTA [*Aside*]   She will not search me, will she,
   Like the forewoman of a female jury?
BEATRICE [*Aside*]
   Glass M: ay, this is it. – Look, Diaphanta,   100
   You take no worse than I do.   [*Drinks*]
DIAPHANTA   And in so doing,
   I will not question what it is, but take it.   [*Drinks*]
BEATRICE [*Aside*] Now if the experiment be true, 'twill
     praise itself,
   And give me noble ease. – Begins already;
                         [DIAPHANTA *gapes*]
   There's the first symptom. And what haste it makes   105
   To fall into the second, there by this time!
                        [DIAPHANTA *sneezes*]
   Most admirable secret! – On the contrary,
   It stirs not me a whit, which most concerns it.
DIAPHANTA
   Ha, ha, ha!
BEATRICE [*Aside*] Just in all things, and in order

91 *quick* i.e., in your reaction; also: too ardent, sexually (cf. H)
92 *urge* provoke
93 *honourable* respectable and chaste
96 *hear't. Then you* hear't then, you Q (followed by some eds)
98–9 *She . . . jury* an allusion to the divorce trial brought by the Countess of Essex in
    1613. She charged that her marriage had not been consummated, and was
    examined by a group of matrons and other women.
102 *it is* Dilke ('tis Q); cf. metre.
103 *praise* appraise, value
107 *admirable* wonderful
108 *which . . . it* i.e., which it most aimed to do
109 *Just* precise

As if 'twere circumscribed; one accident   110
Gives way unto another.
DIAPHANTA   Ha, ha, ha!
BEATRICE
How now, wench?
DIAPHANTA   Ha, ha, ha! I am so – so light
At heart! Ha, ha, ha! – so pleasurable!
But one swig more, sweet madam.
BEATRICE   Ay, tomorrow;
We shall have time to sit by't.
DIAPHANTA   Now I'm sad again.   115
BEATRICE [*Aside*]
It lays itself so gently too! [*To* DIAPHANTA] Come,
    wench;
Most honest Diaphanta I dare call thee now.
DIAPHANTA
Pray tell me, madam, what trick call you this?
BEATRICE
I'll tell thee all hereafter; we must study
The carriage of this business.
DIAPHANTA   I shall carry't well,   120
Because I love the burden.
BEATRICE   About midnight
You must not fail to steal forth gently,
That I may use the place.
DIAPHANTA   O fear not, madam;
I shall be cool by that time. [*Aside*] The bride's place,
And with a thousand ducats! I'm for a justice now: 125
I bring a portion with me; I scorn small fools.   *Exeunt*

---

110 *As ... circumscribed* as though it were written in a circle (as on a coin), so: with its
    specific sequence neatly displayed
    accident symptom
114 *tomorrow* i.e., when more convenient: 'Beatrice is anxious to get away from
    Alsemero's apartment, where a fiancée's presence is unconventional' (Black).
115 *sad* Cf. IV. ii. 147.
116 *lays itself* subsides
117 *honest* (also) chaste
120 *carriage* how to carry out; with play on the carrying of a sexual *burden*, and
    business as 'copulation'
124 *cool* i.e., no longer sexually 'hot'
125–6 *I'm ... fools* 'I'm for a big fool, a justice' (Spencer). Cf. I. ii. 131.
126 *portion* dowry, with play on 'virginity' and 'pudend' (H)

[Act IV, Scene ii]

Enter VERMANDERO *and* SERVANT

VERMANDERO
  I tell thee, knave, mine honour is in question,
  A thing till now free from suspiciön,
  Nor ever was there cause. Who of my gentlemen
  Are absent? Tell me, and truly, how many and who.
SERVANT
  Antonio, sir, and Franciscus.   5
VERMANDERO
  When did they leave the castle?
SERVANT
  Some ten days since, sir, the one intending to Briamata,
  th'other for Valencia.
VERMANDERO
  The time accuses 'em. A charge of murder
  Is brought within my castle gate, Piracquo's murder;   10
  I dare not answer faithfully their absence.
  A strict command of apprehensiön
  Shall pursue 'em suddenly, and either wipe
  The stain off clear, or openly discover it.
  Provide me wingëd warrants for the purpose.   15
                                          Exit SERVANT
  See, I am set on again.

Enter TOMAZO

TOMAZO
  I claim a brother of you.
VERMANDERO   Y'are too hot;
  Seek him not here.
TOMAZO   Yes, 'mongst your dearest bloods,
  If my peace find no fairer satisfaction.
  This is the place must yield account for him,   20
  For here I left him; and the hasty tie
  Of this snatched marriage gives strong testimony
  Of his most certain ruin.
VERMANDERO   Certain falsehood!

Scene ii   author: Rowley ll. 1–16, Middleton ll. 17–150; place: Vermandero's castle
  7 *Briamata* in Reynolds, Vermandero's country house, ten leagues from Alicante
  11 *answer faithfully* explain with confident knowledge of the truth
  14 *discover* lay bare
  15 sd In Q this follows l. 16.
  16 *set on* harassed (by Tomazo)
  18 *bloods* near relatives. Cf. ll. 34–5.

This is the place indeed: his breach of faith
Has too much marred both my abusèd love –   25
The honourable love I reserved for him –
And mocked my daughter's joy. The prepared morning
Blushed at his infidelity; he left
Contempt and scorn to throw upon those friends
Whose belief hurt 'em. O, 'twas most ignoble   30
To take his flight so unexpectedly,
And throw such public wrongs on those that loved him!
TOMAZO
    Then this is all your answer?
VERMANDERO   'Tis too fair
    For one of his alliance, and I warn you
    That this place no more see you.   *Exit*

                Enter DE FLORES

TOMAZO   The best is,   35
    There is more ground to meet a man's revenge on. –
    Honest De Flores?
DE FLORES   That's my name indeed.
    Saw you the bride? Good sweet sir, which way took she?
TOMAZO
    I have blest mine eyes from seeing such a false one.
DE FLORES [*Aside*] I'd fain get off, this man's not for my
        company: 40
    I smell his brother's blood when I come near him.
TOMAZO
    Come hither, kind and true one; I remember
    My brother loved thee well.
DE FLORES   O purely, dear sir!
    [*Aside*] – Methinks I am now again a-killing on him,
    He brings it so fresh to me.
TOMAZO   Thou canst guess, sirrah –   45
    One honest friend has an instinct of jealousy –
    At some foul guilty person?

25 *marred* injured
30 *belief* i.e., mistaken confidence in him
34 *alliance* kindred
34–5 *I . . . you* Vermandero is doubtless concerned about his 'bloods' (l. 18).
36 'There is another way to find out whom I must take vengeance on' (Black). He
    clearly notes De Flores, whose entrance is ironic. Tomazo's praise cannot be mere
    flattery, for cf. ll. 57–8.
43 *purely* absolutely
46 The idea appears to be that De Flores is the one honest friend amongst unreliable
    people and as such will have a useful intuitive suspicion as to who may have killed
    Alonzo. Dyce plausibly read 'An' for Q's 'One'.

DE FLORES

    'Las, sir, I am so charitable, I think none
    Worse than myself. – You did not see the bride then?

TOMAZO

    I prithee, name her not. Is she not wicked?   50

DE FLORES

    No, no: a pretty, easy, round-packed sinner,
    As your most ladies are (else you might think
    I flattered her), but, sir, at no hand wicked,
    Till th'are so old their chins and noses meet,
    And they salute witches. – I am called, I think, sir.   55
    [*Aside*] – His company ev'n o'erlays my conscience. *Exit*

TOMAZO

    That De Flores has a wondrous honest heart;
    He'll bring it out in time, I'm assured on't.
    O, here's the glorious master of the day's joy.
    'Twill not be long till he and I do reckon.   60

Enter ALSEMERO

    Sir!

ALSEMERO You are most welcome.

TOMAZO   You may call that word
        back:
    I do not think I am, nor wish to be.

ALSEMERO

    'Tis strange you found the way to this house then.

TOMAZO

    Would I'd ne'er known the cause! I'm none of those, sir,
    That come to give you joy, and swill your wine;   65
    'Tis a more precious liquor that must lay
    The fiery thirst I bring.

51 *easy* of easy virtue (*PSB*)
    round-pack'd curvaceous and fleshly
53 *at no hand* by no means
54 *chins and noses* Dyce conj. (sins and vices Q); the emendation is generally accepted
    as technically likely and giving good sense.
55 *salute* greet and make the acquaintance of (as they then look like witches them-
    selves)
56 *o'erlays my conscience* oppresses my mind
58 Perhaps there are three iambs and two trochees here.
    bring it out i.e., reveal (1) his good heart, and (2) the identity of the killer
59 *glorious* i.e., vainglorious (*OED*, 1)
    day's possibly disyllabic (dayes Q)
60 *'Twill* Dilke (I will Q)
    reckon 'settle our accounts'
66 *liquor* liquid – i.e., blood
    lay allay

ALSEMERO   Your words and you
  Appear to me great strangers.
TOMAZO   Time and our swords
  May make us more acquainted. This the business: –
  I should have [had] a brother in your place;   70
  How treachery and malice have disposed of him
  I'm bound to enquire of him which holds his right,
  Which never could come fairly.
ALSEMERO   You must look
  To answer for that word, sir.
TOMAZO   Fear you not;
  I'll have it ready drawn at our next meeting.   75
  Keep your day solemn. Farewell, I disturb it not;
  I'll bear the smart with patience for a time.   *Exit*
ALSEMERO
  'Tis somewhat ominous, this: a quarrel ent'rëd
  Upon this day. My innocence relieves me;

Enter JASPERINO

  I should be wondrous sad else. – Jasperino,   80
  I have news to tell thee, strange news.
JASPERINO   I ha' some too,
  I think as strange as yours. Would I might keep
  Mine, so my faith and friendship might be kept in't!
  Faith, sir, dispense a little with my zeal,
  And let it cool in this.
ALSEMERO   This puts me on,   85
  And blames thee for thy slowness.
JASPERINO   All may prove nothing,
  Only a friendly fear that leapt from me, sir.
ALSEMERO
  No question it may prove nothing; let's partake it,
     though.

70 *had* Dilke; cf. metre and sense.
71 *malice* wickedness
74 *that word* i.e., your accusation
75 *it* 'my sword; as if it were an official answer, "drawn" up' (Williams)
76 *Keep . . . solemn* proceed with the solemnity of your wedding day
77 *smart* painful loss
83 *so* 'provided that'. But he feels he must report.
84–5 *dispense . . . this* 'i.e. if you would allow the vigor of my friendship and service to
    grow somewhat slack ("cool"), I should not have to pass on this news' (Williams)
85 *puts me on* urges me onward
88 *partake* share

JASPERINO
    'Twas Diaphanta's chance – for to that wench
    I pretend honest love, and she deserves it –   90
    To leave me in a back part of the house,
    A place we chose for private conference;
    She was no sooner gone but instantly
    I heard your bride's voice in the next room to me,
    And, lending more attention, found De Flores   95
    Louder than she.
ALSEMERO   De Flores? Thou art out now.
JASPERINO
    You'll tell me more anon.
ALSEMERO   Still I'll prevent thee;
    The very sight of him is poison to her.
JASPERINO
    That made me stagger too, but Diaphanta
    At her return confirmed it.
ALSEMERO   Diaphanta!   100
JASPERINO
    Then fell we both to listen, and words passed
    Like those that challenge interest in a woman –
ALSEMERO
    Peace, quench thy zeal; 'tis dangerous to thy bosom.
JASPERINO
    Then truth is full of peril.
ALSEMERO   Such truths are. –
    O, were she the sole glory of the earth,   105

---

89 ff. It seems unlikely that Jasperino and Diaphanta overheard III. iv, as some eds
    suggest, for in IV. i Diaphanta's conduct shows that she considers Beatrice sex-
    ually innocent and in love with Alsemero. We are to imagine that they have over-
    heard a more recent conversation, presumably after IV. i and on this wedding day
    (cf. 'your bride's voice', l. 94). In the theatre, an audience would hardly ask itself
    just when the incident took place.
90 *pretend* offer (?'prétend')
    honest i.e., genuine and honourable – ?chaste (despite his bawdy talk in I. i Dia-
    phanta is still a virgin in IV. i)
    she . . . it an ironic error
92 *private conference* Both words suggest – but do not prove – that copulation may
    have been intended (cf. H), though apparently it did not materialize anyway; more
    likely Jasperino simply means 'private rendezvous'.
96 *out* in error
97 *prevent* forestall
99 *Diaphanta* who knows De Flores' voice
102 *challenge* claim. Her *interest* as a woman is no doubt the greater in view of her
    meeting with Beatrice in IV. i.

Had eyes that could shoot fire into kings' breasts,
And touched, she sleeps not here! Yet I have time,
Though night be near, to be resolved hereof;
And prithee do not weigh me by my passions.
JASPERINO
I never weighed friend so.
ALSEMERO   Done charitably.   110
That key will lead thee to a pretty secret,   [*Gives key*]
By a Chaldean taught me, and I've [made]
My study upon some. Bring from my closet
A glass inscribed there with the letter M,
And question not my purpose.
JASPERINO   It shall be done, sir.   *Exit* 115
ALSEMERO
How can this hang together? Not an hour since,
Her woman came pleading her lady's fears,
Delivered her for the most timorous virgin
That ever shrunk at man's name, and so modest,
She charged her weep out her request to me,   120
That she might come obscurely to my bosom.

Enter BEATRICE

BEATRICE [*Aside*]
All things go well. My woman's preparing yonder
For her sweet voyage, which grieves me to lose;
Necessity compels it, I lose all else.
ALSEMERO [*Aside*]
Push, modesty's shrine is set in yonder forehead.   125
I cannot be too sure, though. [*To her*] – My Joanna!
BEATRICE
Sir, I was bold to weep a message to you;
Pardon my modest fears.

---

106 *fire* Cf. III. iv. 151; 'fire' here no doubt means the passions of love, and conversely
    'love' is thought of as a fire in 'love-shooting'.
    into probably 'intó'
107 *touched* (were she) tainted (for all that)
108 *resolved* i.e., satisfied
111 *pretty* ingenious
112 *Chaldean* i.e., a seer or wizard (Daniel 2:2)
    made Bawcutt; cf. sense and metre.
113 *some* i.e., secrets
118 *Delivered her for* described her as
121 *obscurely* in the dark (and perhaps veiled)
123 *sweet voyage* i.e., her pleasant love-making. Cf. I. i. 89.

ALSEMERO [*Aside*]   The dove's not meeker;
  She's abused, questionless.

               Enter JASPERINO [*with glass*]

                         – O, are you come, sir?
BEATRICE [*Aside*]
  The glass, upon my life! I see the letter.   130
JASPERINO
  Sir, this is M.
ALSEMERO   'Tis it.
BEATRICE [*Aside*]   I am suspected.
ALSEMERO
  How fitly our bride comes to partake with us!
BEATRICE
  What is't, my lord?
ALSEMERO   No hurt.
BEATRICE   Sir, pardon me,
  I seldom taste of any composition.
ALSEMERO
  But this, upon my warrant, you shall venture on.   135
                              [*Gives her the glass*]
BEATRICE
  I fear 'twill make me ill.
ALSEMERO   Heaven forbid that.
                              [*Talks apart to* JASPERINO]
BEATRICE [*Aside*]
  I'm put now to my cunning. Th' effects I know –
  If I can now but feign 'em handsomely.   [*Drinks*]
ALSEMERO
  It has that secret virtue it ne'er missed, sir,
  Upon a virgin.
JASPERINO   Treble-qualitied?   140
                      [BEATRICE *gapes, then sneezes*]
ALSEMERO
  By all that's virtuous, it takes there, proceeds!

129 In Q the sd follows the line.
     She's . . . questionless she has undoubtedly been misrepresented and wronged
131 *'Tis* Q: T's; perhaps pronounced unemphatically
134 *composition* made-up drink
135 *warrant* guarantee
137 *effects* symptoms
138 *handsomely* aptly
139 *that virtue* i.e., such good quality (and cf. *virtuous*, l. 141)
140 *treble-qualitied* Alsemero has obviously told him that the mixture has a threefold
     effect.
141 *virtuous* (1) efficacious; (2) chaste   *takes* takes effect as intended (*OED*, 11)

JASPERINO
    This is the strangest trick to know a maid by.
BEATRICE
    Ha, ha, ha!
    You have given me joy of heart to drink, my lord.
ALSEMERO [*To her*]
    No, thou hast given me such joy of heart   145
    That never can be blasted.
BEATRICE   What's the matter, sir?
ALSEMERO [*To* JASPERINO]
    See, now 'tis settled in a melancholy
    Keep[s] both the time and method. – [*To her*]
        My Joanna,
    Chaste as the breath of heaven, or morning's womb
    That brings the day forth, thus my love encloses thee!   150
                            [*Embraces her*] *Exeunt*

[Act IV, Scene iii]

Enter ISABELLA *and* LOLLIO

ISABELLA
    O heaven! Is this the waxing moon?
    Does love turn fool, run mad, and all [at] once?
    Sirrah, here's a madman, akin to the fool too,
    A lunatic lover.
LOLLIO
    No, no! – Not he I brought the letter from?   5
ISABELLA
    Compare his inside with his out, and tell me.
                            [*Gives him the letter*]

142 *maid* virgin
148 *Keeps* Dyce's emendation; sense: which keeps
Scene iii   author: Rowley; place: Alibius' madhouse
    1 *waxing* Williams (waiting Q). As *waiting* (= ominous?) gives no satisfactory sense,
        several emendations have been suggested, of which this seems the best: techni-
        cally likely, and logical in meaning (= growing bigger and thereby causing an
        increase in lunacy).
    2 *at* Dilke
    3 The madman is Franciscus, who is related to the fool, Antonio, in that both turn
        out to be lovers in disguise.
    6 *inside . . . out* (1) the true nature of Franciscus and his disguise; (2) the letter and its
        (*his*) superscription

LOLLIO

The out's mad, I'm sure of that; I had a taste on't.
[*Reads*] 'To the bright Andromeda, chief chambermaid to
the Knight of the Sun, at the sign of Scorpio, in the middle
region, sent by the bellows-mender of Aeolus. Pay the   10
post.' This is stark madness.

ISABELLA

Now mark the inside. [*Takes the letter and reads*] 'Sweet
lady, having now cast off this counterfeit cover of a
madman, I appear to your best judgement a true and
faithful lover of your beauty.'   15

LOLLIO

He is mad still.

ISABELLA

'If any fault you find, chide those perfections in you which
have made me imperfect: 'tis the same sun that causeth to
grow and enforceth to wither, –'

LOLLIO

O rogue!   20

ISABELLA

' – Shapes and transshapes, destroys and builds again. I
come in winter to you, dismantled of my proper ornaments: by the sweet splendour of your cheerful smiles I
spring and live a lover.'

LOLLIO

Mad rascal still!   25

ISABELLA

'Tread him not under foot, that shall appear an honour to
your bounties. I remain – mad till I speak with you, from
whom I expect my cure, yours all, or one beside himself,
Franciscus.'

LOLLIO

You are like to have a fine time on't. My master and I may   30

7 *The … on't* Lollio is convinced that Franciscus is mad when disguised, as he
remembers being harassed in III. iii (cf. l. 86, sd).

8–11 Andromeda-Isabella is to be rescued from the dragon Alibius (or Lollio) by
Perseus-Franciscus. Franciscus addresses the letter to Isabella as *bright* (beautiful
but also clever) in the hope that she will get this general idea. However, he also
jocularly describes her as a chambermaid, supposedly lascivious (like Diaphanta,
cf. V. i. 16; *chambering* also has the sense of copulating, cf. *PSB*) and the typical
reader of a romance like *The Mirror of Knighthood*, in which the Knight of the Sun
(i.e., he) is the hero. She lives (he hopes) at the zodiacal sign of Scorpio because
that governs the private parts ('the middle region'). He is the bellows-mender of
Aeolus, ruler of the winds, because he wants to get things moving (*bellows* clearly = phallus). 'Pay the post' (= courier) is absurdly 'normal' in this 'mad' attempt
at seduction.

9–10 *middle region* also: the fifth to eighth months of the astrological year

give over our professions; I do not think but you can cure
fools and madmen faster than we, with little pains too.

ISABELLA
Very likely.

LOLLIO
One thing I must tell you, mistress. You perceive that I am
privy to your skill: if I find you minister once and set up   35
the trade, I put in for my thirds; I shall be mad or fool else.

ISABELLA
The first place is thine, believe it, Lollio,
If I do fall –

LOLLIO
I fall upon you.

ISABELLA
So.   40

LOLLIO
Well, I stand to my venture.

ISABELLA
But thy counsel now, how shall I deal with 'em?

LOLLIO
Why, do you mean to deal with 'em?

ISABELLA
Nay, the fair understanding – how to use 'em.

LOLLIO
Abuse 'em! That's the way to mad the fool and make a fool   45

33 *Very likely* in that (1) Antonio and Franciscus would be 'cured' if she gave in to
     them; (2) Alibius and Lollio could not do that job; (3) Alibius is, to her, a madman,
     and Lollio a fool (III. iii. 17).
35 *privy . . . skill* i.e., am a sharer of the secret of your profession
35–6 *if . . . trade Minister* = administer something healing, and *trade* = our trade, as
     keepers – the superficial, respectable senses; also: 'if I find you once serving some-
     one's need by copulation and setting up the trade of whore' (cf. H).
36 *my thirds* (1) my one-third share of our medical business (in which she is new); (2)
     my share of what you offer as whore (the other two share-holders being Alibius
     and her lover). Technically, *thirds* = a third of captures, etc., otherwise due to the
     crown, and the share of the personal property of a deceased husband allowed to his
     widow; for *put in* cf. II. ii.60.
37–8 *The . . . fall* Isabella means that Lollio would be the first recipient of her favour
     if she did copulate; before she can say 'But I won't do so' Lollio interrupts her.
40 *So* i.e., indeed – but it won't happen
41 'I will abide by my enterprise' (involving risk or gain).
43 *Why* Dilke (We Q)
     deal with (1) treat; (2) copulate with
44 *fair understanding* i.e., the decent sense which I intended – but *use* also could mean
     'copulate with' as well as 'treat'!
45 *Abuse 'em* (1) deceive them (by disguising yourself and pretending that you are in
     love with them); (2) play on 'make a cuckold of (each of) them' (*PSB*); (3) perhaps
     'abuse' = 'ab-use', i.e., deprive them of copulation

of the madman, and then you use 'em kindly.

ISABELLA

'Tis easy; I'll practise. Do thou observe it.
The key of thy wardrobe.

LOLLIO

There; fit yourself for 'em, and I'll fit 'em both for
you.   [*Gives her the key*]   50

ISABELLA

Take thou no further notice than the outside.   *Exit*

LOLLIO

Not an inch: I'll put you to the inside.

Enter ALIBIUS

ALIBIUS

Lollio, art there? Will all be perfect, think'st thou?
Tomorrow night, as if to close up the solemnity,
Vermandero expects us.   55

LOLLIO

I mistrust the madmen most. The fools will do well
enough; I have taken pains with them.

ALIBIUS

Tush, they cannot miss. The more absurdity,
The more commends it, so no rough behaviours
Affright the ladies. They are nice things, thou know'st.   60

LOLLIO

You need not fear, sir; so long as we are there with our
commanding pizzles, they'll be as tame as the ladies themselves.

ALIBIUS

I will see them once more rehearse before they go.

LOLLIO

I was about it, sir. Look you to the madmen's morris, and   65
let me alone with the other; there is one or two that I
mistrust their fooling. I'll instruct them, and then they
shall rehearse the whole measure.

46 *kindly* according to their natures
47 *practise* execute a (deceitful) plot
49 *fit* (1) dress; (2) prepare; (3) prepare sexually
52 *I'll . . . inside* I'll make you have intercourse (subject you to sexual ingression; cf.
   PSB and H for 'put to' and 'inside')
59 *so* provided that
60 *nice* delicate
62 *pizzles* whips made from dried bulls' penises (meant to keep tame both the
   performers and the ladies)
65 *morris* grotesque dance
66 *one or two* i.e., Antonio
68 *measure* dance

ALIBIUS

Do so; I'll see the music prepared. But, Lollio,
By the way, how does my wife brook her restraint?   70
Does she not grudge at it?

LOLLIO

So, so. She takes some pleasure in the house, she would
abroad else. You must allow her a little more length, she's
kept too short.

ALIBIUS

She shall along to Vermandero's with us: 75
That will serve her for a month's liberty.

LOLLIO

What's that on your face, sir?

ALIBIUS

Where, Lollio? I see nothing.

LOLLIO

Cry you mercy, sir, 'tis your nose: it showed like the trunk
of a young elephant.   80

ALIBIUS

Away, rascal! I'll prepare the music, Lollio. *Exit* ALIBIUS

LOLLIO

Do, sir, and I'll dance the whilst. – Tony, where art thou,
Tony?

Enter ANTONIO

ANTONIO

Here, cousin. Where art thou?

LOLLIO

Come, Tony, the footmanship I taught you.   85

ANTONIO

I had rather ride, cousin.

71 *grudge* complain
72–3 *She . . . else* (also) Isabella can find some sexual pleasure here; otherwise she
would want to be at large and spread her legs (cf. H, *abroad*)
73–4 *You . . . short* play on *length* = 'latitude' and 'length of penis', and *short* = (1)
confined; (2) not gratified (sexually); (3) deprived of penis length (H)
76 *month's* moneth's Q – perhaps disyllabic
liberty without sexual innuendo. This 'liberty' would not only be short but hardly
a change, given her company.
79 *your nose* (1) enlarged because Lollio leads him by it; (2) perhaps = the equivalent
of a cuckold's horns; (3) probably = your very large penis (cf. *nose* and *trunk-work*
in *PSB,* and *trunk* in *PDS*). Chiefly, Lollio jokes about Alibius' huge sexual
appetite (for Isabella, here).
86 *ride* a pun all too obvious to Lollio, who came to know him as a rival in III. iii (cf.
ll. 177 ff.)

LOLLIO

    Ay, a whip take you! But I'll keep you out. Vault in – look
    you, Tony: fa, la, la, la, la.   [*Dances*]

ANTONIO

    Fa, la, la, la, la.   [*Dances*]

LOLLIO

    There, an honour.   [*Bows*]   90

ANTONIO

    Is this an honour, coz?   [*Bows*]

LOLLIO

    Yes, and it please your worship.

ANTONIO

    Does honour bend in the hams, coz?

LOLLIO

    Marry does it, as low as worship, squireship, nay, yeo-
    manry itself sometimes, from whence it first stiffened.   95
    There, rise, a caper.

ANTONIO

    Caper after an honour, coz?

LOLLIO

    Very proper: for honour is but a caper – rise[s] as fast and
    high, has a knee or two, and falls to th' ground again. You
    can remember your figure, Tony?   *Exit*   100

ANTONIO

    Yes, cousin; when I see thy figure I can remember mine.

           Enter ISABELLA [*like a madwoman*]

ISABELLA

    Hey, how he treads the air!

---

87 *out* i.e., from Isabella. Instead of riding her, Antonio is to *Vault* (i.e., jump, with
    play on 'copulate') into the dance.

90 *honour* a curtsey, which Antonio probably (but not necessarily) tries to ape

92 *and* if

93 Antonio wonders whether this is the way to bow, whether people humiliate them-
    selves when they do it, and whether this is the way to copulate. There may also be
    the familiar pun *honour* = 'on her' (cf. H).

94 *Marry does it* by Mary it does

95 *stiffened* (1) grew formal; (2) became an erection (cf. *rise*, l. 96)

96 *caper* 'leap' and 'brief frolic' (Frost)

98 *rises* Dilke's emendation

99 *has . . . two* 'Is curtsied to once or twice' (Black)

100 *figure* (1) dance pattern; (2) appearance

102 ff. Isabella compares Antonio to Icarus, the son of Daedalus, builder of the laby-
    rinth at Crete. Having been imprisoned there, they fled over the sea on artificial
    wings. However, Icarus came too close to the sun, the wax in his wings melted,
    and he fell into the sea.

102 *he* Dilke (she Q)
    treads the air i.e., flies (dances/copulates on air)

Shough, shough, t'other way – he burns his wings else!
Here's wax enough below, Icárus – more
Than will be cancellëd these eighteen moons.   105

                                        [ANTONIO *falls*]

He's down, he's down! What a terrible fall he had!
Stand up, thou son of Cretan Daedalus,
And let us tread the lower labyrinth;
I'll bring thee to the clue.   [*Grabs him*]

ANTONIO

Prithee, coz, let me alone.   [*Rises*]   110

ISABELLA

Art thou not drowned?
About thy head I saw a heap of clouds
Wrapped like a Turkish turban; on thy back
A crookt chameleon-coloured rainbow hung
Like a tiara down unto thy hams.   115
Let me suck out those billows in thy belly:

                              [*Kneels and listens*]

Hark how they roar and rumble in the straits!
Bless thee from the pirates.

ANTONIO

Pox upon you, let me alone!

ISABELLA

Why shouldst thou mount so high as Mercury,   120
Unless thou hadst reversion of his place?
Stay in the moon with me, Endymion,
And we will rule these wild rebellious waves
That would have drowned my love.

103 *Shough* 'shoo' – an exclamation to drive him away (like a bird)

105 *cancellëd* i.e., destroyed, as sealing-wax

108 A mocking sexual invitation (*tread* implies 'copulate') under the guise of madness;
     lower labyrinth suggests both the madhouse and the loins, the sexual zone.

109 The *clue* of thread, given by Ariadne to Theseus, was to lead him out of the
     labyrinth – here it must be an image of sexual release. She does not know how to
     leave the madhouse.

111 Isabella expresses her surprise at things not working out as in the legend; she
     pretends that 'Icarus' has ended up in the labyrinth, not the sea, but then imagina-
     tively moves towards that.

115 *tiara* a headdress with a long tail

116 *billows* 'great waves' supposedly in his belly as a result of drowning, but with pun
     on 'bellows' (an alternative spelling) = phallus (cf. l. 10)

117 *straits* Dyce (streets Q); narrow duct (singular) through which the roaring waves
     seek escape – geographically, this would be between Crete and Greece.

120 *Mercury* winged messenger of the gods

121 *reversion* right of succession

122 *Endymion* a youth beloved by the moon goddess (here Isabella), who controls the
     tides

ANTONIO
    I'll kick thee if again thou touch me,   125
    Thou wild unshapen antic; I am no fool,
    You bedlam!
ISABELLA   But you are, as sure as I am, mad.
    Have I put on this habit of a frantic,
    With love as full of fury, to beguile
    The nimble eye of watchful jealousy,   130
    And am I thus rewarded?   [*Reveals herself*]
ANTONIO
    Ha, dearest beauty!
ISABELLA   No, I have no beauty now,
    Nor never had, but what was in my garments.
    You a quick-sighted lover? Come not near me!
    Keep your caparisons, y'are aptly clad;   135
    I came a feigner, to return stark mad.   *Exit*

Enter LOLLIO

ANTONIO
    Stay, or I shall change conditiön,
    And become as you are.
LOLLIO
    Why, Tony, whither now? Why, fool?
ANTONIO
    Whose fool, usher of idiots? You coxcomb!   140
    I have fooled too much.
LOLLIO
    You were best be mad another while then.
ANTONIO
    So I am, stark mad: I have cause enough,
    And I could throw the full effects on thee,
    And beat thee like a fury!   145
LOLLIO
    Do not, do not. I shall not forbear the gentleman under
    the fool if you do – alas, I saw through your fox-skin

126 *antic* grotesque figure (also: theatrical performer)
127 *bedlam* lunatic
    am, mad The comma is in Q but absent in some eds.
128 *frantic* lunatic
135 *caparisons* clothes fit for a beast (like you)
136 *mad* i.e., with rage
137 *conditiön* my temper
140 *usher* door-keeper and assistant-teacher
146–7 *I . . . do* i.e., I shall not put up with your aggression even though it comes from a
    gentleman disguised as fool
147 *fox-skin* clever disguise

before now! Come, I can give you comfort. My mistress
loves you, and there is as arrant a madman i' th' house as
you are a fool, your rival, whom she loves not. If after the   150
masque we can rid her of him, you earn her love, she says,
and the fool shall ride her.

ANTONIO
May I believe thee?

LOLLIO
Yes, or you may choose whether you will or no.

ANTONIO
She's eased of him; I have a good quarrel on't.   155

LOLLIO
Well, keep your old station yet, and be quiet.

ANTONIO
Tell her I will deserve her love.   [Exit]

LOLLIO
And you are like to have your desire.

Enter FRANCISCUS

FRANCISCUS [*Sings*]
'Down, down, down a-down a-down'; and then with a
    horse-trick
To kick Latona's forehead, and break her bowstring.   160

LOLLIO [*Aside*]
This is t'other counterfeit; I'll put him out of his humour.
[*Takes out letter and reads*] 'Sweet lady, having now cast
[off] this counterfeit cover of a madman, I appear to your
best judgement a true and faithful lover of your beauty.'
This is pretty well for a madman.   165

FRANCISCUS
Ha! What's that?

148 *before now* Cf. I. ii. 115–16.
149 *arrant* Cf. I. ii. 136.
151 *rid her of* set her free from
152 *ride her* i.e., sexually. Note play on *rid her*.
155 *eased* relieved. Cf. III. iv. 97–9.
     I . . . on't 'I have every reason to quarrel with him' (Black)
156 *station* 'position', as fool
159 *Down . . . a-down* Cf. Ophelia, *Hamlet* IV. v. 167, 'You must sing "A-down,
     a-down"' – R's allusion is fitting, given her madness.
     horse-trick (1) horse-play, in imitation of a horse's action; (2) copulation (H).
     Franciscus continues the bawdiness of his song.
160 *Latona* 'The mother of Artemis/Diana, here confused with Artemis herself, com-
     monly depicted as a huntress with a bow. Rowley may have written
     "Latonia" = daughter of Latona' (Frost). Clearly, Franciscus means Isabella,
     whose chastity he hopes to terminate (cf. III. iii. 81).
163 *off* Dyce; cf. l. 13.

LOLLIO

'Chide those perfections in you which [have] made me imperfect.'

FRANCISCUS

I am discovered to the fool.

LOLLIO

I hope to discover the fool in you, ere I have done with   170
you. 'Yours all, or one beside himself, Franciscus.' This
madman will mend sure.

FRANCISCUS

What do you read, sirrah?

LOLLIO

Your destiny, sir. You'll be hanged for this trick, and
another that I know.   175

FRANCISCUS

Art thou of counsel with thy mistress?

LOLLIO

Next her apron-strings.

FRANCISCUS

Give me thy hand.

LOLLIO

Stay, let me put yours in my pocket first [*Puts away the
letter*]. Your hand is true is it not? It will not pick? I partly 180
fear it, because I think it does lie.

FRANCISCUS

Not in a syllable.

LOLLIO

So; if you love my mistress so well as you have handled
the matter here, you are like to be cured of your madness.   185

FRANCISCUS

And none but she can cure it.

167 *have* Dyce; cf. l. 18.
169 *discovered to* found out by
170 *discover* expose
171–2 *This . . . sure* Antonio is a fool gone mad, while Franciscus is a lunatic who turns
       out to be a fool, according to this kind of hypallage.
174 *this trick* fraud. The other trick which Lollio knows through the letter is intended
       copulation (cf. *horse-trick*, l. 159) with a married woman.
176 *of counsel with* in the confidence of
179 *yours* (1) hand; (2) handwriting
180 *true* honest
     pick i.e., my pocket
184–5 *madness* (also) infatuation

LOLLIO

  Well, I'll give you over then, and she shall cast your water
  next.

FRANCISCUS

  Take for thy pains past.   [*Gives him money*]

LOLLIO

  I shall deserve more, sir, I hope. My mistress loves you,   190
  but must have some proof of your love to her.

FRANCISCUS

  There I meet my wishes.

LOLLIO

  That will not serve: you must meet her enemy and yours.

FRANCISCUS

  He's dead already!

LOLLIO

  Will you tell me that, and I parted but now with him?   195

FRANCISCUS

  Show me the man.

LOLLIO

  Ay, that's a right course now: see him before you kill him
  in any case. And yet it needs not go so far neither. 'Tis but
  a fool that haunts the house and my mistress in the shape
  of an idiot. Bang but his fool's coat well-favouredly, and   200
  'tis well.

FRANCISCUS

  Soundly, soundly!

LOLLIO

  Only reserve him till the masque be past, and if you find
  him not now in the dance yourself, I'll show you. In, in!
  My master!   [*Dances*]   205

FRANCISCUS

  He handles him like a feather. Hey!   [*Exit dancing*]

Enter ALIBIUS

ALIBIUS

  Well said. In a readiness, Lollio?

LOLLIO

  Yes, sir.

187 *cast your water* examine your urine in diagnosis
199 *shape* disguise
200 *well-favouredly* soundly
202 *Soundly* i.e., 'soundly advised', and 'I'll hit him soundly'
203 *reserve* spare
204 *In* Lollio guides Franciscus towards the inner stage because he has suddenly seen
    Alibius.
206 *him* himself
207 *Well said* well done

ALIBIUS

    Away then, and guide them in, Lollio;
    Entreat your mistress to see this sight.   [*Exit* LOLLIO]   210
    Hark, is there not one incurable fool
    That might be begged? I have friends.

LOLLIO [*Within*]

    I have him for you: one that shall deserve it too.

ALIBIUS

    Good boy, Lollio.

       [*Enter* ISABELLA, *then* LOLLIO *with* MADMEN *and* FOOLS]
               The MADMEN *and* FOOLS *dance*

ALIBIUS

    'Tis perfect. Well, fit [we] but once these strains,   215
    We shall have coin and credit for our pains.   *Exeunt*

Act V [, Scene i]

Enter BEATRICE. *A clock strikes one*

BEATRICE

    One struck, and yet she lies by't! – O my fears!
    This strumpet serves her own ends, 'tis apparent now,
    Devours the pleasure with a greedy appetite,
    And never minds my honour or my peace,
    Makes havoc of my right. But she pays dearly for't: 5

212 *That ... begged* The lands and profits of a fool – who was considered a Minor of
    Law – were during his life held by the King, who could farm out the lands, and
    give custody, to another party. Such a party could 'beg a fool', i.e., apply to be his
    guardian, and thus enjoy the profits of his lands. A different, less lucrative
    arrangement applied to lunatics. Applications were heard by the Court of Wards
    and Liveries, and the situation could thus be highly profitable to lawyers as well as
    successful applicants. When Alibius talks about 'friends' he might mean a helpful
    lawyer (the fool first was to be legally proved a congenital idiot); as he received
    payment for his 'care' the arrangement would benefit him even if he was not the
    guardian himself, though more so if he was.
213 Lollio presumably means Alibius, who may deserve to be declared an incurable
    fool rather than a guardian. If pressed to explain further, Lollio could say 'me', or
    'Antonio' or 'Franciscus'.
215 *we* Craik; gives better metre and the sense 'provided that we fit ...'
    these strains i.e., these efforts, which are to be matched as yet to the strains of the
    music (cf. l. 69)
Act V, Scene i author: Middleton; place: Vermandero's castle
  1 *and ... by't* and still she is having intercourse (cf. H, *it*)
  2 *ends* with possible innuendo of pudendum (H). The language (e.g., in 'Devours'
    and 'appetite', l. 3) is certainly full of sexual suggestiveness.
  4 *honour* reputation for chastity

No trusting of her life with such a secret,
That cannot rule her blood to keep her promise.
Beside, I have some suspicion of her faith to me,
Because I was suspected of my lord,
And it must come from her. – Hark, by my horrors,   10
Another clock strikes two.   *Strike[s] two*

Enter DE FLORES

DE FLORES   Pist, where are you?
BEATRICE
    De Flores!
DE FLORES   Ay. Is she not come from him yet?
BEATRICE
    As I am a living soul, not.
DE FLORES   Sure the devil
    Hath sowed his itch within her. Who would trust
    A waiting-woman?
BEATRICE   I must trust somebody.   15
DE FLORES
    Push, they are termagants,
    Especially when they fall upon their masters
    And have their ladies' first-fruits; th'are mad whelps,
    You cannot stave 'em off from game royal. Then,
    You are so harsh and hardy, ask no counsel;   20
    And I could have helped you to a[n] apothecary's
        daughter
    Would have fall'n off before eleven, and thank[ed] you
        too.
BEATRICE
    O me, not yet? This whore forgets herself.
DE FLORES
    The rascal fares so well. Look, y'are undone:

7 *blood* sexual passion
9 *of* by
11 sd *Strikes* Dilke's emendation
14 *itch* inclination to evil (Spencer); sexual urge (*PDS*)
    would Dyce ('d Q); cf. metre.
15 *waiting-woman* female servant and personal attendant
16 *termagants* 'violent women, hence presumably lustful' (Black)
17 *fall upon* happen to meet – in bed
19 *stave . . . royal* 'divert them from hunting game which are a royal preserve' (Frost)
    Then as well
20 *harsh and hardy* 'rough and tough', over-bold (Black)
21 *an* Dilke's emendation
22 *thanked* Dilke: thank'd; some defend Q's 'thank'.

The day-star, by this hand! See Phosphorus plain
   yonder.   25
BEATRICE
Advise me now to fall upon some ruin;
There is no counsel safe else.
DE FLORES   Peace! I ha't now,
For we must force a rising; there's no remedy.
BEATRICE
How? Take heed of that.
DE FLORES
Tush, be you quiet, or else give over all.   30
BEATRICE
Prithee, I ha' done then.
DE FLORES   This is my reach: I'll set
Some part a-fire of Diaphanta's chamber.
BEATRICE
How? Fire, sir? That may endanger the whole house.
DE FLORES
You talk of danger when your fame's on fire?   ·
BEATRICE
That's true; do what thou wilt now.
DE FLORES   Push, I aim   35
At a most rich success, strikes all dead sure:
The chimney being a-fire, and some light parcels
Of the least danger in her chamber only,
If Diaphanta should be met by chance then
Far from her lodging (which is now suspicious),   40
It would be thought her fears and affrights then
Drove her to seek for succour; if not seen
Or met at all, as that's the likeliest,
For her own shame she'll hasten towards her lodging.
I will be ready with a piece high-charged,   45

---

25 *Phosphorus* (Dilke; Bosphorus Q) the morning star, or Lucifer – the Devil (ironic
   in De Flores' mouth; cf. also l. 13)
26 *to .. ruin* how to hit upon some method of destruction (of Diaphanta, as she
   thinks)
27 *There . . . else* there is no other safe scheme
28 *force a rising* make everyone get up (so as to include Diaphanta)
31 *reach* plan
34 *fame* reputation
36 *success* outcome
   strikes all dead which will (1) amaze everyone (De Flores); (2) kill everyone (M)
37–8 *light . . . danger* insubstantial things least likely to cause a major fire
40 *which . . . suspicious* because, under present circumstances, she should not be far
   from her bedroom (*lodging*)
44 *towards* Read 't'wards'.
45 *piece high-charged* heavily loaded hand-gun

As 'twere to cleanse the chimney; there 'tis proper,
But she shall be the mark.
BEATRICE   I'm forced to love thee now,
'Cause thou provid'st so carefully for my honour.
DE FLORES
'Slid, it concerns the safety of us both,
Our pleasure and continuance.
BEATRICE   One word now,   50
Prithee. How for the servants?
DE FLORES   I'll despatch them
Some one way, some another in the hurry,
For buckets, hooks, ladders. Fear not you;
The deed shall find its time. – And I've thought since
Upon a safe conveyance for the body too.   55
How this fire purifies wit! Watch you your minute.
BEATRICE
Fear keeps my soul upon't; I cannot stray from't.

Enter ALONZO'*s ghost*

DE FLORES
Ha! what art thou, that tak'st away the light
'Twixt that star and me? I dread thee not;
'Twas but a mist of conscience. – All's clear again.   *Exit*   60
BEATRICE
Who's that, De Flores? Bless me! It slides by!
                                        [*Exit ghost*]
Some ill thing haunts the house; 't has left behind it
A shivering sweat upon me. I'm afraid now.
This night hath been so tedious! O, this strumpet!
Had she a thousand lives, he should not leave her   65

46 *proper* Craik (proper now Q; its *now* is superfluous and no doubt results from
   confusion with *now* in l. 47). De Flores means that it is common to use a gun when
   attempting to put out a chimney-fire. Hence the presence of a gun near Diaphanta's chimney will be appropriate – but she will be its target.
49 '*Slid* 'by God's eyelid' (contracted)
50 *Our . . . continuance* our sexual enjoyment and its continuance, as well as our
   continued existence
54 *The deed* i.e., the killing of Diaphanta
55 *conveyance* removal; trick
56 *your minute* i.e., for action, as a participant in our plot
59 *that star* no doubt the morning star (l. 25) with its devilish light, from which De
   Flores is momentarily separated by what he calls 'a mist of conscience'. Pyrotech-
   nics were probably used to represent the star in the theatre.
62 *Some ill thing* Beatrice is probably less aware than De Flores of the nature of the
   ghost, and even more inclined not to see it for what it is, i.e., what Hamlet calls an
   'honest' ghost – not evil, but a reminder of it.
64 *tedious* painful and long

Till he had destroyed the last. List! O my
    terrors!   *Struck three o'clock*
Three struck, by Saint Sebastian's!
[VOICES] *within*
  Fire, fire, fire!
BEATRICE
  Already! How rare is that man's speed!
  How heartily he serves me! His face loathes one,   70
  But look upon his care, who would not love him?
  The east is not more beauteous than his service.
[VOICES] *within*
  Fire, fire, fire!

      Enter DE FLORES; SERVANTS *pass over, ring a bell*

DE FLORES
  Away, despatch! Hooks, buckets, ladders! That's well
    said! –
  The fire-bell rings, the chimney works; my charge,   75
  The piece is ready.   *Exit*
BEATRICE   Here's a man worth loving! –

        Enter DIAPHANTA

  O, y'are a jewel!
DIAPHANTA   Pardon frailty, madam;
  In troth I was so well I ev'n forgot myself.
BEATRICE
  Y'have made trim work.
DIAPHANTA   What?
BEATRICE   Hie quickly to your
    chamber;
  Your reward follows you.
DIAPHANTA   I never made   80
  So sweet a bargain.   *Exit*

        Enter ALSEMERO

ALSEMERO   O my dear Joanna!

66 sd This follows l. 67 in Q.
70 *loathes one* is loathsome to one
74 *well said* well done
75–6 *the chimney . . . ready* the chimney works, my charge; / The piece is ready, Q.
    But presumably De Flores means: 'The chimney is working as planned, being
    afire (cf. l. 37); and the load of powder, i.e., the gun, is ready for Diaphanta.'
77 *jewel* (1) a gem; (2) ironically: 'chastity itself'. Cf. III. iv. 36.
79 *trim* (1) proper, neat; (2) play on *trim* v., to copulate – strengthened by *work*, which
    could mean 'intercourse' (H)
80 *Your reward* (1) your money; (2) your death

Alas, art thou risen too? I was coming,
My absolute treasure.
BEATRICE   When I missed you
I could not choose but follow.
ALSEMERO   Th'art all sweetness!
The fire is not so dangerous.
BEATRICE   Think you so, sir?   85
ALSEMERO
I prithee, tremble not; believe me, 'tis not.

Enter VERMANDERO, JASPERINO

VERMANDERO
O, bless my house and me!
ALSEMERO   My lord your father.

Enter DE FLORES *with a piece*

VERMANDERO
Knave, whither goes that piece?
DE FLORES   To scour the
   chimney.   *Exit*
VERMANDERO
O, well said, well said!
That fellow's good on all occasiöns.   90
BEATRICE
A wondrous necessary man, my lord.
VERMANDERO
He hath a ready wit; he's worth 'em all, sir.
Dog at a house on fire – I ha' seen him singed ere now.
                              The piece goes off
Ha, there he goes.
BEATRICE [*Aside*]   'Tis done.
ALSEMERO   Come, sweet, to bed now;
Alas, thou wilt get cold.
BEATRICE   Alas, the fear keeps that out!   95
My heart will find no quiet till I hear
How Diaphanta, my poor woman, fares;
It is her chamber, sir, her lodging chamber.
VERMANDERO
How should the fire come there?

---

84 *I . . . follow* ironically echoed in V. iii. 108
93 *Dog at* skilled in. Cf. 'To be (old) dog at it' (*ODEP*, p. 194).
    on fire Dilke (of fire Q)
95 *Alas . . . Alas* It has been suggested that the word should occur only once, but
    there is no agreement as to whether the first *Alas* is superfluous or the second.

BEATRICE

As good a soul as ever lady countenanced,   100
But in her chamber negligent and heavy.
She 'scaped a ruin twice.

VERMANDERO   Twice?

BEATRICE   Strangely, twice, sir.

VERMANDERO

Those sleepy sluts are dangerous in a house,
And they be ne'er so good.

Enter DE FLORES

DE FLORES   O poor virginity!
Thou hast paid dearly for't.

VERMANDERO   Bless us! What's that?   105

DE FLORES

A thing you all knew once – Diaphanta's burnt.

BEATRICE

My woman! O my woman!

DE FLORES   Now the flames
Are greedy of her: burnt, burnt, burnt to death, sir.

BEATRICE

O my presaging soul!

ALSEMERO   Not a tear more!
I charge you by the last embrace I gave you   110
In bed, before this raised us.

BEATRICE   Now you tie me:
Were it my sister, now she gets no more.

Enter SERVANT

100 *countenanced* favoured

101 *heavy* sluggish

102 *ruin* Craik (Mine Q). Although the image of a *mine* fits in with that of De Flores'
gun (and, referring to a hidden explosive, could signify 'danger'), the word would
be puzzling to Vermandero, as it is to most readers. Craik's *ruin* is technically
likely, gives clear sense at any level, and fits the metre. Diaphanta almost came to
ruin, presumably, when she passed the virginity test, and when she deceived
Alsemero. (Beatrice herself would have failed on both occasions.) The word has
already been used in a similar and relevant way in l. 26.

104 *And . . . good* no matter how good they otherwise are

104–5 *O . . . for't* De Flores (the deflowerer) pretends that Diaphanta's virginity has
cost her her life; with a husband, she might have survived (like Beatrice) – now,
instead, the flames are 'greedy' of her (l. 108).

105 *that* There is no sign that De Flores is carrying anything other than Diaphanta's
body, and it would be theatrically effective for him to do so, especially as a means
of 'explaining' what has happened and thus of removing the body; his dishonesty
here contrasts with his love for Beatrice when he brings her in later (V. iii).

109 *O . . . soul* Cf. *Hamlet* I. v. 40, 'O my prophetic soul!'

112 The sd follows 'How now?' (l. 113) in Q.

VERMANDERO
How now?

SERVANT   All danger's past; you may now take
Your rests, my lords. The fire is throughly quenched.
Ah, poor gentlewoman, how soon was she stifled!   115

BEATRICE
De Flores, what is left of her inter,
And we as mourners all will follow her.
I will entreat that honour to my servant
Ev'n of my lord himself.

ALSEMERO   Command it, sweetness.

BEATRICE
Which of you spied the fire first?

DE FLORES   'Twas I, madam.   120

BEATRICE
And took such pains in't too? A double goodness!
'Twere well he were rewarded.

VERMANDERO   He shall be. –
De Flores, call upon me.

ALSEMERO   And upon me, sir.

                Exeunt [all but DE FLORES]

DE FLORES
Rewarded? Precious! Here's a trick beyond me!
I see in all bouts, both of sport and wit,   125
Always a woman strives for the last hit.   *Exit*

[Act V, Scene ii]

Enter TOMAZO

TOMAZO
I cannot taste the benefits of life
With the same relish I was wont to do.
Man I grow weary of, and hold his fellowship
A treacherous bloody friendship; and because
I am ignorant in whom my wrath should settle,   5
I must think all men villains, and the next
I meet, whoe'er he be, the murderer
Of my most worthy brother. – Ha! What's he?

Enter DE FLORES, *passes over the stage*

---

114 *throughly* thoroughly
125 *sport* Cf. I. ii. 173; but here chiefly = (1) fencing, (2) amorous sport (*PSB*); *hit*
    (l. 126) has the subsidiary sense of copulation.
Scene ii   author: Middleton; place Vermandero's castle

O, the fellow that some call honest De Flores.
But methinks honesty was hard bested   10
To come there for a lodging – as if a queen
Should make her palace of a pest-house.
I find a contrariety in nature
Betwixt that face and me; the least occasion
Would give me game upon him. Yet he's so foul,   15
One would scarce touch [him] with a sword he loved
And made account of; so most deadly venomous,
He would go near to poison any weapon
That should draw blood on him. One must resolve
Never to use that sword again in fight,   20
In way of honest manhood, that strikes him.
Some river must devour it; 'twere not fit
That any man should find it. – What, again?

Enter DE FLORES

He walks a' purpose by, sure, to choke me up,
To infect my blood.
DE FLORES   My worthy noble lord!   25
TOMAZO
Dost offer to come near and breathe upon me?
                                    [*Strikes him*]
DE FLORES
A blow!   [*Draws his sword*]
TOMAZO   Yea, are you so prepared?
I'll rather like a soldier die by th' sword
Than like a politician by thy poison.   [*Draws*]
DE FLORES
Hold, my lord, as you are honourable.   30
TOMAZO
All slaves that kill by poison are still cowards.
DE FLORES [*Aside*]
I cannot strike: I see his brother's wounds

---

10 *hard bested* hard put to it ('bestéd')
12 *pest-house* hospital for those suffering from infectious diseases, especially the
   plague
15 *give . . . him* ?incite me to fight him (Sampson)
   foul loathsome (perhaps with reference to disease)
16 *him* Dilke
   he i.e., one
22 *it* Dyce ('t Q); cf. metre.
24 *choke me up* i.e., to suffocate me to death with his contagious presence
29 *politician* schemer
31 *still* always

Fresh bleeding in his eye, as in a crystal.
[*To* TOMAZO] I will not question this: I know y'are
    noble.   [*Sheathes his sword*]
I take my injury with thanks given, sir,   35
Like a wise lawyër, and as a favour
Will wear it for the worthy hand that gave it.
[*Aside*] Why this from him, that yesterday appeared
So strangely loving to me?
O, but instínct is of a subtler strain!   40
Guilt must not walk so near his lodge again –
He came near me now.   *Exit*

TOMAZO

All league with mankind I renounce for ever
Till I find this murderer. Not so much
As common courtesy but I'll lock up,   45
For in the state of ignorance I live in
A brother may salute his brother's murderer,
And wish good speed to th'villain in a greeting.

Enter VERMANDERO, ALIBIUS, *and* ISABELLA

VERMANDERO

Noble Piracquo!
TOMAZO   Pray keep on your way, sir;
I've nothing to say to you.
VERMANDERO   Comforts bless you, sir.   50
TOMAZO

I have forsworn compliment; in troth I have, sir.
As you are merely man, I have not left
A good wish for you, nor [for] any here.

---

33 *Fresh bleeding* perhaps an allusion to the belief that the victim's wounds started
    bleeding again if the murderer was near (Bawcutt)
    as in a crystal clearly, as in a crystal ball
36 *Like . . . lawyër* Cf. 'A good lawyer must be a great liar' (*ODEP*, p. 447).
38–9 The change in Tomazo's behaviour is indeed odd, but he is a dramatic charac-
    ter, not a real one, and De Flores provides an adequate explanation in l. 40:
    Tomazo's instinct (intuitive and unconscious) is *subtler* (= more perceptive) than
    what we usually call reason. His instinct has now revealed to him a truth about De
    Flores of which he was previously unaware.
41 *his* Tomazo's
42 'He was very near to sensing my guilt just now' (Black).
43 *league* i.e., alliance
44–5 *Not . . . up* i.e., 'I'll display no more than something less than common courtesy'
48 *speed* success
51 *forsworn* (perhaps 'fórsworn') renounced
    compliment formal courtesy (cf. ll. 43–8)
53 *for* Dyce; cf. metre.

VERMANDERO
   Unless you be so far in love with grief
   You will not part from't upon any terms,   55
   We bring that news will make a welcome for us.
TOMAZO
   What news can that be?
VERMANDERO   Throw no scornful smile
   Upon the zeal I bring you; 'tis worth more, sir.
   Two of the chiefest men I kept about me
   I hide not from the law, or your just vengeance.   60
TOMAZO
   Ha!
VERMANDERO
   To give your peace more ample satisfaction,
   Thank these discoverers.
TOMAZO   If you bring that calm,
   Name but the manner I shall ask forgiveness in
   For that contemptuous smile [I threw] upon you: 65
   I'll pérfect it with reverence that belongs
   Unto a sacred altar.   [*Kneels*]
VERMANDERO   Good sir, rise.
   Why, now you overdo as much a' this hand,
   As you fell short a' t' other. – Speak, Alibius.
ALIBIUS
   'Twas my wife's fortune – as she is most lucky   70
   At a discovery – to find out lately
   Within our hospital of fools and madmen
   Two counterfeits slipped into these disguises;
   Their names, Franciscus and Antonio.
VERMANDERO
   Both mine, sir, and I ask no favour for 'em.   75
ALIBIUS
   Now that which draws suspicion to their habits:
   The time of their disguisings agrees justly
   With the day of the murder.
TOMAZO   O blest revelation!

56 *will* i.e., that will
58 *zeal* (1) good will; (2) zeal in my pursuit
60 *or . . . vengeance* Many saw private revenge as a satisfactory substitute for a legal
   process; Tomazo is offered a choice.
63 *discoverers* informants who have found out a secret (Alibius and Isabella)
65 *I threw* Dyce; cf. metre and l. 57.
73 *these disguises* Presumably Vermandero has them with him as evidence.
75 *favour* lenient treatment
76 *habits* clothes (of madman and fool)
77 *justly* exactly

VERMANDERO

Nay more, nay more, sir – I'll not spare mine own
In way of justice – they both feigned a journey   80
To Bramata, and so wrought out their leaves;
My love was so abused in't.

TOMAZO   Time's too precious
To run in waste now. You have brought a peace
The riches of five kingdoms could not purchase.
Be my most happy conduct. I thirst for 'em: 85
Like subtle lightning will I wind about 'em,
And melt their marrow in 'em.   *Exeunt*

[Act V, Scene iii]

Enter ALSEMERO *and* JASPERINO

JASPERINO

Your confidence, I'm sure, is now of proof.
The prospect from the garden has showed
Enough for deep suspicion.

ALSEMERO   The black mask
That so continually was worn upon't
Condemns the face for ugly ere't be seen –   5
Her despite to him, and so seeming bottomless.

---

81 *Bramata* so Q (cf. *Briamata*, IV. ii. 7). Perhaps the spelling indicates the pronun-
    ciation here.
    so . . . leaves that way worked out their requests for leave of absence
85 *conduct* guide
86–7 'Lightning was held capable of melting marrow without damaging the skin, and
    so became an image for sudden, undetectable murder' (Frost).
Scene iii author: Rowley; place: Vermandero's castle
   1 *of proof* (1) based on firm evidence; (2) armoured against attack. Previously,
      Alsemero had lacked complete *confidence* in Jasperino's judgement; now, it is
      fortified against any trial.
   2 *prospect* 'what we have viewed' or 'the spectacle offered'. Either way, it seems that
      they have themselves been in the garden (cf. ll. 9–11) and have there seen a
      meeting between De Flores and Beatrice which they agree justifies grave (*deep*)
      suspicion, allowing but one conclusion.
   3 *The black mask* the mask which Alsemero feels Beatrice has worn deceitfully –
      black because it is evil
   5 Her true *face*, which he has not seen because she has hidden it, inevitably must be
      judged to be ugly (morally) before it is revealed. As for her *despite* (l. 6) to De
      Flores, which seemed to be unlimited: the false mask condemns that, too, before
      anything further is found out, as it can only be dishonest.

JASPERINO
    Touch it home then. 'Tis not a shallow probe
    Can search this ulcer soundly: I fear you'll find it
    Full of corruptiön. – 'Tis fit I leave you.
    She meets you opportunely from that walk;   10
    She took the back door at his parting with her.
                                                Exit JASPERINO
ALSEMERO
    Did my fate wait for this unhappy stroke
    At my first sight of woman? – She is here.

                            Enter BEATRICE

BEATRICE
    Alsemero!
ALSEMERO   How do you?
BEATRICE   How do I?
    Alas, [sir], how do you? You look not well.   15
ALSEMERO
    You read me well enough. I am not well.
BEATRICE
    Not well, sir? Is't in my power to better you?
ALSEMERO
    Yes.
BEATRICE   Nay, then y'are cured again.
ALSEMERO
    Pray resolve me one question, lady.
BEATRICE   If I can.
ALSEMERO
    None can so sure. Are you honest?   20
BEATRICE
    Ha, ha, ha! That's a broad question, my lord.
ALSEMERO
    But that's not a modest answer, my lady.

---

7 *Touch it home* examine it all the way – obviously by confronting Beatrice
9–11 *'Tis . . . her* Jasperino leaves Alsemero so as to give him an opportunity to
    address her privately; she appears to have returned from the garden after them,
    and now happens to be coming Alsemero's way.
12–13 *Did . . . woman* Cf. his first speech (I. i. 1–12), in which he thinks of her as Eve;
    he had known no women before, and now wonders whether his fate had waited
    intentionally to deliver this blow.
13 *is* Dyce ('s Q); cf. metre.
15 *sir* Craik (Dyce had inserted it after 'you'); cf. metre, and resulting emphasis on
    you.
19 *resolve* answer, satisfy me concerning
20 *honest* (1) truthful; (2) chaste
22 *modest* bashful and chaste

Do you laugh? My doubts are strong upon me.
BEATRICE
  'Tis innocence that smiles, and no rough brow
  Can take away the dimple in her cheek.   25
  Say I should strain a tear to fill the vault,
  Which would you give the better faith to?
ALSEMERO
  'Twere but hypocrisy of a sadder colour,
  But the same stuff. Neither your smiles not tears
  Shall move or flatter me from my belief: 30
  You are a whore.
BEATRICE   What a horrid sound it hath!
  It blasts a beauty to deformity;
  Upon what face soever that breath falls,
  It strikes it ugly. O, you have ruined
  What you can ne'er repair again!   35
ALSEMERO
  I'll all demolish, and seek out truth within you,
  If there be any left. Let your sweet tongue
  Prevent your heart's rifling; there I'll ransack
  And tear out my suspiciön.
BEATRICE   You may, sir,
  'Tis an easy passage. Yet, if you please,   40
  Show me the ground whereon you lost your love.
  My spotless virtue may but tread on that
  Before I perish.
ALSEMERO   Unanswerable!
  A ground you cannot stand on: you fall down
  Beneath all grace and goodness when you set   45

---

23 *doubts* (also) fears
26 *strain . . . vault* i.e., force enough out of a tear to fill the arch of heaven
27 *Which* i.e., smiling or crying
28 *a sadder colour* a more solemn, darker hue than appears at present. Although
  Alsemero has already described her face to Jasperino as having a 'black' mask
  (l. 3), he has not yet used such epithets in Beatrice's presence – so long as she
  laughs, her hypocrisy does not, superficially, seem as 'sad' as it would if she cried.
37–8 *Let . . . rifling* 'make sure that your sweet tongue tells the truth and thus fore-
  stalls my forceful search of your heart'; or – if Q's semi-colon after *rifling* is
  mistaken – 'no matter how that sweet tongue of yours may try to forestall my
  forceful search of your heart . . .'
38 *there* in your heart
  ransack search aggressively
40 *passage* i.e., to the truth in my heart
41 *ground* i.e., basis
42 *may . . . that* can only crush it
43 *Unanswerable* i.e., it is a basis so strong that you cannot begin to argue with it

Your ticklish heel on it. There was a visor
O'er that cunning face, and that became you;
Now impudence in triumph rides upon't.
How comes this tender reconcilement else
'Twixt you and your despite, your rancorous loathing,   50
De Flores? He that your eye was sore at sight of,
He's now become your arms' supporter, your
Lips' saint!

BEATRICE   Is there the cause?

ALSEMERO   Worse; your lust's devil,
Your adultery!

BEATRICE   Would any but yourself say that,
'Twould turn him to a villain.

ALSEMERO   It was witnessed   55
By the counsel of your bosom, Diaphanta.

BEATRICE
Is your witness dead then?

ALSEMERO   'Tis to be feared
It was the wages of her knowledge. Poor soul,
She lived not long after the discovery.

BEATRICE
Then hear a story of not much less horror   60
Than this your false suspicion is beguiled with.

46 *ticklish* (1) unsteady (on the ground) (2) lascivious
   it Dyce ('t Q); cf. metre.
   visor i.e., the *black mask* (l. 3) which has now been removed (he feels), revealing
   her *cunning face*
47 *that ... you* it was a 'becoming' mask of modesty, but it also ironically fitted her in
   that it, like her true nature, was false
48 *impudence* shamelessness
49–51 *How ... De Flores* i.e., in what other way than by assuming that you were
   wearing a *visor* can one explain this reconciliation between you and the man you
   seemed to scorn and hate so much?
52 *arms' supporter* Williams explains: (1) the man or beast that stands beside the
   shield of arms in heraldic blazoning; (2) physical sustainer of your arms.
53 *Lips' saint* 'spiritual sustainer to whom the prayers of your spirit are voiced'
   (Williams) as well as 'lover' (cf. I. i. 153)
   there 'in what you have just told me'
   the cause Cf. l.41.
   devil Cf. I. i. 223, etc.
54 *Your adultery* ?your partner in adultery (Black)
55 *It was* Dyce ('Twas Q); cf. metre.
56 *the ... bosom* your confidante

To your bed's scandal, I stand up innocence,
Which even the guilt of one black other deed
Will stand for proof of: your̈ love has made me
A cruel murd'ress.

ALSEMERO   Ha!

BEATRICE   A bloody one;   65
I have kissed poison for it, stroked a serpent:
That thing of hate – worthy in my esteem
Of no better employment, and him most worthy
To be so employed – I caused to murder
That innocent Piracquo, having no   70
Better means than that worst, to assure
Yourself to me.

ALSEMERO   O, the place itself e'er since
Has crying been for vengëance: the temple
Where blood and beauty first unlawfully
Fired their devotiön, and quenched the right one;   75
'Twas in my fears at first, 'twill have it now:
O, thou art all deformed!

---

62 'In answer to your bed's scandal, I stand up (set up, put forward) innocence'
(Bawcutt). The interpretation makes sense and is generally endorsed, though
Williams suggests the reading 'innocent' and points out that the transitive force of
'stand' which Bawcutt advocates is not recognized by *OED* before the nineteenth
century. That may well be *OED*'s shortcoming rather than Bawcutt's, and cf.
Antony and Cleopatra I. i. 40 (Frost).

64 *your̈* A monosyllable is possible, though unlikely if the line has five metrical
stresses.
your̈ love i.e., my love for you. She argues that her willingness to be a murderess
for the sake of that proves her innocent of adultery; indeed, in l. 66 she claims that
she has 'kissed poison' (i.e., De Flores) out of love for Alsemero.

65 *bloody* ironically also signifying 'driven by sexual passion'

66 *it* Dyce ('t Q); cf. metre – though *for't* is possible.
stroked almost certainly with ironic sense of 'copulated with' (cf. H), which contrasts with her claim in l. 82

74 *blood* sexual desire

75 *Fired* set on fire, sexually and destructively
the right one i.e., religious devotion – not only proper in a temple anyway, but the
more necessary because Beatrice was already engaged (cf. *unlawfully*)

76 Unclear. Often *'twill ... now* is interpreted as 'the temple will have vengeance'.
But *'Twas ... first* cannot refer to the temple, and rather seems to mean 'A sense of
foreboding was in my fears at first' (cf. I. i. 1–4); if so, the remainder perhaps
means 'and that feeling insists on having its outcome now', i.e., the fact that you
have changed from beauty to ugliness (l. 77). He realizes that this outcome was
inevitable after he allowed her beauty and his desire to create within him a mistaken devotion to her – he should have paid attention to his fear instead.

BEATRICE   Forget not, sir,
  It for your sake was done. Shall greater dangers
  Make the less welcome?
ALSEMERO   O, thou shouldst have gone
  A thousand leagues about to have avoided   80
  This dangerous bridge of blood! Here we are lost.
BEATRICE
  Remember I am true unto your bed.
ALSEMERO
  The bed itself's a charnel, the sheets shrouds
  For murdered carcasses. It must ask pause
  What I must do in this. Meantime you shall   85
  Be my prisoner only. Enter my closet;
                    Exit BEATRICE [*into closet*]
  I'll be your keeper yet. – O, in what part
  Of this sad story shall I first begin? – Ha!

          Enter DE FLORES

  This same fellow has put me in. – De Flores?
DE FLORES
  Noble Alsemero!
ALSEMERO   I can tell you   90
  News, sir. My wife has her commended to you.
DE FLORES
  That's news indeed, my lord; I think she would
  Commend me to the gallows if she could,
  She ever loved me so well. I thank her.
ALSEMERO
  What's this blood upon your band, De Flores?   95
DE FLORES
  Blood? No, sure; 'twas washed since.
ALSEMERO   Since when, man?
DE FLORES
  Since t'other day I got a knock
  In a sword-and-dagger school; I think 'tis out.

78–9 *Shall ... welcome* shall the greater dangers I have dared for you make my welcome the less? (Black)
80 *about* out of your way
81 *This ... blood* this dangerous bridge between us, based on blood
83 *charnel* vault for dead bodies (charnel-house)
84 *pause* i.e., for consideration
86 *closet* Cf. IV. i. 17.
87 *yet* 'for the time being' (Black); otherwise: 'as yet – in contrast to what I thought
  when I reassured myself about your virginity / to the role of keeper which I
  imagined I would have as a husband (before you became *my prisoner only*)'
89 *put me in* given me the cue (Sampson) – i.e., as to where to start: with him
95 *band* cuff (*OED, sb.*², 3; 'collar' is possible but less likely)

ALSEMERO
  Yes, 'tis almost out, but 'tis perceived though. –
  I had forgot my message. This it is: 100
  What price goes murder?
DE FLORES   How, sir?
ALSEMERO   I ask you, sir.
  My wife's behindhand with you, she tells me,
  For a brave bloody blow you gave for her sake
  Upon Piracquo.
DE FLORES   Upon? 'Twas quite through him, sure.
  Has she confessed it?
ALSEMERO   As sure as death to both of you,   105
  And much more than that.
DE FLORES   It could not be much more:
  'Twas but one thing, and that she is a whore.
ALSEMERO
  I[t] could not choose but follow. O cunning devils!
  How should blind men know you from fair-faced saints?
BEATRICE *within*
  He lies, the villain does belie me!   110
DE FLORES
  Let me go to her, sir.
ALSEMERO   Nay, you shall to her. –
  Peace, crying crocodile, your sounds are heard!
  Take your prey to you. – Get you into her, sir.
                    Exit DE FLORES [*into closet*]
  I'll be your pander now: rehearse again
  Your scene of lust, that you may be perféct   115

102 *behindhand with* indebted to
103 *brave* courageous; splendid
107 Editors generally introduce a punctuation mark after *that*. But the sense is plainer
    without it: 'There was only one thing to be confessed, i.e., the murder of Alonzo,
    and, additionally, the fact that she is a whore ("adulterous" – or even "prepared to
    pay for the murder by giving her body to me").'
    she is Dyce (she's Q); cf. metre.
108 *It* Dilke's emendation (but Q's 'I' could be correct, in an ironic echo of V. i. 84,
    meaning 'it was inevitable that I, too, would become a victim')
    devils In becoming De Flores' partner, Beatrice, too, has become a 'devil'; or else
    Alsemero is generalizing about women.
112 *crocodile* believed to weep hypocritically while taking its prey – first Alsemero,
    now ironically De Flores
113 *into* so Q – correctly, with an allusion to sexual ingression (they are to rehearse
    again their 'scene of lust', l. 115)
115 *perféct* i.e., perfected (participle)

When you shall come to act it to the black audience
Where howls and gnashings shall be music to you.
Clip your adult'ress freely – 'tis the pilot
Will guide you to the Mare Mortuum,
Where you shall sink to fathoms bottomless.   120

Enter VERMANDERO, ALIBIUS, ISABELLA, TOMAZO,
FRANCISCUS, *and* ANTONIO

VERMANDERO
O Alsemero, I have a wonder for you.
ALSEMERO
No sir, 'tis I, I have a wonder for you.
VERMANDERO
I have suspicion near as proof itself
For Piracquo's murder.
ALSEMERO   Sir, I have proof
Beyond suspicion for Piracquo's murder.   125
VERMANDERO
Beseech you, hear me. These two have been disguised
E'er since the deed was done.
ALSEMERO   I have two other
That were more close disguised than your two could be,
E'er since the deed was done.
VERMANDERO
You'll hear me – these mine own servants –   130
ALSEMERO
Hear me – those nearer than your servants,
That shall acquit them, and prove them guiltless.
FRANCISCUS
That may be done with easy truth, sir.

---

116 *black audience* i.e., of devils, to whom their evil will inevitably lead them. The
     language of l. 117 clearly derives from the Bible: in Hell 'there shall be wailing and
     gnashing of teeth' – cf. Matthew 13:42.
118 *Clip* embrace
118–19 *'tis . . . Mortuum* Beatrice is the pilot who will guide De Flores to the Mare
     Mortuum, the Dead Sea, bottomless like Hell – with which it is here imaginatively
     identified (cf. the entrance to the underworld in Greek mythology).
126 *These two* Antonio and Franciscus; Vermandero points to them, as (1) Alsemero
     does not know them, and (2) they are without their disguises and thus might not be
     recognized by the audience.
128 *close* covertly
129 *the deed* (1) the murder; (2) their sexual act
131–2 Beatrice and De Flores are closer to Vermandero's person than Antonio and
     Franciscus, whom they will prove guiltless by their confession.
131 *me* here, as often, an indirect object ('for me'). Cf. Abbott, §220.

TOMAZO
>How is my cause bandied through your delays!
>'Tis urgent in [my] blood, and calls for haste: 135
>Give me a brother alive or dead –
>Alive, a wife with him; if dead, for both
>A recompense, for murder and adultery.

BEATRICE *within*
>O, O, O!

ALSEMERO   Hark! 'Tis coming to you.

DE FLORES *within*
>Nay, I'll along for company.

BEATRICE *within*   O, O!   140

VERMANDERO
>What horrid sounds are these?

ALSEMERO
>Come forth, you twins of mischief!

>*Enter* DE FLORES *bringing in* BEATRICE [*wounded*]

DE FLORES
>Here we are. If you have any more
>To say to us, speak quickly; I shall not
>Give you the hearing else. I am so stout yet,   145
>And so, I think, that broken rib of mankind.

VERMANDERO
>An host of enemies ent'rëd my citadel

---

134 *bandied* tossed to and fro; neglected

135 *my* Dilke. The syllable seems needed, and could easily have been omitted in transcription after *my* in l. 134. It gives good sense too, although 'urgent in blood' is possible.

136 *alive* Dilke: or alive – perhaps this 'or' is metrically necessary, but it otherwise seems rather weak and superfluous. Maybe the line is octosyllabic (with 'broth'r' and four stresses).

138 *adultery* As Beatrice and Alonzo were engaged, Tomazo regards her marriage to Alsemero as adulterous.

139 *'Tis . . . you* i.e., the requital you seek – in the form of another murder and adulterous act (Beatrice's 'O, O, O!' reacts to the combination of sex and violence which De Flores offers)

140 *Nay . . . company* De Flores has just fatally wounded Beatrice, and now wounds himself because he wishes to join her in death. Of course the scene is invisible to the audience, which, however, can at least partly infer from the words what has happened.

145 *so . . . yet* still strong enough (despite his wound) to listen, as is Beatrice. It must now be visually clear to the audience that both are wounded.

146 *that . . . mankind* Beatrice, described as though she were Eve, created from Adam's rib (cf. Genesis 2:21–3), now 'broken'

Could not amaze like this. Joanna! Beatrice! Joanna!
BEATRICE

O come not near me, sir; I shall defile you.
I am that of your blood was taken from you   150
For your better health. Look no more upon't,
But cast it to the ground regardlessly;
Let the common sewer take it from distinction.
Beneath the stars, upon yon meteor
                              [*Pointing to* DE FLORES]
Ever hung my fate, 'mongst things corruptible;   155
I ne'er could pluck it from him. My loathing
Was prophet to the rest, but ne'er believed;
Mine honour fell with him, and now my life. –
Alsemero, I am a stranger to your bed:
Your bed was coz'nëd on the nuptial night,   160
For which your false bride died.
ALSEMERO   Diaphanta!
DE FLORES

Yes; and the while I coupled with your mate
At barley-break. Now we are left in hell.

148 *amaze* put one out of one's wits (stupefy/craze); perplex; alarm. It is now Ver-
    mandero's turn to be in a 'maze' or labyrinth, wondering whether his daughter is
    Beatrice ('she who makes happy')' or *Joanna* ('the Lord's grace'), while in truth she
    is neither. Cf. *labyrinth* in III. iv. 71 and IV. iii. 108.
150–1 *I . . . health* I am that part of your blood which, in purging, has been taken
    away from you to improve your health. Vermandero finds that his child, instead of
    being beautiful as he thought, turns out to be mentally ugly – a quintessential
    changeling.
151–3 *Look . . . distinction* 'Behold it no more, but throw it to the ground uncaring. Let
    the common sewer swallow its identity' (Black). The *common sewer* is the main
    drain, or else 'the common shore' (Q has *shewer*), being originally the 'no-man's-
    land' by the water-side, where filth was allowed to be deposited for the tide to
    wash away (cf. *OED*, shore, *sb.*⁴). Beatrice sees herself as bad blood that should be
    washed away, amazed though Vermandero may be to behold it.
154 *stars; meteor* The realm of the stars is one of eternal purity, while such things as
    meteors belong to the sublunary area of change, decay, evil, etc.; Beatrice is part of
    this inferior world, her fate having depended, not upon an eternal power of good,
    but the transitory and bad one of the meteor De Flores (cf. II. i. 36).
155 *hung* Dyce (hang Q)
156 This is a decasyllabic line, but difficult to scan.
156–7 *My . . . believed* She seems to reason that her loathing for De Flores was a
    warning she persistently ignored; but if it was 'prophet to the rest' it must have
    been bound up with the sexual urge which she now concedes she was led by.
160 *coz'nëd* Cf. II. i. 127; likely pun on *cousin* = mistress, strumpet.
162–3 Cf. III. iii. 166. De Flores and Beatrice were players from opposite ends in
    barley-break, trying to rush past the central area called 'hell' while forming a
    couple, but eventually they ended up there.

VERMANDERO

We are all there; it circumscribes [us] here.

DE FLORES

I loved this woman in spite of her heart;   165
Her love I earned out of Piracquo's murder.

TOMAZO

Ha! My brother's murderer!

DE FLORES   Yes, and her honour's prize
Was my reward, I thank life for nothíng
But that pleasure; it was so sweet to me
That I have drunk up all, left none behind   170
For any man to pledge me.

VERMANDERO   Horrid villain!
Keep life in him for further tortures.

DE FLORES   No: –
I can prevent you, here's my penknife still.
It is but one thread more, [*Stabs himself*] – and now 'tis
     cut.
Make haste, Joanna, by that token to thee   175
Canst not forget, so lately put in mind;
I would not go to leave thee far behind.   *Dies*

BEATRICE

Forgive me, Alsemero, all forgive!
'Tis time to die, when 'tis a shame to live.   *Dies*

VERMANDERO

O, my name is ent'rëd now in that record   180

---

164 They are now all in the central circle of 'barley-break', i.e., hell, which circum-
    scribes them. There is a clear echo of *Dr Faustus* (ed. Roma Gill, 2nd ed., 1989),
    sc. 5, 121–2, 'Hell hath no limits, nor is circumscribed / In one self place; for where
    we are is hell'. Hell encloses one in an unexpected place.
    us Dilke; required for metre and sense
165 *heart* disposition (towards me)
167 *her . . . prize* i.e., her maidenhead, the prize of her chastity
168 *nothíng* This accentuation is frequent.
169 *pleasure* sexual enjoyment
173 *prevent* forestall
174 *one . . . more* i.e., for an additional and fatal cut
175–7 The meaning has been much disputed. I take it to be: 'Make haste in dying,
    Joanna, in keeping with the promise which I made to you when I first wounded
    myself, and which you cannot forget, having been reminded of it so recently now
    that I have wounded myself a second time; I should not be keen to go (and will not
    go) while I leave you far behind me.' The *token* is the wound which De Flores gave
    himself in the closet, as a sign to her that he wished to join her in death (cf. l. 140),
    and she should now join him, the first to die.
180 *recórd* The book in heaven in which our misdeeds are recorded, and where his
    name so far had not appeared because he had not been guilty of any; or more
    simply, his reputation had so far been spotless and is so no longer – it is this idea
    which Alsemero appears to have in mind.

Where till this fatal hour 'twas never read.

ALSEMERO

Let it be blotted out; let your heart lose it,
And it can never look you in the face,
Nor tell a tale behind the back of life
To your dishonour. Justice hath so right   185
The guilty hit, that innocence is quit
By proclamation, and may joy again.
Sir, you are sensible of what truth hath done;
'Tis the best comfort that your grief can find.

TOMAZO [*To* VERMANDERO]

Sir, I am satisfied; my injuries   190
Lie dead before me. I can exact no more,
Unless my soul were loose, and could o'ertake
Those black fugitives, that are fled from thence,
                              [*Pointing to the bodies*]
To take a second vengeance. But there are wraths
Deeper than mine, 'tis to be feared, about 'em.   195

ALSEMERO

What an opacous body had that moon
That last changed on us! Here is beauty changed
To ugly whoredom; here, servant-obedience
To a master-sin, imperious murder;
I, a supposed husband, changed embraces   200
With wantonness, but that was paid before;
[*To* TOMAZO] Your change is come too, from an ignorant
   wrath
To knowing friendship. Are there any more on's?

ANTONIO

Yes, sir, I was changed too, from a little ass as I was to a
great fool as I am; and had like to ha' been changed to the   205

186–7 *innocence . . . proclamation* the innocent have been cleared of suspicion by public
   proclamation of the truth (Bawcutt)

188–9 Some think these lines are addressed to Tomazo, but they seem at least as
   applicable to Vermandero, who is newly aware (*sensible*) of 'what truth hath done'.
   While that may be no more than the best comfort that his grief can find, it is not
   negligible, as it has shown a clear distinction between the innocent and the guilty
   which had so far remained obscure.

190 *my injuries* the wrongs done to me – dead because the culprits are

193 *black fugitives* the wicked souls of Beatrice and De Flores, on their way to hell

195 *about 'em* about to punish them

196 *opacous* clouded and ominous

197 *is* Dilke ('s Q); cf. metre.

201 *wantonness* i.e., of Diaphanta, whose sin was paid by her murder

gallows but that you know my innocence always excuses
me.

FRANCISCUS

I was changed from a little wit to be stark mad,
Almost for the same purpose.

ISABELLA [*To* ALIBIUS]   Your change is still behind,
But deserve best your transformatiön: 210
You are a jealous coxcomb, keep schools of folly,
And teach your scholars how to break your own head.

ALIBIUS

I see all apparent, wife, and will change now
Into a better husband, and never keep
Scholars that shall be wiser than myself.   215

ALSEMERO [*To* VERMANDERO]

Sir, you have yet a son's duty living;
Please you, accept it. Let that your sorrow,
As it goes from your eye, go from your heart.
Man and his sorrow at the grave must part.

EPILOGUE

ALSEMERO

All we can do, to comfort one another,   220
To stay a brother's sorrow for a brother,
To dry a child from the kind father's eyes,
Is to no purpose; it rather multiplies.
Your only smiles have power to cause re-live
The dead again, or in their rooms to give   225
Brother a new brother, father a child;
If these appear, all griefs are reconciled.   *Exeunt* OMNES

FINIS

206 *innocence* (1) guiltlessness; (2) idiocy (which makes one innocent)

209 *behind* to come

212 *break . . . head* to put cuckold's horns on your forehead

215 *wiser* i.e., cleverer and saner – less stupid and less paranoid

216 *a . . . living* the duty which I owe you as a living son

217 *that your sorrow* that grief which you feel on account of Beatrice's death (and
which is pointless)

221 *stay* 'bring under control' or 'comfort' (cf. *OED* stay, *v.*¹ and *v.*²)

222 *kind* related by kinship, and loving

223 *it . . . multiplies* i.e., any such action rather increases grief

224 *Your only smiles* only your smiles (those of the audience)

225 *in their rooms* i.e., instead of the dead

226 Tomazo will have Vermandero as a new brother, and Vermandero Alsemero as a
new child, if the audience shows its approval of this performance.

APPENDIX: PROSODY

This Appendix consists of three parts:

(a) General;
(b) Lineation;
(c) Verbal forms with suffix -*ed*.

(a) **General**

The metre of the verse passages in the play is established from the outset as that of iambic pentameter:

> 'Twas in the temple where I first beheld her,
> And now again the same. What omen yet
> Follows of that? None but imaginary:
> Why should my hopes of fate be timorous?

We may first observe that the lines are – and characteristically – either ten or eleven syllables in length. The longer lines have an extra 'weak' (unaccented) syllable, a so-called feminine ending. Although the decasyllabic line (of which line 2 above is a perfect example) is the norm, hendecasyllabic lines like 1 and 3 are perfectly common. Lines of a different length occur: for example 'half lines' like 'Than making choice of him' (II. i. 9), or 'headless' ones such as 'With man's first creation, the place blest' (I. i. 8), where the first – theoretically weak – syllable has been 'omitted' from a line of nine syllables. However, the vast majority of lines consist of ten or eleven syllables, and most often, if our initial impression is that the line is of a different length, we do not read it correctly.

There is no particular difficulty about the four lines above. The underlying stress pattern is unambiguous in line 2, where it coincides with the stresses of speech so as to show a perfect weak-strong-weak-strong regularity. The other lines, too, reveal the iambic pattern readily enough when pronounced, although at times it is not at once obvious. For example, in line 3 we must not be tempted to pronounce 'imaginary' as though it were tetrasyllabic, and should realize that the fourth syllable has metrical stress even though we do not need to accentuate it markedly in speech. The stress pattern of 'Follows' is inverted in speech though the metre leads us to expect an iambic (weak-strong) formation, but such 'trochaic substitution' (strong-weak) is not uncommon in iambic verse, even though its subsequent occurrence in 'None but' does create an impression of irregularity. The line has five feet (two trochees and three iambs).

Much of the verse of Middleton and Rowley, which is often thought of as remarkably rough or irregular, can be analyzed this way without much trouble as syllabically quite regular (though with variation in line length), and not conspicuously irregular when we consider the relation between the line as spoken and the underlying iambic sequence. At the same time, it may be admitted that the stresses of a good many lines when delivered both naturally and with attention to the metre seem to 'clash' with our expectation of regularity. Rowley, in particular, is known to surprise his readers/listeners. He opens the play in a way which is prosodically intelligible enough, but if we try to impose a metrical pattern on 'With man's first creation, the place blest' we shall find that quite at odds with the stresses of speech, even allowing for the notion of a 'headless' line. The friction between speech rhythm and metre in cases like this is no doubt intentional, and not to be seen as an inadequacy in Rowley's writing or our perception. As I have argued elsewhere,[1] notoriously (or famously) 'rough' writers like Wyatt or Donne often alternate accentually regular and highly irregular lines in a way which is perplexing to us but apparently natural to them, while they maintain great syllabic regularity. Middleton and Rowley appear to have had a similar approach, which is not at all untypical of the English Renaissance, and very characteristic of much Jacobean verse.

As readers, we must first make sure that we get the number of syllables right in as many lines as we can. Often this means that the number of syllables is reduced. The text indicates in a number of places how this is to be done, by printing 'that's', 'I'm', 'e'en', 'ne'er', etc. From such forms, and from experience, one learns also how to omit syllables where the text gives no indication. Thus in 'And lively refresher of the countenance' (I. i. 122), 'refresher' becomes 'r'fresher' (disyllabic), which is in no sense an unnatural pronunciation and secures the right number of syllables (as well as the correct accentual pattern). 'Of some harm towards me: danger's in my mind still' (II. i. 90), which seems to have twelve syllables and to be irregular accentually, comes to sound more normal when we read 't'wards' and 'dang'r's', although the stress pattern will still not be quite smooth. Sometimes the line becomes much shorter than it looks at first, as for example in II. i. 153: 'How much w'are bound to heaven to depart lovingly'. The line appears to have thirteen syllables but probably is to be read as having ten, with the last iamb replaced by a trochee: 'How much w'are bound to heav'n to d'part lov'ngly'. I have refrained from indicating such elisions in the text, as they are a matter of argu-

[1] 'Wyatt's Prosody Revisited', *Language and Style* 10 (1977), 3–15; 'The Prosodic Significance of Donne's "Accidentals"', *Parergon* n.s. 4 (1986), 87–101

ment rather than undisputed fact. It would not have been possible to record them exhaustively in the notes. However, it is essential to be aware that elisions (or pronunciations like monosyllabic 'ne'er') do occur; otherwise verse becomes confused with prose, and an injustice is done to the art of the dramatists.

The opposite situation to the one just discussed also occurs, viz. that the line should be interpreted as having more syllables than current pronunciation would suggest. Again it is not possible to provide comprehensive guidance, but the phenomenon must at least be noted here, with a number of examples. Many of the more striking examples are indicated by marks in the text. Sometimes these are likely to be complete for the category involved. Thus, for example, I think it will be clear when final -ed in verbs will have to be pronounced for metrical reasons, as in the case of 'deceivëd' (I. i. 15), where the -ed is printed in Q; but I believe that in unmarked cases (where -ed in my text merely represents forms like 'stretcht' in Q) there will be no case for reading the ending as syllabic. This reasoning does not necessarily apply to words like 'devotiön' (I. i. 35), where the diaeresis is a sign that the word has four syllables. It is quite possible that there are words ending in -ion, etc., where that ending is disyllabic although I have not felt inclined to mark it as such. One of the hardest problems concerns words where r is 'syllabic' in that there is likely to be a 'glide' between the preceding vowel or diphthong and r: thus in places (either fewer or more than I have marked) a word like 'or' may be disyllabic although it is no doubt monosyllabic in others. I feel no doubt, however, that at least in some instances the introduction of a glide on our part is justified on both linguistic and metrical grounds.[2] Again, the reader should be at least aware of the possibility of such occurrences.

It is generally accepted that the accentuation of words in the early seventeenth century was not identical to ours, particularly in words of 'Romance' origin. Most of us are aware of the fact that even now not all people stress words like 'controversy' in the same way. Generally variations around 1620 appear to have been confined to words derived from Latin or its descendants, but pronunciations like 'fárewell' and 'nothíng' also appear. I have marked what appear to me to be telling cases by adding an accent mark, as in 'survéy' (noun), but it must be pointed out that occasionally I

---

[2] Concerning linguistic aspects of the matter, see Helge Kökeritz, *Shakespeare's Pronunciation* (1953), notably p. 291. The book is still useful for anyone wishing to become acquainted with pronunciation in Shakespeare and somewhat later dramatists; but cf. especially Fausto Cercignani, *Shakespeare's Works and Elizabethan Pronunciation* (1981), for criticisms of aspects of Kökeritz's work, and for further information.

may have marked a word where the stress is not certain, while perhaps in other cases it did occur. The matter is controversial, in that there may be an unwarranted inclination for one to base one's choice of a stressed syllable on the metre, while accentual regularity should not be too readily assumed. Nevertheless, there are a good many words which we may confidently suppose to have been stressed in an unexpected way, as 'survéy' (noun) not only appears to fit the metre in Shakespeare but also occurs in eighteenth-century books which provide stress marks.[3] There is, of course, always the possibility that Middleton did not have the same pronunciation as Rowley (or Shakespeare), and caution is necessary. But, if 'survéy' survived into the eighteenth century, its pronunciation in the seventeenth appears likely, and, at least in such a case, the Shakespearean pronunciation (as it seems) may well be called on in further support. I certainly hope I have marked all the words which are of this kind – particularly those which even in the eighteenth century still had a stress that is to us surprising, and they are the majority of the ones which I have selected.

From this account, it will be evident that it is not in every instance easy to determine exactly how a line is to be pronounced. On the other hand, the difficulties should not be exaggerated. On the whole, editors have shown remarkable agreement in the way they have re-lined Q where that was presented as prose or unsatisfactory verse although one can sense the prosodic intensions of the dramatists. No such consensus would have been achieved if the divisions of the lines, and the way we are to pronounce them, had not been fairly clear from a careful reading of Q. Thus I hope that my general remarks here, and the presentation of the text, will guide the reader towards a pronunciation which, at least syllabically and accentually, will not be far removed from that of Middleton and Rowley.

(b) Lineation

The following list indicates how the lineation in this edition differs from that in Q.

---

[3] Kökeritz has a valuable Appendix on 'Shakespearean Accentuation', though his list is perhaps too much based on metrical assumptions. Stress marks occur in, for example, Thomas Dyche's *A Guide to the English Tongue* (2nd ed., 1710) and *New General English Dictionary* (3rd ed., 1740).

This edition

Q (modernized spelling)

I.i

36–9:	Lover ... was / Found ... nor / Best ... ay / And ... way	Lover ... stoic / Was ... mother / Nor ... beauty / Ay ... way
42–4:	Somewhat ... this / Violence ... Compared / With ... yesterday	Somewhat ... temple / Is ... idleness / Compared ... yesterday
151–2:	O ... thee / Your ... ended	*one line*
167–8:	Alsemero? ... son / Of ... Alsemero	*one line*
169–71:	He ... wont / To ... most / Unfeignëd truth	He ... speaks / A ... truth
215–16:	He's much / Bound ... sir	*one line*
217–18:	As ... want / My ... else	*one line*
229–31:	Here's ... know / She ... pair / Of ... fingers	Here's ... now / I ... tanned / In ... fingers

I. ii

30–1:	You ... into't	You ... by / One ... into't
33–4:	Must ... be / At home	*one line*
84–5:	Ay ... sir / 'Tis ... patient	*one line*
86–90:	And ... defrayed	And ... commodious / To ... sick / And ... are / But ... pieces / That ... charge / Of ... necessaries / Fully defrayed
92–3:	Sir ... hands	Sir ... something / The ... hands
98–9:	His ... Tony	His ... half / To ... Tony
105–6:	Well, sir / If ... height	*one line*
123–4:	O ... enough	O ... shorter / Will ... enough
175–6:	Yes ... Tony	Yes ... say't / Once ... Tony
207–9:	There's ... for't	There's ... madman / Was ... permasant / Lost ... for't

II.i

9–10:	Than ... him / For ... choose	*one line*
52–3:	Again / This ... me	*one line*
56–7:	Soft ... fair / I ... now	*one line*
57–8:	The ... fixed / Thou ... toad-pool	*one line*
60–1:	My ... deliver / A ... you	*one line*
61–2:	What ... since / Do't ... thee	*one line*
64–5:	Let ... patience / You ... all	*one line*
66–7:	Signor ... lady / Sole ... Piracquo	*one line*
69–70:	The ... Alonzo / With ... Tomazo	*one line*
73–4:	My ... father / Charged ... out	*one line*
74–5:	Is ... other / To ... by	*one line*
75–6:	It ... luck / To ... still	*one line*
76–7:	So / Why ... ways	*one line*
121–2:	May ... ever / Meet ... sirs	May ... still / Y'are ... sirs

137–8:	She … passions / And … dangerous	*one line*
142–3:	Nay … that / Be …enough	*one line*

II. ii

5–6:	This … well / These cabinets	*one line*
12–13:	W'are … like / In … borrow	*one line*
25–6:	Pray … sir / What … happy	*prose*
48–9:	I … sir / The …side	*one line*
51–2:	As … now / Till … opens	*one line*
63–4:	One … thousand / Proves … royal	*one line*
69–70:	And … here / De Flores	*one line*
72–3:	What … done / To … physician	*one line*
75–6:	Not I / 'Tis … pimple	*one line*
77–8:	Which … ago / How … this	*one line*
79–80:	Turn … see / Faugh … perceive't	*one line*
81–2:	Her … me / She … amber	*one line*
83–4:	I'll … this / Within … fortnight	*one line*
85–6:	Yes … cure / I'll … other	*one line*
86–7:	'Tis … pleasure / To … me	*one line*
87–8:	When … used / To … unpleasing	*one line*
89–90:	It … mends / I … experience	*one line*
90–1:	I … blest / To … on't	*one line*
93–4:	It … manhood / If … employment	*one line*
94–5:	'Twould … seen / If … it	*one line*
96–7:	I … service / So … to	*one line*
98–9:	How's that / She … De Flores	*one line*
101–2:	There … again / The … on't	*one line*
106–7:	For … yet / Beat … bosom	*one line*
109–10:	O … freedom / I … one	*prose*
112–13:	Then … 'em / For … sight	*one line*
113–14:	O … occasion / Without … wishes	*prose*
115–16:	In … De Flores / There's … that	*one line*
116–17:	Put … me / It's … you	*one line*
120–1:	If … knew / How … employed	*one line*
124–5:	This … methinks / Belike … such	*one line*
127–8:	Possible … need / Is … thee	*one line*
130–2:	That … on / I … beforehand/ And … ravishes	*prose*
134–5:	His … him / He … more	*one line*
135–7:	How … now / Dost … man / Dearlier … rewarded	How … me / Never … rewarded
141–3:	When … done / I'll … flight / Thou … country	*prose*
144–5:	I … myself / Of … time	*one line*
146–7:	O … blood / Methinks … already	*one line*
157–8:	Thou … me / The … castle	*one line*
159–61:	And … straits / Of … you / I … lord	*prose*

| 162–4: | I'm ... then / 'Tis ... rising / I'll ... me | *prose* |

III.i

| 9–10: | Here ... lord / To ... purpose | *one line* |

III.ii

1–2:	All ... anon / A ... on	*one line*
2–3:	I ... glad / I ... house	*one line*
10–14:	Ay ...sir / No ... bells / At ... lord / Take ... you / There ... awhile	*prose*
15–16:	De Flores ... De Flores / Whose ... on	*one line*
16–17:	Do ... question / A ... secrecy	*one line*

III.iii

29–31:	If ... fool	If ... show / You ... may / Call ... fool
46–8:	For ... neither	For ... mistress / He ...first / The ... chambermaid / Yet ... neither
49–53:	Hail ... Titania / Why ... banks / Oberon ... Dryadës / I'll ... violets/ And ... poesy	*prose*
55–7:	O ... Diomed / Thou ... thee / Get ... kneels	*prose*
64–5:	Didst ... Tiresias / A ... poet	*prose*
69–70:	Yes ... man / Seven ... ago	*prose*
80–6:	Luna ... room / For ... Hecatë / I'll ... sphere / And ... bush / That ... night / The ... round / We'll ... sheep	*prose*
90–1:	Sweet ... me / Give ... thee	*one line*
111–12:	Hark ... room / Are ... order	*one line*
123–4:	O ... strange / Love ... all	*one line*
125–8:	The ... poet / Catches ... knowledge / Yet ... mystery / Into ... in	The ... like / A ... quantity / Of ... home / Into ...secret / That ... in
139–40:	Take ... acquaintance / Of ... within	*one line*
141–3:	When ... him / I'll ... keep / Your ... enough	When ... meantime / Keep ... enough
148–9:	And ...cousin / I'll ... morning	And ... Valentine / Tomorrow morning
153–4:	If ... like / To ... something	*one line*
155–7:	Ay ... six	Ay ... begins / To ... is / Five ... six

159–60:	What … seven	What … is / One …seven
167–9:	Again … together	Again … home / I … together
173–4:	How …freeze / Lives … alone	*one line*
179–81:	How … that	How … Lipsius / He's … harder / Questions … that
182–3:	What … fear / Having … smile	*one line*
192–3:	Of … us / Yet … lunatics	*one line*
228–9:	What … fear / Having … smile	*one line*
235–9:	Becomes … not / [*prose*] And … on't	Becomes … more / Foolish … Lacedaemonian / Let … thing / About … on't
245–6:	I'll … and / Be … it	I'll … purpose / And … it
249–50:	Fie … sweetheart / No … that	*one line*
277–8:	Y'have … on't / Madmen … commodity	*prose*

III.iv

29–30:	Why … more / Than … heart-strings	*prose*
48–50:	It … sir / Why … given / In … recompense	*prose*
50–1:	No … lady / You … then	*prose*
60–1:	'Tis … then / Look … florins	*one line*
68–9:	I … hired / A … rate	*one line*
70–1:	And … had / The … home	And … might have / And … home
73–4:	You … course / To … do	*one line*
89–90:	How … sir / This … well	*one line*
90–1:	What … strange / This … us	*one line*
94–5:	Take … forgetfulness / 'Twill … us	*one line*
97–8:	I … you / Of … pain	*one line*
101–2:	O … shall / Speak … lose	*one line*
104–5:	I … again / For … deed	*one line*
105–6:	Soft … soft / The … act	*one line*
124–5:	I … it / With … modesty	*one line*
125–6:	Push … yourself / A … modesty	*prose*
137–8:	Y'are … lost / Your … you	Y'are … name / You … you
159–60:	The … buy / My … me	*one line*

IV.i

30–1:	If … C	If … not / Give … C
32–4:	Where's … now/ [*prose*] and … not	Where's … child / She … not
50–1:	Where … been / I … bedtime	?*prose; one line*
55–6:	Would … cause / To … madam	Would … too / Why … madam
80–1:	Nay … madam / Shall … maid	*prose* (with break after 'madam')
81–2:	You … else / Because … me	*one line*
101–2:	And … doing / I … it	*one line*
110–11:	As … accident / Gives … another	*one line*

112–13:	Ha ... light / At ... pleasurable	*one line*
114–15:	Ay, tomorrow / We ... by't	*one line*
116–17:	It ... wench / Most ... now	It ... Diaphanta / I ... now
119–20:	I'll ... study / The ... business	*prose*
120–1:	I ... well / Because ... burden	*one line*
121–2:	About midnight / You ... gently	*one line*

IV.ii

3–4:	Nor ... gentlemen / Are ... who	Nor ... absent / Tell ... who
7–8:	Some ... Valencia	Some ... Briamata / Th'other ... Valencia
17–18:	Y'are ... hot / Seek ... here	*one line*
33–4:	'Tis ... fair / For ... you	*one line*
35–6:	The ... is / There ... on	*one line*
43–4:	O ... sir / Methinks ... him	*one line*
60–1:	'Twill ... reckon / Sir	*one line*
67–8:	Your ... you / Appear ... strangers	*one line*
68–9:	Time ... swords / May ... business	Time ... acquainted / This ... business
73–4:	You ... look / To ... sir	*one line*
74–5:	Fear ... not / I'll ... meeting	*one line*
85–6:	This ... on / And ... slowness	*one line*
97–8:	Still ... thee / The ... her	*one line*
104–5:	Such ... are / O ... earth	*one line*
110–11:	Done charitably / That ... secret	*one line*
133–4:	Sir ... me / I ... composition	*one line*
143–4:	Ha ... ha / You ... lord	*one line*

IV.iii

87–8:	Ay ... la	Ay ... out / Vault ... la
94–6:	Marry ... caper	Marry ... yeomanry / Itself ... stiffened / There ... caper
98–100:	Very ... Tony	Very ... high / Has ... again / You ... Tony
102–9:	Hey ... air / Shough ... else / Here's ... more / Than ... moons / He's ... had / Stand ... Daedalus / And ... labyrinth / I'll ... clue	Hey ... way / He ... Icarus / More ... moons / He's ... up / Thou ... lower / Labyrinth ... clue
205–6:	In ... master	*separate line*

V.i

14–15:	Hath ... trust / A waiting-woman	*one line*
31–2:	This ... set / Some ... chamber	*one line*
35–6:	Push ... aim / At ... sure	*one line*
50–1:	One ... now / Prithee ... servants	*one line*
51–2:	I'll ... them / Some ... hurry	*one line*
76–7:	Here's ... loving / O ... jewel	*one line*
79–80:	Hie ... chamber / Your ... you	*one line*
80–1:	I ... made / So ... bargain	*one line*

83–4:	When … you / I … follow	*one line*
84–5:	Th'art … sweetness / The … dangerous	*one line*
94–5:	Come … now / Alas … cold	*one line*
104–5:	O … virginity / Thou … for't	*one line*
107–8:	Now … flames / Are … sir	Now …are / Greedy … sir
109–11:	Not … more / I … you / In … us	Not … embrace / I … us
113–15:	All … take / Your … quenched / Ah … stifled	All … Lords / The … gentlewoman / How … stifled
122–3:	He … be / De Flores … me	*one line*

V.iii

14–15:	How … I / Alas … well	*one line*
39–40:	You … sir / 'Tis … please	*one line*
52–3:	He's … your / Lips' saint	*one line*
53–4:	Worse … devil / Your adultery	*one line*
55–6:	It … witnessed / By … Diaphanta	*one line*
90–1:	I … you / News … you	*one line*
172–3:	No / I …still	*one line*
209–10:	Your … behind / But … transformation	*one line*
214–15:	Into … keep / Scholars … myself	Into … scholars / That … myself

Almost all of the re-lining of Q was done by the earliest editors, Dilke and Dyce. The lineation which appears in Dyce has been substantially accepted by all later editors, but departures from it are not uncommon. Thus, in the present edition I have reverted to Q in a number of unlisted instances, and I have adopted the following departures from Q which do not occur in Dyce: I. ii. 84–5: Bawcutt; II. i. 9–10: Bawcutt; II. i. 137–8: Black; III. iv. 70–1: Gomme; IV. ii. 3–4: Neilson; IV. iii. 102–9: this ed.; V. i. 50–1: Neilson. All other departures from Q as listed above occur in Dyce, although Dilke was often the first to think of them.

(c) **Verbal forms with suffix *-ed***

The suffix *-ed* in verbal forms, used to indicate a past tense or a past participle, is in modern English sometimes pronounced (as in 'discarded') and sometimes silent ('deceived'), depending on the word in question. This distinction also occurs in *The Changeling*, where forms like 'discarded' are spelled with *-ed*, while silent forms are spelled without *-ed* ('lov'd', 'stretcht'). By itself, this difference is not of great interest, as the modern reader/actor would pronounce the words as presumably intended by the dramatists even if 'lov'd' were changed to 'loved' (as has happened in this edition).

However, forms like 'lov'd' were used to indicate a contrast not so much with 'discarded' as with disyllabic 'loved', in which the -*ed* was sounded. That pronunciation had been quite normal, and the very fact that the 1653 text of *The Changeling* has so many forms like 'lov'd' shows that the spelling 'loved' might still indicate a disyllabic word. In several instances we see just that, for example in 'deceived' (I. i. 15), which is so spelled in Q, and which fits the metre if pronounced as a trisyllabic word. Such Q spellings are of great importance and must be kept distinct from disyllabic 'deceiv'd'. Many earlier editions indicate the difference by using 'deceived' for the trisyllabic word and 'deceiv'd' for the disyllabic one. As forms like 'deceiv'd' constitute a massive majority in *The Changeling*, I have modernized them into 'deceived' and marked syllabic -*ed* (in cases other than 'discarded') as follows: 'deceivëd'.

In general this method works well, as in most instances the modern pronunciation is the correct one, but there are a number of words which pose somewhat of a problem – at least in theory – and which I list here, using Q spellings:

I. i. 174: continued; I. i. 180: Swallowed; I .i. 183: followed; I. ii. 9: married; I. ii. 28: borrowed; I. ii. 58: answered; I. ii. 90: defrayed; I. ii. 158: answered; II. i. 49: tumbled; II. i. 127: cousened (2x); II. ii. 31: ventured; II. ii. 39: dried; II. ii. 121: imployed; III. iii. 80: bellied; III. iii. 240: discovered; III. iv. 5: married; III. iv. 67: valued; III. iv. 110: sued; III. iv. 163: followed; IV.i [*Dumb show*] accompanied; IV.i. 5: ennobled; IV.ii. 140: qualited (misprint for 'qualitied' or a 'French' form); IV. ii. 147: setled; IV. iii. 22: dismantled; IV. iii. 95: stiffened; IV. iii. 183: handled; IV. iii. 200: favouredly; V. i. 115: stifled; V. i. 120: spied; V. ii. 16: loved; V. iii. 84: murdered; V. iii. 134: bandied; V. iii. 161: died; V. iii. 162: coupled; V. iii. 190: satisfied.

The words ending in -*led* ('tumbled', 'ennobled', etc.) were pronounced either with a final -*ed* or as now, with a 'syllabic' *l*. The number of syllables, at any rate, does not seem in doubt. This is not necessarily so with the other forms. At first, it seems tempting to decide that -*ed* after a vowel ('continued', 'married') has no syllabic significance, but forms like *apply'd* are used in Q (III. iv. 40; IV. i. 41), which may suggest that, for example, *married* could (at least at times) be trisyllabic. However, from a metrical point of view no such instances appear to occur, and it seems probable that neither *apply'd* nor *married* is indicative of syllabic variation. Similarly, although in theory *Swallowed* could be either trisyllabic or disyllabic in more than one way ('Swallow'd' or 'Swall'wëd'), I have in practice found the normal modern pronunciation as likely as any other. This also appears to be true of words like 'answered' and 'discovered', although, for example, *cousened*, which seems disyllabic in II. i. 127, may have been pronounced 'coz'nëd' rather than 'cozen'd', as in V. iii. 160 Q has 'coz'ned'.

The truth seems to be that, where Q's spelling does not so indicate, we shall never really know whether the pronunciation was intended to be 'cozen'd' or 'coz'nëd'. Nevertheless, the reader should be aware of the problem, and that is one reason for the existence of this section of the Appendix. More importantly, inasmuch as we can envisage that 'cousened' might represent a trisyllabic pronunciation, the reader must be given the Q spelling where such a possibility exists. I myself believe that in each case the modern pronunciation is at the least defensible, and in keeping with what appear to be the dramatists' prosodic intentions.